C.

Withdrawn

DONATED

The Genius of Alexander the Great

The Genius of Alexander the Great

N.G.L. Hammond

The University of North Carolina Press
Chapel Hill

First published in the United States in 1997 by
the University of North Carolina Press

First published in 1997 by
Gerald Duckworth & Co. Ltd.
The Old Piano Factory
48 Hoxton Square, London N1 6PB
Tel: 0171 729 5986
Fax: 0171 729 0015

Library of Congress Cataloging-in-Publication Data

Hammond, N. G. L. (Nicholas Geoffrey Lemprière), 1907–
    The genius of Alexander the Great / N.G.L. Hammond.
        p.   cm.
    Includes bibliographical references and index.
    ISBN 0-8078-2350-3 (cloth : alk. paper)
    ISBN 0-8078-4744-5 (pbk. : alk. paper)
    1. Alexander, the Great, 356-323 B.C.—Psychology. 2. Philip II.
King of Macedonia, 382–336 B.C.—Influence. 3. Greece—History—
Macedonian Expansion, 359-323 B.C. 4. Greece—Kings and rulers—
Biography. 5. Generals—Greece—Biography. I. Title.
DF234.3.H35 1997
938′ .07′092—dc21   96-46881
                                                                                          CIP

07 06 05 04 03   7 6 5 4 3

Contents

Preface   ix
List of illustrations   xi
Bibliography   xiii

I. The boyhood of Alexander   1

II. The world of Philip as king and Alexander as prince   9
  1. The setting of Alexander's birth and boyhood   9
  2. The Macedonian State   12

III. The influence of Philip   15
  1. From weakness to strength in 346   15
  2. Philip's policy towards the city-states   18
  3. Relations between Philip and his grown-up son   21
  4. The invasion of Asia and the death of Philip   24

**IV. Alexander establishes his position in Macedonia,
Greece and the Balkans**   27
  1. The succession and the trial of conspirators   27
  2. The funeral of Philip and the march to Corinth   29
  3. Arrangements in the kingdom   31
  4. The campaign in Thrace and the organisation of the
    empire   32
  5. The campaign in Illyria   36

**V. Sources of information, a rising in Greece and
preparations for Persia**   41
  1. The sources of information for the Balkan campaign 41
  2. The revolt and capture of Thebes, and the sources of
    information   44
  3. The judgement passed on Thebes by the Council of
    the Greeks   47
  4. Alexander prepares for the campaign against Persia 50
  5. Coinage and culture in 336-335   53

VI. The crossing of the Hellespont and the first victory 59
  1. Arrangements in Europe and calculations for Asia 59
  2. The crossing of the Hellespont 62
  3. The battle of the river Granicus 65

VII. The winning of Asia Minor 71
  1. Alexander's policy and advance to Ephesus 71
  2. The war at sea and the siege of Halicarnassus 73
  3. The division of forces and the advance of Alexander to Pamphylia 76
  4. Anatolia and Gordium 80

VIII. The battle of Issus and the capture of the Mediterranean coast 83
  1. War at sea and the advance to Tarsus 83
  2. The campaign of Issus 86
  3. The winning of the coast and the siege of Tyre 90
  4. The advance to Egypt and the establishment of thalassocracy 96

IX. Advance to the East and the battle of Gaugamela 99
  1. Events in Egypt in early 331 99
  2. The campaign and the battle of Gaugamela 103

X. Advance to Persepolis and the situation in Greece 111
  1. Babylon, Susa and military reorganisation 111
  2. Persepolis and the future of Persia 114
  3. The situation in Greece 116

XI. The death of Darius and the decision to advance to the east 119
  1. The advance to Ecbatana and the pursuit of Darius 119
  2. Alexander's concept of 'Asia' and the preliminaries to the advance eastwards 121

XII. From Parthyaea to Kabul in Afghanistan 129
  1. Forward planning by Alexander 129
  2. Campaigning in Afghanistan 130
  3. The trial of Philotas and others 132
  4. Operations in Afghanistan and Baluchistan 135

XIII. The advance to the river Jaxartes 139
  1. The system of supply and the crossing of the Hindu Kush 139

2. The crossing of the Oxus, the Branchidae and the failure of Bessus   140
3. Risings in Sogdiana and Bactria in 329   144

XIV. The subjugation of the northeastern area in 328-327   149
1. Operations against rebels and the Cleitus episode   149
2. Operations in the northeastern area   153
3. The conspiracy of the Pages   155

XV. The Indus valley   161
1. The advance to and the crossing of the river Indus   161
2. The battle of the Hydaspes   164
3. Advance to and halt at the Hyphasis   167

XVI. Southern Asia   169
1. To the delta of the Indus   169
2. The conquest of the southern regions   175
3. Southwestern Asia   178

XVII. The Kingdom of Asia and the Macedonians   181
1. The organisation of the Kingdom of Asia   181
2. Macedonians and Asians   187

XVIII. The plans and personality of Alexander   191
1. Arrangements affecting the Macedonians and Macedonia   191
2. Arrangements affecting the city-states   192
3. Preparations for the Mediterranean campaign   195
4. Events leading to the death of Alexander   196
5. Alexander's beliefs and personal qualities   198

Appendix of references to the author's studies   203
Notes on illustrations   205
Chronological table   207
Index   209

MARGARET
UXORI DILECTISSIMAE

Preface

In 1980 when I published a book on Alexander I wrote that my aim was 'to state most of the evidence and bring the reader into the task of evaluation'. Thus, to take as an example the Battle of the Granicus, I reported the incompatible versions of the ancient writers (Diodorus, Plutarch and Arrian in particular), added some topographical details, and put forward my reconstruction, which rested on my own evaluation of the worth of the rival accounts. The reader was thereby equipped to make his own assessment of what actually happened, and he was enabled to carry his study further by consulting the works of other scholars to which reference was provided. Thus it was a book designed to provoke inquiry into and estimation of Alexander's achievements.

Since 1980 I have carried my researches very much further. In particular I have published two books (*Three Historians of Alexander* and *Sources for Alexander*) on the central problem which faces any Alexander-historian. It may be summarised as follows. The narratives which survive were written between three and five centuries after Alexander's career, and their portrayals of Alexander vary widely not only in what might be regarded as matters of fact but also in interpretations of Alexander's personality. The latter range from intellectual brilliance and statesmanlike vision to unbridled lust for conquest and drunken debauchery. The temptation for the modern writer is to pick and choose from these narratives what suits his own conception of Alexander's personality and to bring the portrayal of Alexander into line with a modern scale of values. This temptation is extremely strong in our modern age which is marked, to cite the words of Thomas Carlyle, 'by a disbelief in great men' because our age has so signally failed to produce statesmen and leaders of such stature. To take an example, it may be more attractive to attribute the burning of the palace at Persepolis to an act of drunken vandalism by an Athenian prostitute and an inebriated king than to a deliberate decision of policy.

In my own work since 1980 I have tried to resist that temptation and to concentrate my attention on a detailed analysis of the surviving narratives, in order to ascertain their historical worth at each stage. Arrian, for instance, tells us that he derived his facts from the narratives of Ptolemy and Aristobulus, who 'campaigned with Alexander' and 'were more trustworthy'. Plutarch on the other hand relied largely on

the account of Cleitarchus, a contemporary but not a campaigner, and
we are told by Quintilian that Cleitarchus' work was 'brilliantly ingen-
ious and notoriously untrustworthy'. Thus, when we find different
versions of an event in Arrian and in Plutarch, we have to ask which
previous author each was using and only then judge what actually or at
least probably happened.

Retirement has given me the opportunity to undertake and complete
thorough studies of these and similar problems, studies of which many
have been republished in my *Collected Studies* II and III. It is to be
hoped that they will open a new era of Alexander-scholarship in the
future. At present it seems appropriate to put my conclusions together
and to write an account of Alexander which may claim to be close to the
actual facts of his career and the nature of his personality. Because the
picture which emerges is of a man who did more than any other
individual to change the history of civilization, I have entitled my book
The Genius of Alexander the Great.

The narrative is designed primarily for the general reader, for it has
no footnotes. Sometimes a passage is in inverted commas, which indicates that it is a translation from an ancient text or inscription. An
Appendix is provided for those who wish to know the basis of my views.
For ease of reference the Appendix is arranged chapter by chapter and
topic by topic, and the reader is directed to those of my studies which
are relevant. In them he will find discussion of other scholars' views.
The Bibliography is limited to relatively few books in English, because
extensive bibliographies are available for instance in *The Cambridge
Ancient History* 6 (Cambridge, 1994). The chronology is as in my earlier
book on Alexander, pp. 312-16, except that I now date his accession to
October 336. I am most grateful to Sonia Argyle for help with the Index,
and to Deborah Blake for guiding the book through the Press.

I owe a debt of gratitude to David Cox of Cox Cartographic Ltd., who
drew the originals of the maps and the plans, and for constant encour-
agement and shrewd criticism to Margaret, to whom this book is
dedicated.

Clare College, Cambridge   N.G.L.H.

Illustrations

Figures

1. (a) Companion Cavalryman (after Hammond *MS* 105)   13
   (b) Pikeman-phalanx (after Hammond *MM* 60)   14
2. Alexander's Kingdom of Macedonia (after Hammond *MS* 50)   16
3. Philip's wives and descendants (after Hammond *Philip* 42)   22
4. The Balkan area (after Hammond *Philip* 116)   33
5. The manoeuvres by Pelium (after Hammond *AG* 51)   38
6. The Palace of Philip and Alexander at Pella (drawn from M.B. Hatzopoulos ed., *Macedonia from Philip II to the Roman Conquest* (Athens, 1993) 88)   57
7. The penteconter (after Hammond *AG* 233)   61
8. The movements of Alexander's forces 336-333 BC (after Hammond *AG* 43)   63
9. Cilicia (after Hammond *AG* 102)   84
10. The Battle of Issus (after Hammond *AG* 102)   88
11. The movements of Alexander's forces 333-331 BC (after Hammond *AG* 114)   93
12. The central satrapies (after Hammond *AG* 133)   104
13. The phases of the Battle of Gaugamela (after Hammond *AG* 142)   107
14. The northeastern satrapies (after Hammond *AG* 175)   124
15. Alexander's world in 327 BC (after Hammond *AG* 177)   126
16. The Alexander-city at Ai Khanoum (drawn from the plan in *Scientific American* 247 (1982) 148 ff.)   158
17. The Battle of the Hydaspes River (after Hammond *AG* 213)   165
18. The southeastern satrapies (after Hammond *AG* 209)   170
19. The administrative divisions of Alexander's territories (after Hammond *MS* 218)   182

Figs 1(b) to 6 and 16 were drawn by the author and Figs 7 to 15 and 17-19 by A. Cox of Cox Cartographic Ltd, Waterstock, Oxon. Acknowledgement is made to Oxford University Press for permission to reproduce Figs 1(a), 2 and 19, and to Sidgwick and Jackson for Fig. 1(b).

Plates
(between pages 114 and 115)

1. (a) Gold medallions of Philip and Olympias (source, Ad. de Longperier in *Rev. Num.* 1868)
   (b) Ivory heads of Olympias and Alexander (source, M. Andronicos)
2. Fresco of a Royal Hunt (source, M. Andronicos)
3. (a) Phalanx of pikemen (source, P. Connolly)
   (b) Alexander in action (source, Mansell Collection)
4. (a) Silver oenochoe with the head of a Silenus (source, M. Andronicos)
   (b) Head of a young Heracles on a silver amphora (source, M. Andronicos)
5. (a) Gold larnax (source, M. Andronicos)
   (b) Gold wreath (source, M. Andronicos)
6. (a) Mosaic of a Lion Hunt (source, Ph. Petsas)
   (b) Mosaic of Dionysus riding on a Panther (source, Ph. Petsas)
7. The righthand half of the Boscoreale fresco (source, C.M. Robertson)
8. (a) Satellite photograph of the Pelium area (source, NASA)
   (b) The plain beside Pelium (source, A. Harding)
9. Alexander in action (source, Hirmer Fotoarchiv)
10. Satellite photograph of Cilicia (source, NASA)
11. The family of Darius before Alexander (source, The National Gallery)
12. The Alexander Mosaic (after Hammond *AG* Fig. 33)
13. The Porus medallion and the Indian archer (source, The Trustees of the British Museum)
14. The Derveni crater (source, The Archaeological Museum, Thessaloniki)
15. A young Alexander riding Bucephalus (source, M. Andronicos)
16. A mature Alexander somewhat idealised (source, The Pella Museum)

Acknowledgement is made to the following: the late M. Andronicos for 1(b), 2, 4, 5 and 15; P. Connolly for 3(a); The Mansell Collection for 3(b); Ph. Petsas for 6; C.M. Robertson for 7; NASA for 8(a) and 10; A. Harding for 8(b); Hirmer Fotoarchiv for 9; The National Gallery for 11; The Trustees of the British Museum for 13; The Archaeological Museum for 14; The Pella Museum for 16.

Bibliography

A short list of books in English only:

Andronicos, M., *Vergina: the Royal Tombs and the Ancient City* (Athens, 1984)

Bosworth, A.B., *Conquest and Empire: the Reign of Alexander the Great* (Cambridge, 1988)

Bosworth, A.B., *From Arrian to Alexander* (Oxford, 1988)

Brunt, P.A., *Arrian with an English translation* I (London, 1976) II (1983)

Cook, J.M., *The Persian Empire* (London, 1983)

Engels, D.W., *Alexander the Great and the Logistics of the Macedonian Army* (Berkeley, 1978)

Fraser, P.M., *Ptolemaic Alexandria* (Oxford, 1972)

Green, P., *Alexander of Macedon* (London, 1974)

Griffith, G.T., *The Mercenaries of the Hellenistic World* (Cambridge, 1935)

Hamilton. J.R., *Alexander the Great* (London, 1973)

Hammond, N.G.L., *Alexander the Great: King, Commander and Statesman* (1st edn. New Jersey, 1980 and London, 1981; 2nd edn. Bristol, 1989; 3rd edn. Bristol, 1994)

Hammond, N.G.L., *The Macedonian State* (Oxford, 1989)

Heisserer, A.J., *Alexander the Great and the Greeks of Asia Minor* (Oklahoma, 1980)

Lane Fox, R., *Alexander the Great* (London, 1973)

Marsden, E.W., *Greek and Roman Artillery* (Oxford, 1969)

Milns, R.D., *Alexander the Great* (London, 1968)

Pickard-Cambridge, A.W., *Demosthenes* (London, 1914)

Price, M.J., *Coins of the Macedonians* (British Museum, 1974)

Sekunda, N., *The Army of Alexander the Great* (London, 1984)

Stein, A., *On Alexander's Track to the Indus* (London, 1929)

Tarn, W.W., *Alexander the Great* I (Cambridge, 1948), II (1948 and 1979)

Wilcken, U., *Alexander the Great* (London, 1932 and New York, 1967).

CHAPTER I

The boyhood of Alexander

Philonicus the Thessalian brought to Philip a stallion 'Bucephalus' at an asking price of thirteen talents. So down they went into the plain to put him to the test. The verdict was that he was savage and quite unmanageable. He would let no one mount him, disregarded the voice of any of Philip's company, and reared up to strike at one and all. Thereupon Philip was angry. He ordered the removal of the animal as utterly wild and undisciplined. Alexander was present. 'What a horse they are losing,' he said. 'They cannot handle him because they lack understanding and courage.' Philip at first was silent. But when Alexander persisted time and again and grew impassioned, Philip said, 'Criticise your elders, do you, on the ground that you yourself have a bit more understanding or are better able to manage a horse?' 'This horse at any rate,' Alexander replied, 'I'd manage better than anyone else would.' 'And if you do not manage him, what price will you pay for your rashness?' 'By Heaven,' he said, 'I shall pay you the price of the horse.' There was an outburst of laughter. Then, as soon as the terms of the bet between them were settled in monetary terms, Alexander ran to the horse, took the bridle-rein, and turned him round to face the sun – realising, so it seems, that the horse was completely upset by the sight of his own shadow dancing about in front of him.

For a while Alexander ran alongside the horse and stroked him. Then on seeing that he was full of zest and spirit, he quietly cast aside his cloak, made a flying jump, and was securely astride him. For a time he held him back, using a touch of the reins to check the bit, but without pulling or tearing his mouth, and when he saw the horse had rid himself of the fear and was eager for the race, he let him go and actually urged him on with a bolder cry and with the pressure of his leg. At first those who were with Philip were agonised and silent. But when he turned the horse in the correct manner and rode back proud and jubilant, all the others cheered, but his father, it is said, wept a little for joy, kissed him when he dismounted, and said. 'My boy, seek a kingdom to match yourself. Macedonia is not large enough to hold you.'

On my interpretation we owe this vivid account to an eyewitness, one Marsyas Macedon, who was an exact contemporary of Alexander and many years later wrote a book called *The upbringing of Alexander*. In accordance with the etiquette of the court, King Philip and his chosen Companions were attended daily by some of the Royal Pages; and on this occasion Alexander and Marsyas, both probably in their fifteenth year, were in attendance. Bucephalus, meaning 'Oxhead', so named from the brand-mark on his haunch, was a stallion some four years old. He was 'of large size and noble spirit', as indeed we see him portrayed in the Alexander Mosaic commemorating the Battle of Issus (Plate 12). He had already been broken by his trainer Philonicus. Now he was bridled and available for bareback riding (stirrups and saddle were not to be invented until our Middle Ages) by anyone who wanted to try his paces. His wild and dangerous behaviour daunted everyone except young Alexander.

In his handling of the situation Alexander showed an independence of judgement, an understanding of the horse, and a degree of courage remarkable in a boy of his age. It is no wonder that the spectators were in an agony of apprehension, for Alexander was risking his life. It is a measure of that apprehension that Philip is said to have wept for joy when his son returned in triumph. To those who lived to see Alexander in Asia, this event foreshadowed many occasions on which his independence, intelligence and courage brought triumph after triumph. At the time the wager was won by Alexander, and we may assume that Philip paid the price of the horse, which became Alexander's personal possession, was trained as a warhorse and would not accept any other rider. The words attributed to Philip as 'a saying' were probably not historical; for when father and son were dead, men liked to draw comparisons between them. But there is this much truth in the account: Alexander was striving to compete with his father and he was willing to risk his life to that end.

The following incidents and sayings were probably also taken by Plutarch from the work of Marsyas. Whenever news came that Philip had captured a famous city or won a remarkable victory, Alexander used to say to his contemporaries: 'My father, boys, will be the first to win everything; and for me he will leave no great and brilliant action to carry out together with you.' What he wanted as a young boy was not the enjoyment of pleasure or the spending of his wealth but the winning of 'excellence and glory', that is to excel and be recognised as excelling, and to win glory and be acclaimed as glorious. He had no doubt that one day he would be king. Indeed he felt he had to act already in a manner worthy of a king. That is the point of the story that, when the boys in his company asked him whether he would compete in the foot-race in the Olympic Games (for 'he was swift of foot'), he said, 'Yes, if I am to have kings as fellow-competitors.' To some of his companions he may have seemed precocious; for as Plutarch observed, probably citing Marsyas, 'his ambition kept him serious in mind and lofty in spirit'. But he had also a great gift for friendship of the finest kind. For instance, he was very deeply attached to Hephaestion, and he was loyal almost beyond reason to Harpalus, as we shall see. He carried his friends with him in his ambitions; that is why he spoke of winning renown 'together with you'.

In stature Alexander was below the average height for a man of his time. His voice was loud and assertive. He was of a strong and untiring physique. On the march he would practise mounting and dismounting from a running chariot; and it was this strength and his athleticism which enabled him to jump onto the back of Bucephalus. Whereas his father had rugged features and a strongly masculine aspect, Alexander as a youth was remarkable for the softness of his features, the slight protuberance and the melting glance of his eyes, a fair skin and a ruddy complexion. He probably inherited his looks less from his father than from his mother, Olympias (see Plates 1(a) and 15). Until the age of fourteen he was educated at home where life was simple; for there were no slaves and the womenfolk of the royal family cooked the meals and made the clothes. He must have been much influenced by his paternal grandmother Eurydice, who as Queen Mother was held in the highest esteem. She dedicated altars in the city-centre of the old capital Aegeae to 'Eukleia', 'Fair Fame', which was the guiding star of young Alexander, and she composed a delightful epigram which accompanied a dedication to the Muses:

> Eurydice, daughter of Sirras, dedicated this (statue probably of Hermes) to her city's Muses, because she had in her soul a longing for knowledge. The happy mother of sons growing up, she laboured to learn letters, the recorders of the spoken word.

Alexander too was devoted to the Muses. The *Iliad* of Homer was his favourite, he delighted in the works of Pindar, the great tragedians and the dithyrambic poets, and he had a natural love of learning and of reading.

When Eurydice died, Alexander was about fourteen years of age. There was a separate area at Aegeae where women of the royal family were buried, and it was there that Professor Andronicos excavated the earliest and largest vaulted tomb yet known. He dated it late in the 340s and identified it as 'The Tomb of Eurydice'. Alexander will have been at the ceremony of cremation and at the placing of Eurydice's ashes in the main chamber of the Tomb. He must have admired the *trompe l'oeil* fresco of a façade on its back wall, which created the illusion of a room beyond.

Alexander's strongest emotional attachment was to his mother, Olympias. We have to remember that not only in Macedonia but also in the city-states, the giving of a girl in marriage was arranged by the man who was 'responsible' for her. Commoners used such marriages to strengthen family ties and connections. Kings normally made marriages with, and arranged a daughter's marriage with a member of another royal house for political purposes (or as a cynical writer, Satyrus, put it, 'for purposes of war'). Thus Eurydice, a princess of the royal house of Lyncus, had been given in marriage to Amyntas and lived thereafter in Macedonia. Nor was she the only queen. For the kings and sometimes other males of the royal house practised polygamy in order to ensure a supply of heirs in the direct line and to extend their political connections. Amyntas, for instance, had at least two wives and from them six sons. In the two years 358 and 357 Philip, now in his mid-twenties, took four wives, of whom at least three bore him children. One of the four was Olympias, a princess of the royal house of Molossia, who was given in marriage to Philip by her uncle, Arybbas, the Molossian king. Later writers invented a love-match, which stemmed from a meeting of the young pair at the shrine of the Cabiri on Samothrace; but that is ruled out by consideration of their respective ages. The four wives were treated as equals in queenly prestige.

Olympias had good looks and a fiery temperament. She was intensely religious, sacrificing to the Olympian gods of the Macedonian state and observing the rites of the mystery cults into which she had been initiated. One was the cult of the Cabiri, which was concerned with the fertility of men and animals and with survival after death in the underworld. Offerings were made to the Cabiri as 'The Great Gods' in a circular pit in Samothrace and just outside the city-wall of Pella. Another cult was that of Orpheus, which laid down rules of conduct and promised a happy afterlife to the faithful. The rape of Persephone by Pluto in accordance with Orphic belief was the subject of frescoes in the Tomb of Amyntas and of a painting in the Tomb of Eurydice. A related cult was that of Dionysus, made famous by the *Bacchae* which Euripides composed and produced in Macedonia. It was remarkable for the orgiastic rites of the women who were possessed by the spirit of the god, and it was said that Olympias was 'inspired and possessed more than any others' and handled huge tame snakes in honour of the god. When Alexander was in Asia, she recommended to him a priestly server who was an expert – like herself – in the Bacchic and Argeadic rites, the latter being those of the Macedonian royal tribe.

Her influence on young Alexander was very great. He grew up profoundly religious with a readiness to believe in the manifestation of the gods in many cults and in many places, and with many names; but as far as we know he did not follow her into the mystery cults of Orpheus and the Cabiri. The bond of affection between them was exceptionally strong. As he was to say later, one tear of his mother cancelled innumerable accusations which had been made in letters by Antipater, his senior marshal. And when a rift developed between his father and his mother, he took her side and together with her left the court. However, strong personality though she certainly was, Alexander was not dominated by her; after he became king he gave her many presents but depended entirely on his own judgement in public affairs.

On attaining the age of fourteen in 342 Alexander entered the School of Royal Pages. Its origin was in the distant past, but such detailed knowledge as we have dates from the reigns of Philip and Alexander. He was one of probably fifty boys, the selected sons of leading Macedonians, who at the age of puberty started on a four-year course and graduated on their eighteenth birthday. During these years they lived at or near the court as boarders, and they received instruction in military matters, especially in horsemanship, and in the liberal arts, of which grammar, rhetoric, dialectic, geometry, arithmetic, astronomy and music were the basic subjects. During the last year they served as the king's Bodyguards in battle and as huntsmen on foot, supporting members of the royal family who were required by law to hunt on horseback. See the fresco of the Royal Hunt in Plate 2 and note the statutory uniform of the Royal Page on the extreme right. Physical fitness was essential, and the boys engaged in athletics, gymnastics and wrestling.

The king acted as headmaster, and he alone administered corporal punishment to offenders. For instance, Philip flogged one boy 'unenviably' for falling out of a paramilitary exercise to visit a public house; and in the last year on military service discipline was very strict, even to the extent that a Page was killed by Philip for disobeying orders and laying aside his armour. Philip employed as trainers and teachers capable freemen (not slaves as was often the case in private education at Athens). One of them, Leonidas, a relation of Olympias, was 'a man of stern character' who was described as Alexander's second father and personal professor. He used to examine Alexander's boxes in case Olympias had packed some delicacy for him, and he reprimanded the boy for being extravagant in throwing too much incense on an altar-fire. Alexander evidently regarded him as a Mr Chips, for he later sent him sixteen tons of incense from Egypt.

In 342 Philip hired Aristotle at a handsome salary to teach 'philosophy', which embraced both practical and theoretical knowledge. Lessons and seminars were held usually in the open air in the sanctuary of the Nymphs near Mieza, a beautiful place with natural grottos in the limestone, which was visited by sightseers in Plutarch's day and still is so visited. The influence of Aristotle on Alexander was profound. Alexander accepted as correct Aristotle's views on cosmology, geography, botany, zoology and medicine and therefore took scientists with his army to Asia, and he was fascinated by Aristotle's lectures on logic, metaphysics, the nature of poetry, and the essence of politics. Above all he learnt from Aristotle to put faith in the intellect. In their personal relationship the boy's admiration developed into a deep affection, and they shared a special interest in establishing the text of the *Iliad*. No doubt Aristotle hoped to guide the future king in the performance of his duties, even as his own teacher, Plato, had tried to guide the younger Dionysius as the ruler of Syracuse. To that end he wrote for Alexander a treatise *On Kingship*, which unfortunately has not survived. Whether it had any effect when Alexander came to the throne may be doubted. But in 336, having been elected to command the joint forces of the Greeks and the Macedonians for the war against Persia, Alexander showed his regard for 'philosophy' during a visit to the ascetic philosopher Diogenes by remarking, 'If I were not Alexander, I would indeed be Diogenes.'

To be the son of the headmaster of the School of Pages cannot have been easy for a young boy who had a strongly competitive spirit. That Philip loved his son and admired his courage is clear from the account of the taming of Bucephalus. Alexander probably reciprocated that love; for his father had strong affections, a charismatic personality and cultured interests. That Alexander admired him exceedingly for his achievements goes without saying, for in 342 Philip was the leading statesman in the Greek world and had made his country the leading military power in Europe. From 342 onwards father and son were in close contact. As headmaster Philip guided and observed Alexander's progress, and he developed complete confidence in his son's abilities.

It was probably late in 342 that Persian envoys came to the court in the absence of Philip and were entertained by Alexander. They were impressed by his geniality and the perceptive nature of his enquiries about their country and its ruler. In 340, when Philip was undertaking a major campaign in Thrace, he appointed Alexander to act as his deputy, thereby indicating that he intended Alexander to be his successor if he himself should be killed during the campaign. We are told that Philip had had several sons by his wives, but that some died a natural death and others died in war, presumably as Pages. It may be that Alexander's only male sibling surviving in 340 was Arrhidaeus, who was much the same age but was intellectually retarded. The advancement of Alexander brought special prestige to Olympias, who was marked out as the prospective Queen Mother.

As deputy for his father Alexander was entrusted with the royal seal. He therefore carried out the routine duties of the king and with the seal validated documents of state. In particular he carried out the daily sacrifices. He had probably participated in these from the age of fourteen, and now he was qualified to conduct them on behalf of the state and on behalf of the royal family which had its own worship of Heracles Patroüs, that is of Heracles as the ancestor of the Temenidae. During 340 there was a rising by the Maedi in the Strymon valley, which Alexander defeated as commander of Macedonian forces. He captured their capital city, expelled the natives, and refounded the city as 'Alexandropolis' with a mixed population of Macedonians, Greeks and Thracians. Therein he followed the example of his father, who had introduced Macedonian settlers into the Greek city 'Crenides' and renamed it 'Philippi'. Alexander did so no doubt with the approval of his father, who was founding similar mixed settlements in central Thrace in the latter part of 341, one being named 'Philippopolis'. Father and son were evidently in complete accord.

In summer 338 Alexander and the contemporaries of his year graduated. They came of age on their eighteenth birthdays, and they knew what their careers were to be. The School of Pages, like Eton and Winchester in Victorian England, was famous as 'a training-ground of great governors and generals'. Physically fit graduates entered the Companion Cavalry as troopers. Those, like Harpalus, whose physique was impaired, entered the service of the king in an administrative capacity. Alexander emerged from the School with flying colours. He had won distinction as a cavalryman mounted on his warhorse Bucephalus, as a fearless huntsman, and as a deputy of the king. His future was assured, and he had every expectation that one day in the future he would be elected by the Assembly of Macedonians to be their king.

The strand in his personality which needs to be emphasised is his religious faith. Since childhood he had worshipped Heracles Patroüs, the son of Zeus and a mortal woman, and through his mother he was descended from Achilles, son of the goddess Thetis and a mortal, Peleus. In his mother's veins there was also the blood of a son and a daughter of Priam, King of Troy. To Alexander, Heracles and Achilles were not fantasies of poetic imagination but real people, who expected their descendants to excel as warriors and as benefactors of mankind. He hoped to rival or even to surpass them. Everything in his upbringing had conspired to instil in him a profound belief in the Olympian gods: daily sacrifice in the company of his father, participation in religious festivals, proximity to the throne of Zeus on Mount Olympus, and the religiosity of the Macedonian people. His father's coins proclaimed a devotion to Zeus, Apollo and Heracles; and as Alexander grew up, he saw his father triumph as the champion of Apollo in a 'Sacred War'. He too hoped that the gods would inspire him to excel in their service.

CHAPTER II

The world of Philip as king and Alexander as prince

1. The setting of Alexander's birth and boyhood

In 356, the year of Alexander's birth, a political pamphleteer called Isocrates wrote of the Greek-speaking world, 'Every part of Greece is filled and obsessed with war and revolutions and massacres and innumerable evils.' This terrible situation was the result of a century of internecine wars between city-state and city-state and of internal revolutions in most city-states, which had bred fierce hatreds and led to atrocities on a scale only too familiar in modern times. Many wars arose from local frontier-disputes, for instance between Athens and Thebes over the possession of Oropus, and were apt to recur with any change in the strength of the contestants. Major wars were initiated by states which wished to exercise leadership over other states, and then competed with one another. Thus in 460 Athens, already in control of many maritime states, started a fifteen-year war against Sparta, the leader of a group of land-powers; and in 431 she embarked on a second such war, which ended disastrously for her in 404. Undaunted, she made two further attempts, one starting in 394 and the other in 377. Her last venture ended with defeat at the hands of some of her subject-states in 356. Sparta fought two successful wars against Athens, but in the fourth century her despotic conduct as an imperial power led to revolts and to defeat by a new rival, Thebes, in 371.

Thereafter Sparta and Athens combined in war against Thebes and her associates. In 362 an indecisive battle was fought at Mantinea in the Peloponnese, in which most city-states of the mainland took part. In 356, when Athens was at war with her subject-states, Thebes tried to discipline her neighbour Phocis, which was a reluctant 'ally', but the result was that the leader of a Phocian political party seized the temple of Apollo at Delphi. That was the beginning of what became 'The Sacred War' in which at first all prisoners were executed. It was destined to last ten years, during which most states of the mainland were involved.

These general wars were in some ways less damaging than internal revolutions in city-states, which were initiated by party-leaders and often led to intervention by an outside power. A terrifying example at

Corcyra in 427 was described by Thucydides. The 'democrats' there had the support of an Athenian fleet, and some four hundred 'oligarchs' sought sanctuary in the temple of Hera. The democrats persuaded fifty to come out and stand trial, and then condemned them all to death.

> The mass of the suppliants slew each other there in the consecrated ground; while some hanged themselves upon the trees, and others destroyed themselves as they were severally able. During seven days the Corcyraeans were engaged in butchering those of their fellow-citizens whom they regarded as their enemies .... Death thus raged in every shape; and as usually happens at such times, there was no length to which violence did not go; sons were killed by their fathers, and suppliants dragged from the altar or slain upon it; while some were walled up in the temple of Dionysus and died there. So bloody was the march of revolution (*stasis*) .... Later on, one may say, the whole Hellenic world was convulsed .... The sufferings which revolution entailed upon the cities were many and terrible, such as have occurred and always will occur, as long as the nature of mankind remains the same. (trs. R. Crawley).

Any civil war of this kind bequeathed a legacy of hatred and a desire for revenge, which frequently led to a further civil war. In 353 Plato, having visited the city-states in Sicily where revolution and counter-revolution were endemic, wrote thus of *stasis*.

> To this there is never any end. What seems to be an end always links on to a new beginning, so that this circle of strife is likely to destroy utterly both factions, those of dictatorship and those of democracy alike. The Greek tongue will almost die out in Sicily as it becomes a province of Carthage and Italy.

How was the decline to be arrested? In 360-350 Plato was composing his last dialogue, *Laws*, in which he described his ideal city-state. He believed that his system of state-education would so inspire the citizens under specified economic and social conditions that they would obey their rulers, namely the laws. This was an intellectual's long-term solution. Other thinkers wanted a quicker reform. In 355 Xenophon, having written his *History of Greek Affairs* from 411 to 362, saw the need to set up in Greece 'Guardians of the Peace' (*eirenophylakes*), and he thought that if Athens abandoned her interventionist policy she might be able to become the mediator of such a peace. As a first step he urged Athens to persuade the Phocians to leave Delphi. Isocrates too advised Athens to abandon her imperial ambitions and to concentrate on a policy of peace, but he did not think her capable of leading the other states towards reconciliation. Instead, in 356-355, he wrote an open *Letter* to Archidamus, the King of Sparta, in which he proposed that Archidamus as reconciler should wean the city-states from 'their madness and contentiousness' and lead them in a crusade against Persia. These proposals went unheeded, and the ensuing Sacred War plunged the states into further confusion and slaughter.

There were two parts of the Greek-speaking world at this time which did not suffer from revolution and did not seek to impose rule over the city-states. In Epirus there were three clusters of tribal states, called Molossia, Thesprotia and Chaonia, and although a tribal state might move from one cluster to another cluster, each state remained a tight-knit community (a *koinon* as it was called). The strongest cluster in 356 was the Molossian state. Its monarchy had exceptional prestige because the royal family, it was believed, was descended from Neoptolemus, son of Achilles. These states held the frontier against the Illyrians, whose institutions were fairly similar. In the fourth century down to 360 they were outfought by a cluster of Illyrian states which formed around the Dardanians (in Kosovo and Metohija), whose king Bardylis developed a strong economy. In 385 the Molossians lost 15,000 men in battle and were saved from subjection only by a Spartan army. They suffered losses again in 360.

The other part of the Greek-speaking world extended from Pelagonia in the north to Macedonia in the south. It was occupied by several tribal states, which were constantly at war against Illyrians, Paeonians and Thracians. Each state had its own monarchy. Special prestige attached to the Lyncestae whose royal family, the Bacchiadae, claimed descent from Heracles, and to the Macedonians, whose royal family had a similar ancestry. Although these tribal states occasionally fought one another, each was close-knit and free from revolution (*stasis*). They suffered most from the Dardanians who raided far and wide, even reaching the Thermaic Gulf where they imposed a puppet-king on the Macedonians from 393 to 391. Thereafter Pelagonia and Lyncus were frequently overrun, and in 359 the Macedonian king Perdiccas and 4,000 Macedonians were killed in battle against the Dardanians.

In the opinion of the city-states these tribal states were backward and unworthy of the Greek name, although they spoke dialects of the Greek language. According to Aristotle, monarchy was the mark of people too stupid to govern themselves. The city-states, on the other hand, with the exception of Sparta, had rid themselves of monarchy centuries ago. They governed themselves democratically or oligarchically, and their citizens were highly individualistic. There were other great differences. The northern states lived largely by transhumant pastoralism, used barter more than currency, and had no basis of slaves, whereas the city-state populations lived largely in cities, had capitalist economies and employed very large numbers of slaves, even in agriculture. Northerners herded their flocks, worked the land, and served as soldiers in person, whereas in the fourth century the most sophisticated southerners, the Athenians, preferred to leave labour to slaves and foreigners, and hired mercenaries for wars overseas.

The Balkan tribes beyond the Greek-speaking world were continually at war. For as Herodotus said of the Thracians, 'to live by war and rapine is the most honourable way of life, and the agricultural worker is the least esteemed'. The well-armed aristocrats of the Thracian tribes engaged in wide-ranging raids, such as that led by Sitalces, the king of the Thracian Odrysae, into Macedonia in 429. The Paeonians (in southeast Yugoslavia) and the Illyrians (in Albania) were equally warlike, and they too engaged in rapine. In the raids they carried off men, women and children as well as goods and livestock. One Illyrian tribal group, the Ardiaei, boasted at this time that it had acquired 300,000 serfs.

2. The Macedonian State

Wars not for conquest but for survival were the lot of the Macedonians. The institutions of the country were therefore designed for military efficiency. The population lived mainly in towns which they called 'cities' (*poleis*), because each had its own citizenship (e.g. *Pellaios*) and its system of government with magistrates, council and assembly. Each city trained its own militia for defence, and the training in the time of Philip was educational as well as military. The cities were subject to the rule of the central government, which consisted of two elements – the king and the King's Men under arms. When a king died, his successor was elected by the King's Men meeting under arms in assembly. If he obtained their confidence, his powers were very extensive. He sacrificed to the gods on behalf of the state, conducted the religious festivals, commanded the forces in person, and initiated diplomatic relations. He owned all mineral deposits, stands of fine timber, large areas of land and hunting grounds. He controlled recruitment into the forces of the King's Men from the city militia, directed promotion and enforced discipline. He brought matters of policy before the assembly of the King's Men, and he had to persuade them that he was conducting their affairs properly. In particular he could go to war only if he was assured of their support. When there was suspicion of treason, the king prosecuted and the defendant spoke before the assembly of the King's Men, which delivered the verdict and put it into effect. Thus the powers of the assembly were sovereign, but they were exercised only rarely. In the critical moments when raiders burst into Macedonia the King's Men went into action at his order.

Citizenship as 'Macedones', and with it membership of the assembly, was held only by the King's Men, who had the honour of being the king's 'Companions'. From them he selected his commanders and administrators, whom he called his 'Friends' and in a special sense his 'Compan-

ions'. On occasion and at his own discretion he consulted a group of
them, but he was not bound to accept their advice and they had no
constitutional standing. Many of them had graduated from the School
of Pages. Outstanding service was rewarded by the king, who granted
the revenues of an estate or other property to the recipient for life. The
Friends could rise no higher, for the Macedones would recognise as king
only a member of the royal family. The King's Men were divided into
two categories. In the reign of Philip the cavalrymen wore a metal
cuirass and a metal helmet, wielded a lance with a blade at either end,
and rode bareback into action. They had a long tradition of excellence
as 'heavy-armed cavalry', which required much training in horsemanship (see Fig. 1 (a)). The infantrymen had been organised as 'heavy-
armed' troops only in 369. Ten years later Philip re-equipped them with
his new weapon, the sixteen-foot pike, a small shield suspended from
the neck, helmet and greaves. They fought, like the 'hoplites' of the
city-states, in a solid phalanx of men, shoulder to shoulder, eight to ten
men deep. The pike outreached the seven-foot spear which the hoplite
wielded with one arm, so much so that a phalanx presented four
pike-heads to a hoplite's single spearhead (see Fig. 1 (b)). Whereas the
'Cavalry Companions' provided their own mounts and equipment, the
king supplied the 'Infantry Companions' (*pezhetairoi*) with pikes and
equipment from his own resources. To wield the pike and to maintain
the formation of the phalanx required intensive training and physical
fitness.

1. (a) A Companion Cavalryman

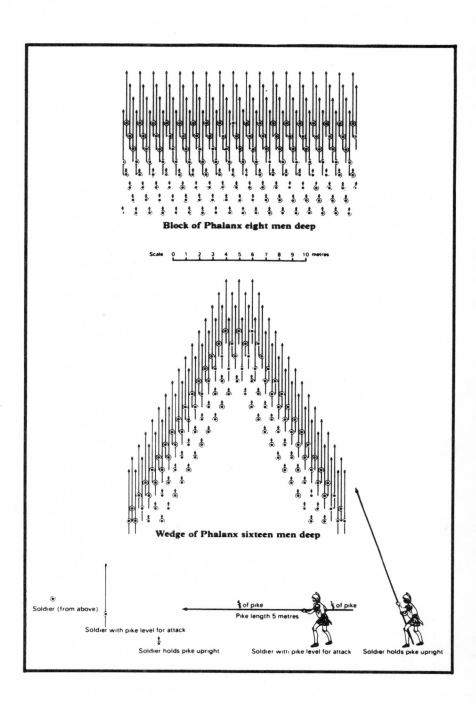

Block of Phalanx eight men deep

Scale 0 1 2 3 4 5 6 7 8 9 10 metres

Wedge of Phalanx sixteen men deep

Soldier (from above)

Soldier with pike level for attack

Soldier holds pike upright

⅓ of pike   ⅔ of pike

Pike length 5 metres

Soldier with pike level for attack

Soldier holds pike upright

1 (b) The pikeman-phalanx

CHAPTER III

The influence of Philip

1. From weakness to strength in 346

Philip took control in 359 not as king but as guardian of his nephew, Amyntas IV, a young boy. His country was on the verge of collapse, having lost 4,000 men in battle, while the victorious forces of Bardylis were in occupation of towns in Pelagonia and Lyncus and threatened to invade Macedonia itself in 358. Philip put heart into his army by holding assembly after assembly, rearming and training his infantry, and inspiring them with his own indomitable spirit. In spring 358 he convinced the assembly of the King's Men that they should take the offensive. In a decisive battle with almost equal numbers he inflicted a crippling defeat on Bardylis, established the east bank of Lake Lychnitis (Ochrid) as his frontier, and confirmed a treaty of peace with Bardylis by marrying his daughter, Audata. His victory freed Pelagonia, Lyncus and the other tribal states of West Macedonia, then called 'Upper Macedonia', from raiding and occupation by the Dardanians. He now invited the peoples of these states to abolish their monarchies and to enter the Macedonian kingdom with equal rights to those of the Macedonians. The invitation was accepted, and Philip showed his respect for his new subjects by marrying Phila, a member of the Elimeote royal family.

By this act, which Philip must have taken with the agreement of the Macedonian assembly, he doubled the resources and the manpower of the kingdom. It was important to raise the standard of life in Upper Macedonia to that of Lower Macedonia, and for that purpose he founded new towns there in which young men received educational and military training. As they graduated he recruited the best of them to enter the king's army and become members of the assembly as 'Macedones'. His innovations were so successful that the number of his Companion Cavalrymen rose from 600 in 358 to 2,800 in 336, and that of the Companion Infantrymen from 10,000 in 358 to 27,000 in 336. Alexander was to inherit the most formidable army in Europe.

By a combination of diplomatic skill and military opportunism Philip defeated Illyrian tribes beyond his western frontier, forced the Paeonians to become his subjects, gained posession of Greek colonies on his coast, defended Amphipolis against the Athenians and Crenides –

2. Alexander's Kingdom of Macedonia

renamed Philippi – against the Thracians, and advanced his eastern
frontier to the river Nestus (Mesta), all by late 354. He was fortunate
in that Athens was distracted by the war against her subject-states
(357-355) and Thebes by the war against Phocis, which became the
Sacred War (355-346); and he managed to make a treaty of alliance with
his powerful neighbour, the Chalcidian League of city-states, on condition that neither party would enter into separate negotiations with
Athens. During these eventful years he confirmed an alliance with the
ruling house of Larissa in Thessaly by marrying a lady of that house,
Philinna, and an alliance with the Molossian royal house by marrying
Olympias in 357, as we have seen (above, p. 4). In that year, 357, he was
elected king in place of Amyntas IV.

The Sacred War was declared by a majority of the members of the
Amphictyonic League, of which the Council laid down rules of conduct
in religious and other matters and in particular administered the
temple of Apollo at Delphi. That majority was formed by the peoples of
Thessaly, Central Greece and Boeotia; but the minority included Athens, Sparta, Achaea, and later Pherae in Thessaly, which all entered
into alliance with Phocis. Other states showed sympathy with one side
or the other. The Phocian occupiers of Delphi survived by looting the
treasures and hiring mercenary soldiers, and in 353 an able leader,
Onomarchus, launched an offensive against Thebes and sent 7,000
mercenaries to support Pherae against the other Thessalians. This was
Philip's opportunity; for the Thessalians asked him for help and he
enabled them to win a victory. But Onomarchus came north and
inflicted two defeats on Philip. He withdrew, as he said, 'like a ram, to
butt the harder'. In 352 Philip and his Thessalian allies won a decisive
victory over Onomarchus' army of 500 cavalry and 20,000 infantry, to
the amazement of the city-states. Philip paraded his championship of
Apollo. For his soldiers went into battle wearing the laurel wreath
associated with the god, and on his orders 3,000 prisoners were
drowned as guilty of sacrilege. He also championed the cause of liberty
and federalism against the dictators of Pherae, whom he now expelled
together with their mercenaries. His reward was election as President
of the Thessalian League, which placed its forces and its revenues at his
disposal. At this time he married Nicesipolis, a member of the leading
family in Pherae.

His chief fear was a coalition of Athens and the Chalcidian League;
for the Athenian fleet could then blockade his coast and the armies of
the two states could invade the coastal plain of Macedonia. In 349, when
the Chalcidian League violated its treaty and entered into alliance with
Athens, Philip invaded Chalcidice and despite the efforts of Athens
captured Olynthus, the capital of the League, in 348. He held the
Olynthians responsible for breaking the religious oaths which had
bound them under the treaty. He razed the city and sold the population

into slavery. He destroyed two other city-states (Apollonia and Stagira) and incorporated the peoples of the Chalcidic peninsula – both Chalcidians and Bottiaeans – into the Macedonian kingdom.

Meanwhile the Phocians were running short of funds and so of mercenary soldiers, and the Thebans had been hammered into a condition of weakness. Who would administer the *coup de grâce*? Envoys from most of the city-states hastened to Pella, hoping to enlist Philip on their side in 346. At that time Alexander, as a boy of ten, will have watched with interest as his father found gracious words for all of them and committed himself to none. When the envoys were on their way home to their respective states, the Macedonian army reached Thermopylae, where the Phocian leader and his 8,000 mercenaries accepted the terms offered by Philip: to surrender their weapons and horses, and to go wherever they wished. The Phocian people were now defenceless. They 'placed themselves in the hands of Philip ... and he sat in council with representatives of the Boeotians and the Thessalians'. He had already made peace and alliance with Athens, and he had invited Athens to send representatives to this council. The invitation was refused on the advice of Hegesippus and Demosthenes.

Philip had acted as the champion of Apollo. It was for him a matter of religious conviction. He therefore entrusted the settlement to the Council of the Amphictyonic League, on which his allies in Thessaly and Central Greece had a majority of the votes, and they no doubt listened to his advice. The terms for the Phocians were mild by Greek standards (one Greek state proposed the execution of all the men): disarmament, division into village-settlements, payment of an indemnity to Apollo and expulsion from the Amphictyony. In their place the Macedonians were elected members. The two votes of Phocis on the Council were transferred to the Macedonian state. On the advice of Philip the Council 'published regulations for the custody of the oracle and for everything else appertaining to religious practice, to common peace and to concord among the Greeks'. Within Boeotia Thebes had a free hand: she destroyed three cities which had been forced to submit to the Phocians and sold their populations into slavery. She would have preferred to treat Phocis similarly.

2. Philip's policy towards the city-states

Philip's aim was to bring the city-states into concord and set up a Treaty of Common Peace, of which Macedonia and they would be members. This was in the spirit of the proposals made by Xenophon and Isocrates in 356-355, and it coincided with the tenor of a political pamphlet, entitled *Philip*, which Isocrates published in 346 just before the capitulation of Phocis. He advised Philip as the ruler of the strongest state in Europe to bring the city-states into concord, lead them against Persia, liberate the Greeks in Asia, and found there new cities to absorb the surplus population of the Greek mainland. The price of concord was acceptance of the *status quo* and the abnegation of any interventionist policy. Despite Philip's offers to set up a Common Peace, Athens, Sparta and Thebes went their own way in the name of 'freedom', and Philip realised in 341 that he might have to use force rather than persuasion if he wanted to exercise control.

Athens depended for her food-supply on imports of grain from South Russia, which had to pass through the Bosporus and the Hellespont. On the European side Byzantium was able to exact 'benevolences' from shipping at the Bosporus, and Athens through her colonies on the Chersonese (the Gallipoli peninsula) could do likewise in the Hellespont. The Asian side was held by Persia, which had put down a series of revolts on the coast of the Mediterranean and could now muster a huge fleet. Philip approached this sensitive area through a conquest of the tribes of eastern Thrace. It was during the Thracian campaign in 340 that he appointed Alexander at the age of sixteen to act as his deputy in Macedonia (above, p. 6). From then on Alexander was fully aware of Philip's plans.

Events moved rapidly. Philip laid siege to Perinthus and Byzantium, whereupon Athens declared war. He was thwarted by Persia and Athens acting in collusion. He summoned Alexander to join him, invaded the Dobruja, defeated a Scythian king there, and extended his control of eastern Thrace to the Danube. During his return to Macedonia in summer 339 he had to fight his way through the land of the Triballi, a powerful tribe which captured some of his booty. In Greece another Sacred War had started, and the command of the Amphictyonic forces was offered to and accepted by Philip in the autumn. The sacrilegious state which he had to discipline was Amphissa. He took his Macedonian army and troops from some Amphictyonic states not towards Amphissa but through Phocis to the border of Boeotia, in order to threaten Thebes, which though his 'friend and ally' had been behaving in a hostile manner, and to act against Athens, with which he was still at war. The envoys which he sent to Thebes were outbid by the envoys of Athens. In violation of her treaty Thebes joined Athens and sided with Amphissa. Philip tried more than once to negotiate terms of peace, but in vain. The decisive battle was fought at Chaeronea in Boeotia in August 338. The troops of Boeotia, Athens, Megara, Corinth and Achaea numbered some 35,000; those of Macedonia and her allies somewhat less.

Alexander, in command of the Companion Cavalry, pitched his tent by the river Cephissus. When his father's tactics created a breach in the opposing phalanx Alexander charged through the gap, and it was he who led the attack on the Sacred Band of 300 Thebans. The Macedonian victory was total. Thebes was treated harshly as the violator of its oaths. Athens was treated generously. Alexander led a guard of honour which brought the ashes of the Athenian dead to Athens – a unique tribute to a defeated enemy – and the 2,000 Athenian prisoners were liberated without ransom. As Philip advanced into the Peloponnese, his enemies submitted and his allies rejoiced. Sparta alone was defiant. He ravaged her territory and he gave some frontier regions to his allies; but he did not attack the city. During his return northwards he left garrisons at Acrocorinth, Thebes and Ambracia. Meanwhile the Council of the Amphictyonic League reduced the restrictions on the Phocians, made the Amphissaeans live in villages and approved the acts of Philip.

The future of the city-states was in Philip's hands. He decided to create the 'Greek Community' (*to koinon ton Hellenon*), in which the states would swear to keep the peace among themselves, maintain existing constitutions, permit changes only by constitutional methods, and combine in action against any violator of the 'Common Peace', whether internal or external. His proposal, made in autumn 338, was accepted by the states in spring 337, and a 'Common Council' was established, of which the members represented one or more states in proportion to their military and naval strengths. The Council was a sovereign body: its decisions were sent to the states for implementation, not for discussion. The military forces and the naval forces at the disposal of the Common Council were defined: the former amounted to 15,000 cavalry and 200,000 infantry, and the number of warships, which is not stated in our sources, was later to be 160 triremes, manned by crews totalling some 30,000 men. Thus the Greek Community far outdid the Macedonian State in the size of the forces it could deploy. The Council had disciplinary, judicial and financial powers which were binding on the member-states. If we look for a modern analogy, we should look rather to the United States of America than to the European Community.

The next step was the creation of an offensive and defensive alliance between the Greek Community and the Macedonian State for all time. Because Macedonia was already at war with Persia, the Council declared war on Persia late in 337 and voted that the commander of the joint forces should be Philip. Within the Community his title was 'Hegemon', and the powers of his office were carefully defined. In the spring of 336 the vanguard of the joint forces crossed to Asia under the command of three Macedonian generals whom Philip appointed, and arrangements were made for the stipulated forces of the coalition to follow in the autumn with Philip as overall commander.

The brilliance of Philip's political initiative, power of persuasion and effective leadership is obvious. He brought into being the combination of a newly created Greek State, self-standing and self-governing, and a Macedonian State which was unrivalled in military power. If that combination should succeed in liberating the Greek cities in Asia and in acquiring extensive territory, it would provide a cure for many of the troubles of the Greek world. Theopompus, critical of Philip in many ways, entitled his history *Philippica* 'because Europe had never produced such a man altogether as Philip, son of Amyntas'.

3. Relations between Philip and his grown-up son

Alexander, who had come of age just before his command at the Battle of Chaeronea, was fully aware of Philip's plans and of the opposition to them; for he was in his father's confidence as his intended successor. The aim of Philip in Asia was revealed when he asked the Pythian priestess at Delphi whether he would 'conquer the king of the Persians'. Whereas the Greek Community intended to liberate the Greeks in Asia and punish Persia for past wrongs, Philip intended to carry his war to the logical conclusion, the defeat of Persia. Within Macedonia there was no doubt some dissent, due not only to the strain of war after war but also to the fear of defeat overseas and of risings in Europe. For it was no secret that many politicians in the city-states were opposed to the very concept of a Greek Community which was in their eyes a violation of city-state independence, and that they regarded the Amphictyonic Council and the Common Council as organs of Macedonian domination in Greece. The Balkan situation was far from secure, with the Odrysians and the Scythians only recently defeated and with the Triballi still defiant. Yet Philip was confident of success in the interest of the Greek-speaking world and of Macedonia in particular.

In battle the king fought as the leading man of his Cavalry Guard or his Infantry Guard. Philip was wounded seven times in action, and he owed his survival as much to the courage of his Bodyguards and his Pages as to his physical strength and his defensive armour. The projected campaign in Asia would put at risk both his life and Alexander's, and the only other surviving son, Arrhidaeus, was not capable of rule. Philip was not alone in wishing that a son of his should succeed him; for the Macedonians believed that the divine favour went from father to son in the royal house. In 341 he married Meda, the daughter of a king of the Getae. By then the four wives of the early years, 358-356, were passing or past the child-bearing age, and he hoped no doubt that Meda would bear him a son. In 339 he may have married a Scythian princess, whose hand had been offered to him by the king in the Dobruja, Atheas. It was probably early in 337 that Philip took in marriage not a member of his own royal house nor a princess of another royal house, but a young Macedonian commoner, Cleopatra. She was the ward of Attalus, a Bodyguard of the king; and this Attalus had been selected to command the Macedonian infantry which was about to invade Asia. Such a marriage was not in the Macedonian tradition, for it introduced a commoner family into the royal circle. It was said by a later writer,

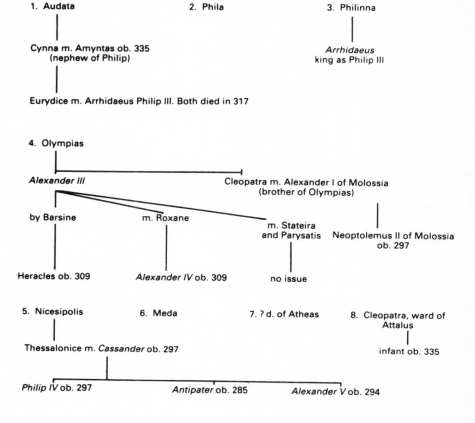

1. Audata

Cynna m. Amyntas ob. 335
(nephew of Philip)

Eurydice m. Arrhidaeus Philip III. Both died in 317

2. Phila

3. Philinna

Arrhidaeus
king as Philip III

4. Olympias

Alexander III

Cleopatra m. Alexander I of Molossia
(brother of Olympias)

by Barsine   m. Roxane   m. Stateira
and Parysatis   Neoptolemus II of Molossia
ob. 297

·Heracles ob. 309   *Alexander IV* ob. 309   no issue

5. Nicesipolis   **6. Meda**   **7. ? d. of Atheas**   **8. Cleopatra, ward of Attalus**

Thessalonice m. *Cassander* ob. 297

infant ob. 335

Philip IV ob. 297   *Antipater* ob. 285   *Alexander V* ob. 294

Note Those who became king of Macedonia are in italics.

3. Philip's wives and descendants

Satyrus, that Philip, now in his mid-forties, had fallen passionately in love with the young girl and so made what was to prove a disastrous marriage.

Whatever Philip's motives, the marriage caused a rift between him and Olympias, and further between him and Alexander. The affairs of royalty were then, as now, of the greatest interest to journalistic writers, for whom scandal-mongering was more important than truthful reporting. Such a writer was Satyrus, who wrote a *Life of Philip* in the middle of the third century. According to his account, of which only a summary survives in secondary sources, the wedding banquet was the scene of the following fracas.

As Attalus toasted the bride, he proclaimed to the assembled guests: 'From now on those born to be our kings will be legitimate sons and not bastards.' Thereupon Alexander threw his tankard at Attalus, and Attalus hit Alexander with his cup. Philip drew his sword to kill his son; but he tripped, fell and collapsed in a drunken stupor. Alexander, turning to the company, said, 'See, you fellows, here is the man who plans to cross from Europe to Asia. Why, he has fallen flat on his face in crossing from one couch to another.' Olympias, already outraged because Philip was bringing one girl after another into her marriage-bed, let fly at Philip for trying to kill her son. Philip responded by divorcing her on a charge of adultery. Alexander sided with his mother. He went with her to Molossia, where she persuaded the young king to mount an invasion of Macedonia. But Philip was too clever. He gave to the Molossian king the hand of his own daughter in marriage. Alexander stayed away until an urbane Corinthian, called Demaratus, brought Philip to see reason and recall his son. Olympias, however, stayed in Molossia.

The setting of the story is Athenian, not Macedonian. Polygamy did not exist at Athens; thus for Philip to marry Cleopatra was to treat Olympias as a cast-off and her son as a bastard, and all other 'wives' of Philip were his mistresses or simply prostitutes. The idea that the Molossians would or even could invade Macedonia in 337 was absurd. The colourful story may confidently be dismissed as a fiction. But the fact remains that the marriage did cause a serious rift. We know this from a digression in the history of Arrian, whose source at this point was Ptolemy or/and Aristobulus, both being contemporaries of Alexander. The passage runs thus:

> When Philip was still king, Harpalus was exiled because he was loyal to Alexander. So too Ptolemy, son of Lagus, Nearchus, son of Androtimus, Erigyius, son of Larichus, and Laomedon his brother on the same charge, because suspicion existed between Philip and Alexander when Philip married Eurydice and dishonoured Alexander's mother, Olympias. On the death of Philip they were restored from the exile they had incurred on his account.

Of what honour had Olympias been deprived? The answer may be provided by Philip's renaming of Cleopatra as 'Eurydice', evidently at the time of the marriage. As we have seen, Eurydice was the name of Philip's mother, who had been held in the highest honour and had been buried in a magnificent tomb in about 340 (above, p. 3). These tributes had been paid to her as Queen Mother, presiding over the women's quarters in the Palace. On her death Olympias evidently succeeded to her position as Queen-Mother-to-be of the son whom Philip was promoting to the position of deputy and so of being his chosen successor in the event of his own death. But to call his new wife 'Eurydice' was surely to demote Olympias and put Cleopatra in her place. In itself that might have been a matter affecting only the women's quarters. But there was the added implication that 'Eurydice' would become Queen-Mother-to-be if she should bear a son to Philip, and that son would displace Alexander as Philip's choice of successor. It is true that such a son would probably be a minor, unless Philip lived on into old age, but Alexander knew that the Macedonians had elected minors in the recent past as their kings – Orestes, Perdiccas and Amyntas. So too the close friends and contemporaries of Alexander realised that he might be superseded and that their chances of promotion in his service would be impaired. Alexander and those friends must have committed some public act of defiance for Alexander to have fallen from favour, and for them to have been exiled, and to have been kept in exile even after Philip and Alexander were reconciled.

4. The invasion of Asia and the death of Philip

A different story about the rift between father and son was given by Plutarch. It also ended with the exiling of Alexander's friends, but this time in connection not with the dishonouring of Olympias as in Arrian's account but with a proposed marriage between Arrhidaeus and the daughter of an Asian satrap. The connection is obviously false; for the statement by Arrian, being derived from Ptolemy and/or Aristobulus, is to be accepted as true. The rest of the story too is false. It is that Pixodarus, the satrap of Caria in the Persian Empire, wanted to marry his daughter to Arrhidaeus, the half-wit son of Philip; that Alexander's friends and Olympias told Alexander he was thereby about to be displaced from the succession; and that Alexander sent a message to Pixodarus that Arrhidaeus was 'a bastard' and Alexander himself was a better match. When Philip heard of this, he upbraided Alexander. Hence the rift and the exiling. When we remember that Pixodarus was a Persian subject, we can see that he would have acted only in complete secrecy, and that a marriage alliance had no value for Philip's purpose while the Persian Empire was intact in Asia.

Whatever ideas Philip may have had about an eventual successor, he had need of Alexander in the immediate future, either as commander of the Companion Cavalry on the Asiatic campaign or as deputy in Macedonia during his own absence on that campaign. In 337 Alexander spent some time 'among Illyrians', i.e. at the courts of Illyrian client kings. That was only possible with the approval of Philip and with a military escort. Alexander may have been negotiating with them as a preliminary to the campaign in autumn 337 which Philip undertook against Pleurias, an Illyrian king (probably of the Autariatae in Bosnia). In any case we may date some form of reconciliation between Philip and Alexander, which included Olympias in some way, to within the year 337, because at that time Philip commissioned chryselephantine (gold and ivory) statues of his parents, himself, Olympias and Alexander for public display in the so-called Philippeum at Olympia.

In 336 the centre of attention was the war in Asia. The advance forces of Macedonia and the Greek Community won striking successes under the command of Parmenio, Attalus and Amyntas. For with a supporting fleet they liberated the Greek cities of the west coast as far south as Ephesus, where a statue of Philip was set up in the temple of Artemis. Persia was slow to react. The defence of Asia Minor was entrusted to Memnon, a Rhodian commander of Greek mercenaries, but there was no Persian fleet in the Aegean to support him. Persian agents may have reached the Greek mainland to subsidise anti-Macedonian politicians such as Demosthenes at Athens; but the politicians would not act unless the Persian fleet was in control of the Aegean. The main forces with Philip in command were to land in the autumn, and it was anticipated that during a winter campaign Philip would become master of western Asia Minor.

While the forces of the Greek Community were gathering, Philip chose to make the October festival at Aegeae an international occasion by inviting as his guests envoys of the city-states and leaders of his Balkan subjects. It was at this festival that weddings were celebrated in Macedonia. The ceremonies began with sacrifices to the gods, weddings which included that of Cleopatra, the daughter of Philip and Olympias, to Alexander, the Molossian king, and lavish state banquets. The guests for their part presented gold wreaths to Philip, some as individuals and others as official delegates of Greek city-states, Athens being one of them. The second day was to begin with a religious procession and with musical and dramatic performances in the theatre just below the palace. So just before dawn the theatre was packed with the leading Macedonians and the official guests of the Macedonian State.

The procession was a dazzling display of wealth. It was headed by richly adorned statues of the twelve Olympian gods and an equally magnificent statue of Philip 'worthy of a god, as the king was showing himself enthroned with the twelve gods'. In Macedonian belief the kings were descended from Zeus, the most distinguished of them were worshipped after their death, and it seems from later instances that 'divine honours' were in outstanding cases conferred on a reigning king by the Macedonians. The best explanation of Philip's statue on this occasion is that 'divine honours' had been so conferred, and that he chose to show his elevation to divinity.

When the procession was over, some of Philip's Friends, headed by Alexander as his chosen successor and by the other Alexander, king of Molossia, entered through the *parodos* and took their designated seats in the front row. Then came the Infantry Guardsmen, who posted themselves at the edge of the *orchestra*. Philip entered alone, wearing a white cloak, and stood in the centre of the *orchestra*, acknowledging the cheers of the spectators. The seven Bodyguards, who had entered behind him, fanned out at some distance. Suddenly one of them, Pausanias, sprang forward, stabbed the king and fled down the *parodos*. Three Bodyguards ran to the king's side. Three others – named as Leonnatus, Perdiccas and Attalus – rushed after Pausanias, who tripped and fell. They killed him with their spears. In the *orchestra* the king lay dead.

CHAPTER IV

Alexander establishes his position in Macedonia, Greece and the Balkans

1. The succession and the trial of conspirators

The sight of his father being killed by a Bodyguard must have haunted Alexander for the rest of his life. The memory made him aware of the constant danger of assassination, and of the fact that in the last resort a king could not trust even a chosen Bodyguard. At the moment the first priority was the election of a successor. As many of the King's Men as could be summoned from the neighbourhood met as an assembly under arms in the theatre, where the corpse of Philip was laid out to witness proceedings. Antipater, Philip's senior Friend, presided. The election was not a foregone conclusion, because there was known to be some support for the claims of Amyntas, who had been king as a minor in 359-357, and some for the sons of Aëropus, king in 397-394. The Friends generally gathered round Alexander. One of them, Alexander Lyncestes, a son of Aëropus, was the first to shout 'Alexander, son of Philip', and the assembly elected Alexander with a resounding acclamation. The Friends put on their cuirasses, the King's Men clashed their spears against their shields, and the new king led a procession to the Palace.

Alexander was a fine orator. When the King's Men took the oath of loyalty, he harangued them and assured them that he would pursue the policies of his father, and he asked the envoys of the Greek Community to show towards himself the goodwill which they had shown towards Philip. His first duty was to conduct an inquiry into the circumstances of the assassination. The personal motive of Pausanias was soon established. It began with a homosexual affair between him and a Royal Page. Such affairs were as acceptable as heterosexual relations (indeed often concurrent with them), and formed part of a military tradition which at this time, for instance, commended the Thebans of the Sacred Band as 'pairs of lovers'. When the affair broke down, Pausanias taunted the boy, who took Attalus into his confidence and revealed his intention to commit suicide, which he did in the battle against Pleurias in summer 337. Attalus avenged the boy by inviting Pausanias to dinner, making him drunk and having him sexually abused by a gang of men. Pausanias complained to Philip, who gave him presents and promotion but took no steps against Attalus. In revenge Pausanias murdered Philip. Although the details may be open to question, the substance is correct, because Aristotle who was then at the court wrote that 'Pausanias attacked Philip because Philip let it pass that Pausanias had been sexually abused by those with Attalus'. But the personal motive of Pausanias did not preclude a conspiracy, of which he would be only a part.

Assassination was a hazard for any Macedonian king. For that reason his person was guarded daily by the seven Bodyguards, who were chosen by him from his leading officers, and by day and night by Royal Pages in relays. In addition the royal quarters were protected by men of the Infantry Guard of Macedonians, and in the latter part of Philip's reign by the Royal Hypaspists in their nearby barracks. But these precautions sometimes failed. Archelaus, for instance, was killed during a Royal Hunt in 399, Amyntas II was murdered by a Royal Page in 394, and Alexander II was assassinated during a festival, probably the *Xandica* of spring 367. The trial of any suspects was conducted before the assembly of Macedonians. In 399 three persons were arraigned, two being Royal Pages and the third an ex-Page, and it seems that the verdict was 'not proven', although Aristotle later held them all guilty. For the murder of Amyntas II we have only the name of the Royal Page, Derdas, and he may have acted alone. Alexander II was killed by more than one person, and one of the killers, a married man with children, was executed. Rumours, of course, proliferated. Marsyas Macedon said that the death of Archelaus was accidental, and that the death of Alexander II was due to 'the party of Ptolemy', who in fact was made guardian of Perdiccas and Philip and was therefore trusted at the time. Later reports even made Ptolemy the killer.

Polygamy bred complications. Any newly elected king was likely to have not only half-brothers but also cousins of varying degrees within the royal house. He tried to win their cooperation, for instance by giving a daughter in marriage, as Archelaus did to a son of the Amyntas who became Amyntas II. On the other hand, if they stood out as pretenders to the throne, he tried to have them condemned as traitors. If a man was found guilty of treason by the assembly of Macedonians, the law was that his relatives be put to death. Plato, for instance, wrote that Archelaus killed an uncle and that uncle's son, as well as a half-brother. When Amyntas III died, he had at least two wives, and each of them had borne him three sons. Thus the sons of Eurydice had three half-brothers. All three survived until the reign of Philip, who arranged the death of one; he captured the other two in Olynthus, and no doubt had them tried for treason and executed. Of Philip's cousins two were supported by foreign powers as pretenders, the death of one was obtained by bribery, and the other was surrendered after a battle.

When Philip was assassinated, there was suspicion of a conspiracy. For in trying to escape Pausanias ran not to one horse but to 'the horses at the gateway which had been provided for the flight'. These horses must have been for more than one killer to use. It seemed then that Pausanias had acted alone on impulse, and that another killer or killers had been thwarted. Who was the other intended victim, or victims? Alexander would surely have been one. For if Philip and Alexander, sitting next to one another, had been killed, the kingdom would have been thrown into utter confusion. The circumstantial evidence pointed towards a conspiracy with such a programme.

The trial of the suspects who were identified by Alexander and his assistants was held before an assembly of the Macedonians. A fragmentary description of it has survived from a Hellenistic history. It may be translated thus.

> Those with him in the theatre and those in attendance they [i.e. the Macedonians] acquitted and those round the throne. X [probably the dead man] he delivered to the Macedonians to punish, and they crucified him. The body of Philip he delivered to courtiers to bury.

'He' was Alexander. The corpses of Pausanias and of Philip were there during the trial. In the preceding part of the text other verdicts were no doubt reported, for we know from other sources that two sons of Aëropus were executed 'at the tumulus' where Philip was buried. A third son of Aëropus, called Alexander Lyncestes, of whom we shall hear later, was acquitted on the intercession of Alexander. The three sons of Pausanias were executed in accordance with Macedonian custom.

2. The funeral of Philip and the march to Corinth

The funeral ceremony after the trial was a military occasion. The King's Men paraded under arms, and the corpse of the king was accompanied by his weapons and his armour. A large pyre of wood had been prepared. Alongside it the horses towards which Pausanias had run and the two sons of Aëropus were killed. Some of the harness and the swords of the two men, together with the weapon used in the assassination, were placed on the pyre alongside the corpse of Philip and the corpse of one of his wives. After the cremation the bones of the king and queen were placed in separate gold coffers. The large tomb was still under construction, but the main chamber was almost complete. The coffer of the king, his weapons and armour, and many other paraphernalia were placed in the main chamber, which was then closed. The objects I have mentioned as being on the pyre were later collected and placed on the vaulted roof of the chamber. The antechamber, in which the coffer of the queen was placed, and the façade were completed at leisure. The corpse of Pausanias, crucified on a plank, was set up on top of the façade as a warning to others, and a beautiful fresco was painted below the cornice. When all was complete, the corpse of Pausanias was burnt and the place where he had hung was purified by fire. A wide tumulus of red soil, brought from elsewhere, was raised over the tomb, so that one end of the tumulus covered the Tomb of Amyntas and the other end was available for later burials. The two corpses of the sons of Aëropus were put into the soil. Sacrifice to the dead kings, Amyntas and Philip, was made at the shrine which lay just outside the tumulus.

The king's chamber was closed prematurely because Alexander had to hasten southwards with all speed. His father's death had occurred in the early stages of three great enterprises: the extension of a Balkan Empire from the lower Adriatic to the west coast of the Black Sea, the leadership of the newly formed Greek Community, and the opening campaign in Asia against the Persian Empire. It was expected that Macedonia would reel under the shock, that the succession might be disputed, and that even if Alexander did succeed he was by Greek standards 'a mere youth' at the age of twenty and would not be able to cope with three enterprises. It seemed to be the moment for the enemies of Macedonia to act. Some Thessalians occupied the Tempe Pass, the people of Ambracia expelled the Macedonian garrison and put the democratic party in power, the Aetolians voted to intervene in Acarnania on behalf of some exiled Acarnanians, the Thebans voted to expel the Macedonian garrison, the opposition in Athens became vociferous, and there were stirrings in the Peloponnese. It seemed that the Greek Community was a dead letter; for the Council had taken no action itself, and it was without a *Hegemon*.

Alexander marched south at the head of the Macedonian army. He outflanked the Thessalians by climbing the cliffs of Mount Ossa and occupied Larissa, where the leading clan, the Aleuadae, was pro-Macedonian. He convened the Council of the Thessalian League and was duly appointed President of the League with the same powers as his father. Advancing to Thermopylae, where he had arranged a meeting of the Council of the Amphictyonic League, he was assured of the League's support in Greece. The democracy at Ambracia was approved by Alexander. Thebes was pardoned. The Athenians voted to bring their property from the countryside into the city, in order to withstand a siege, but they also sent envoys to meet Alexander and apologise. He accepted the apology with all politeness, bypassed Attica and halted at Corinth, to which he had summoned the Councillors of the Greek Community.

He knew already that he could count on the support of the Councillors of the northern and central Greek tribes and city-states, and the presence of the Macedonian army was not unnoticed by the other Councillors. Alexander made a charming speech to the Council, and in response it appointed him *Hegemon* with full powers, which were duly specified in writing, and promised him full cooperation in the war against Persia. At Corinth he met Diogenes (above, p. 6). His remark 'if I were not Alexander, I would indeed be Diogenes' carried the meaning 'if I were not already king of Macedonia, President of Thessaly, the favourite of the Amphictyonic League and *Hegemon* of the Greek Community'. His successes had been meteoric, but he knew that they were not assured.

3. Arrangements in the kingdom

Returning to Macedonia for the winter Alexander appointed his own Bodyguards, Friends and Commanding Officers, and 'he busied his soldiers with constant training in the use of their weapons and with tactical exercises'. Some evidence was found that Amyntas was involved in a conspiracy. He had been loyal to Philip, who had given him his daughter Cynna in marriage and had sent him as an envoy to Thebes; and he was both older than Alexander and the son of a king senior to Philip. Whatever the evidence, Amyntas was executed for treason. Reports came from friends in Athens that Demosthenes was receiving subsidies from Persia and was in correspondence with Attalus, the commander of the Macedonian infantry in Asia, with whom he was very popular. Alexander was apprehensive, and it may be that Attalus admitted that he had been in touch with Demosthenes and expressed repentance. In any event Alexander decided to put him on trial for treason. He sent an officer to arrest Attalus, and if he should resist arrest to kill him, as indeed happened. The corpse was probably brought back for trial and condemned. The relatives of Attalus were executed, among them his ward Cleopatra, renamed Eurydice, and her child by Philip.

Within the kingdom Alexander made arrangements which would last during his intended absence first in the Balkans and then in Asia. Inscriptions have been published recently revealing actions which are probably to be dated not to this winter but to that of 335/4. One reads: 'King Alexander gave to Macedonians Calindoea and the places around Calindoea – Thamiscia, Camacaea and Tripoatis' (these three being the territories of three towns). Alexander was continuing the policy of Philip, who had created a number of 'cities of Macedonians' (we know of such at Oesyme renamed 'Emathia', Apollonia in Mygdonia and Pythion in Perrhaebia). It was a gift because the king owned spear-won land and disposed of it and its inhabitants as he thought fit. The Calindoeans – a Bottiaean people – were planted as a community elsewhere in the kingdom. The Macedonian assembly decided which Macedonian population was to be transplanted *en bloc* to Calindoea, where they took over the city installations and received the revenues levied upon the three territories, which were worked by the townsmen who continued to live in their towns. The Macedonians of Calindoea were engaged not in farming but in military duties and in administration; and in particular they guarded the arterial road which ran along the south side of Lake Bolbe in Mygdonia.

Philippi was treated in diplomacy as an independent ally. The actuality was that it had to follow the policy of the king and accept his final arrangements. A dialogue was conducted by envoys from Philippi who put their case to Alexander about his disposal of reclaimed land in the vicinity. Here also the land and its Thracian inhabitants were spearwon. Alexander gave some land to Philippi 'to possess' and some to rent, and he confirmed the right of the Thracians to cultivate some land, a right which Philip had granted. Two Macedonian officers were to redraw the boundaries. We see here that Alexander dealt personally and directly with the spear-won land and its people, whereas at Calindoea he invoked the Macedonian assembly to arrange the transplantation of a Macedonian community; and that he listened to the requests which Philippi made through its envoys.

The entire area of land between the Axius and the Nestus, except for Amphaxitis, was spear-won land. By redistributing the Macedonian communities and planting some in that area Philip and Alexander were tightening their grip on communications, placing King's Men at strategic points and spreading the use of Greek language and Macedonian ideas. The spear-won peoples provided the economic substructure and paid tribute on the land they cultivated. The Paeonians in the north and the Illyrians in the northwest of the kingdom fulfilled the same function. Small forces of light-armed cavalry, archers and slingers were recruited from these peoples and trained as specialists. We hear also of Companion Cavalry squadrons from Apollonia, i.e. from the 'Macedonian city' in Mygdonia, and from Amphipolis, where Philip had introduced some settlers of his choice and given substantial estates to deserving Companions.

4. The campaign in Thrace and the organisation of the empire

In 335, 'as soon as it was spring Alexander set off for Thrace against the Triballi and the Illyrians, who, he had learnt, intended to revolt'. He had already in person made provision for the manning of the northwestern frontier of the kingdom. He did not take Philip's most experienced general, Antipater, an expert on Illyrian affairs, but left him to act as his deputy in Macedonia. Alexander alone was to exercise command.

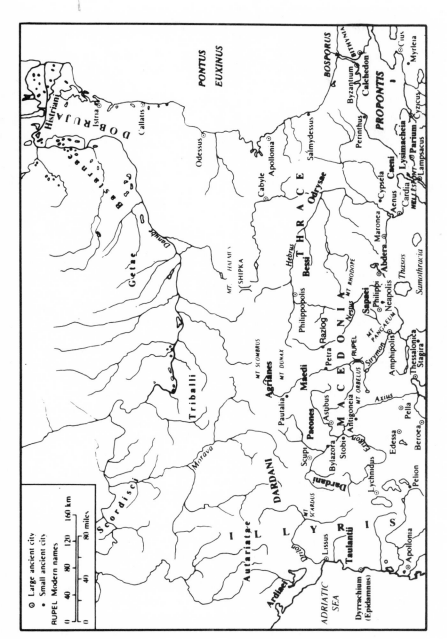

4. The Balkan area

PONTUS
EUXINUS

BOSPORUS

BITHYNIA

PROPONTIS

Cius
Myrleia

Byzantium
Calchedon

Perinthus
Lysimacheia
Parium
Cyzicus
Lampsacus

Cardia
Acnus
MELLES(?)

Cypsela
Caeni

Salmydessus

Apollonia

Odessus

Callatis

HISTRIANI

Istria

DOBRUJA

Basternae

Danube

Getae

Triballi

Morava

Scordisci

MT SCARDUS

Autariatae

ILLYRIS

DARDANI

Ardiaei

Lissus

Taulantii

Dyrrachium
(Epidamnus)

Apollonia

ADRIATIC
SEA

Drilo

Lychnidus

Pelion

DARDANI

Scupi

Bylazora

Stobi

Astibus

Antigoneia

MACEDONIA

Edessa

Pella

Beroea

Paeones

Maedi

Pautalia

MT DUNAX

MT SKOMBRUS

Agrianes

Petra

Razlog

Philippopolis

MT HAEMUS

SHIPKA

Cabyle

Apollonia

THRACE

Odrysae

Hebrus

Bessi

MT RHODOPE

Nestus

Sapaei

Philippi

Abdera

Maronea

Thasos

Samothracia

Neapolis

MT PANGAEUM

Amphipolis

Thessalonica

Stagira

MT ORBELUS

RUPEL

Strymon

Axius

Erigon

- Large ancient city
• Small ancient city

RUPEL Modern names

0   40   80   120   160 km

0   40   80 miles

The army consisted perhaps of 25,000 men, 5,000 horses, and a baggage-train which included siege-engines. He met no serious opposition until he reached the pass over Mount Haemus, which was defended by local tribesmen and Thracian troops, who had fled before his advance. Above the steepest part of the pass the enemy had placed a number of wagons, which, as Alexander surmised, they intended to launch against the infantry phalanx and smash its formation, so that they could defeat the phalangites in hand-to-hand fighting, in which the long pike was a disadvantage. It was a good plan, but Alexander had a better one. He instructed his phalangites to open ranks where there was room, and to lie down with their shields over their heads where they were restricted to close order. The wagons were let loose, and Alexander's orders were obeyed. Not a man was killed. The phalanx, aided by the enfilading fire of the archers, routed the enemy infantrymen, who were by comparison lightly armoured and had inferior weapons. Of them 1,500 fell. Their women, children and gear were captured and sent via the Aegean coast to Macedonia, where they were drafted into city populations.

A few days later Alexander surprised a force of Triballians, who were camping inside a wooded glen. He sent his archers and slingers ahead to fire at the enemy, who, as Alexander had anticipated, attacked and pursued onto open ground where his main force was awaiting them. Squadrons of Companion Cavalry charged into the exposed flanks, and a screen of light-armed cavalry and the phalanx in close order, led by Alexander, drove the enemy centre back and put them to flight. The enemy losses were estimated at 3,000, while 'Alexander is said by Ptolemy to have lost eleven cavalrymen and forty infantrymen'. Descending to the Danube, he found a small Macedonian fleet of warships, which had come through the Bosporus and up the river. The king of the Triballians had taken the tribe's women and children to an island, which was already a refuge for some Thracian troops. Alexander's attempts to force a landing failed. On the far bank of the Danube he could see a force of Getae, estimated at some 4,000 cavalry and more than 10,000 infantry, and it was obvious that they would be able to reinforce and supply the Triballians and the Thracians on the island.

Alexander decided to cross the river at night. It was a bold but logical plan. Some of those nearest to him thought that he acted also from 'a desire' (*pothos*) to set foot on the far side of the Danube, something which his father had not done. Adding to his warships many dug-outs and rafts supported by leather tent-covers filled with straw, he transported 1,500 cavalry and 4,000 infantry and landed them in a field of standing corn, which helped to conceal them. At dawn they set off, the infantry leading and parting the corn with their pikes at an angle. Once on open ground the cavalry, led by Alexander, moved to the right, and the phalanx formed a hollow rectangle in close order and advanced with pikes at the ready. The enemy, amazed at this bold crossing of the river and terrified by the bristling pikes of the phalanx, broke before the violent charge of the cavalry squadrons, each in wedge formation. Alexander pursued at speed, his infantry close to the river bank in order to protect that flank and his cavalry in extended line, until he turned towards the city of the Getae, some six kilometres inland. The Getae fled into the steppe country, taking some women and children on their horses' cruppers. Alexander razed the city and sacrificed to Zeus the Saviour and to Heracles and to Ister for permitting the crossing. On this same day he returned with his men all safe to the south bank. The booty was sent under the command of two officers towards the Aegean coast.

Syrmus and the Thracians on the island sent envoys and gifts to Alexander and asked for friendship. This was granted with mutual pledges. Other tribes along the south bank did likewise. The most westerly of these tribes were Celts near the head of the Adriatic Sea. According to Ptolemy, Alexander asked their envoys what they feared most, in the hope that they would say 'Alexander', but they replied 'the falling of the sky upon us'. He concluded a pact of friendship and alliance with the Celts, remarking to his Friends 'What boasters Celts are!' For four months Alexander was engaged in consolidating the work of his father, who had reduced the Thracian tribes to acceptance of Macedonian rule by many campaigns in summer and in winter. The key to Philip's success was the demonstration of military superiority, the pursuit and decimation of the Thracian aristocratic cavalry, and the enforcement of the peace. Alexander's campaign now set the seal on that success.

The Empire of the Macedonians in the Balkans was unlike that of Athens, for instance, in the Aegean area. The subjected tribes were left to govern themselves, maintain their own laws and customs, and arm their own militia. There was no imposition of a party system of rule, such as 'democracy' or 'oligarchy' which would lead to bitter party-strife (*stasis*), and no occupation in the form of a garrison. Rather, each tribal state kept its own traditions, character and self-respect. The Macedonians required the payment of a fixed tribute (probably a tenth of production), the provision of troops and labour on demand, and the acceptance of Macedonian foreign policy. The centuries-old system of inter-tribal wars and 'living by rapine' (above, p. 12) was to be replaced by an era of peace and prosperity, in which the agricultural workers would play an important part. To that end Philip had founded 'important towns in appropriate places and put an end to the unruly ways of the Thracians'. The population of the new towns, of which Philippoupolis (Plovdiv) was the largest, was 'mixed', in that it consisted of Macedonians, Greeks and the leading local people, and their purpose was to promote agriculture and trade and the spread of Greek as the official language of administration. The mixture of ideas and culture was the beginning of what modern scholars have called 'Hellenisation'. Other beneficiaries of peaceful conditions were the Greek city-states of the Thracian coasts, which 'entered most eagerly into the alliance of Philip' and now of Alexander.

The change in the fortunes of the Greek city-states was very great. Alexander now controlled both sides of the Hellespont, the Sea of Marmara and the Bosporus. The fleets of Macedonia and the Greek Community had complete thalassocracy in these waters and in the Black Sea, and they could sail up the Danube. They were able to put down piracy and to offer protection to city-states there against the native peoples. The result was a rapid expansion of commercial exchange and maritime trade. Philip and Alexander confiscated the rich mineral resources of Thrace as conquered territory, and they issued a fine coinage which became current in central Europe. The city-states of the Greek Community benefited greatly from the increase in trade and from the security of the corn-route from the Black Sea, on which Athens and many other states depended.

5. The campaign in Illyria

In late summer Alexander led his army southwards towards the land of the Agrianians (round Sofia) and the Paeonians (round Skopje). 'There messengers arrived reporting that Cleitus, son of Bardylis (in Kosovo-Metohija), was in revolt and that Glaucias, king of the Taulantii (round Tirana) had joined him; and also that the Autariatae (in Bosnia) would attack him on the march.' Such a combination was extremely formidable. The king of the Agrianians, who was a personal friend of Alexander and had led an embassy to him, undertook to attack the Autariatae; and when Alexander gave the order, he did so successfully. Meanwhile Alexander led his army through Pelagonia, Lyncus and Orestis, in order to protect the kingdom, and then swung north to reach the river Eordaicus, where he encamped close to an Illyrian fortified city, Pelium, which Cleitus had garrisoned. He had moved so fast that Cleitus was still waiting for Glaucias, in order to make a combined onslaught on the Macedonian kingdom. Next day he advanced to the walls of Pelium. The troops of Cleitus on the hills nearby made a sacrifice of three boys, three girls and three black rams, and then came down to attack the Macedonians. They were defeated so roundly that they abandoned their original positions and left the sacrificial victims there on the ground.

Alexander was now able to lay siege to Pelium. But next day the large army of Glaucias arrived and Alexander withdrew into his fortified camp. The pressing problem for Alexander was supply for his 25,000 men and 5,000 horses, because he had already drawn on his own territory to the south. He therefore sent Philotas, the son of Parmenio, with the horse-drawn wagons and an escorting force of Companion

Cavalry northwards into the fertile plain of Koritsa, where harvested grain and pasture were abundant. On the way they went through the Tsangon Pass, which is commanded by hills on either side. These hills were occupied by Glaucias, in order to intercept Philotas on his return. Alexander in person led a force of 400 cavalry, together with the Hypaspists, Archers and Agrianians, at speed to the Tsangon Pass, which he cleared of the enemy in time for the loaded wagons of Philotas' party to return. The relief was only temporary. Alexander's army had to move or starve, and movement seemed very difficult, because the route of retreat southwards would bring his army through country already stripped of supplies and eventually onto broken, hilly ground, where his phalanx could be shot down by the greatly superior numbers of the enemy's light-armed forces. 'Those with Cleitus and Glaucias seemed still to have caught Alexander on difficult ground', a comment which Arrian derived probably from Ptolemy. See Plate 8(a) and (b).

Alexander paraded his army with its siege-train but not its baggage on the level ground beside his camp. His orders were to keep absolute silence and obey each command smartly. The phalanx in close formation with a depth of 120 men went through a series of manoeuvres: with pikes upright, then pikes at the ready, advancing and retiring, wheeling this way and that, and finally forming into a wedge and charging at the enemy on the foothills. Squadrons of cavalry, each 200 strong, moved in concert to protect the flanks of the phalanx. The Dardanians fled to higher ground. The phalanx then turned about, raised the battle-cry and clashed their pikes against their shields as the preliminary to a charge against the Taulantians, who had come down from Pelium but now fled to the protection of the city's walls. Alexander had now cleared both flanks for his line of advance, which was into the very narrow pass which lay beween the Dardanian forces and the Taulantian forces.

The enemy positions are shown in Fig. 5. By advancing into the Wolf's Pass Alexander would keep those forces divided, but within the Pass he had to capture the steep-sided hill K2, before his phalanx arrived and came under fire. To this end he ordered his seven Body-guards and his personal Companions to take their shields, mount their horses and charge towards the hill. On reaching it they were to fight, half on foot and half mounted, against the enemy. In fact the enemy fled at the sight of Alexander charging at the head of his élite cavalry, and Alexander strengthened his hold by bringing up 2,000 Agrianians and Archers. He ordered the Hypaspists and the phalanx brigades to ford the river and form into line in close order along the far bank. When this was done, Alexander's force was isolated on the hill K2, and the Tau-lantians came down the mountain side to attack it as it withdrew. But Alexander led his men in a counter-attack, the phalangites raised their battle-cry, and the enemy withdrew. Thereupon Alexander led his men at the double towards the river, was himself the first to cross, and

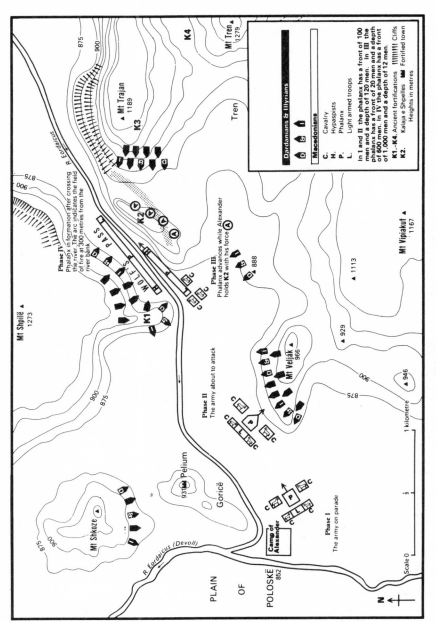

5. The manoeuvres by Pelium

ordered the catapultists on the bank and the Archers in mid-river to lay down a barrage of fire which covered the escape of the rearguard. 'The Macedonians crossed the river safely, so much so that not a single man was killed in the withdrawal.'

Pasture was now available on the swampy shores of Lake Little Prespa, and supplies were obtained from the Macedonian villages near the head of the Lake. Alexander waited out of sight of the enemy for three days, but his scouts noted the disposition of the enemy, the undefended camp and the lack of sentries. On the next night Alexander gave orders for an attack which he led in person with the Hypaspists, the Agrianians, the Archers and two brigades of phalangites as the vanguard. The surprise was complete. Alexander and his men in deep formation broke through one wing of the enemy position and set the rest in flight. Alexander now led the pursuit by his cavalry across the plains 'right up to the mountains of the Taulantians', a distance of about 100 kilometres. 'As many as did escape (i.e. of the enemy cavalry) did so by throwing away their arms.' Cleitus took refuge in Pelium. When the pursuit was over, Alexander led his army south to deal with a rising at Thebes.

The genius of Alexander as a commander is indisputable. To break his way through the Haemus Pass, to cross the Danube and rout the Getae, and to withdraw his army through the Wolf's Pass without the loss of a single man in all three operations is unparalleled. Nor were his opponents weak; for the Thracians were greatly feared by the Greek city-states, and the Dardanians had inflicted very heavy losses on the Molossians and the Macedonians in the period 390-360. The Macedonian army excelled now in its professional expertise. The squadrons of heavy cavalry, each in wedge formation and armed with the long lance, and the phalanx in close order with pikes at the ready were as deadly in action as they were terrifying to behold. Provided they were on level ground and were coordinated in action, they were almost unstoppable. The supporting troops were equally professional: the catapultists, the archers and the slingers, the Agrianians armed with a long spear and a long sword and carrying a small shield, and the light-armed cavalrymen, some armed with the long lance and others with javelins. The 3,000 Hypaspists were particularly versatile; for they fought with the pike in phalanx formation, being stationed next to the phalangites proper, and they were trained to use hoplite equipment (large shield and seven-foot spear) and other weapons. Whereas the phalangites wore a metal cuirass or half-cuirass, only the officers of the Hypaspists were so equipped.

Alexander led the way into every action. He intended to outdo his seven Bodyguards in fighting, for he had a strongly competitive spirit. He encouraged competition throughout the army of the king's men. There was an order of precedence among the Bodyguards and the

Friends, and a similar order in the swearing to confirm diplomatic agreements. The élite units were the Royal Squadron of Companion Cavalry, the Royal Guard of Macedones (earlier called Pezhetairoi), the Royal Brigade of the Hypaspists, and the Royal Pages in their last year. There was the usual ladder of rank for officers and for those below officer level. Every one of the King's Men took an oath of loyalty to the king and depended on his favour for promotion. He was the centre of their world. He intended to act in accordance with his favourite line in the *Iliad* (3.179): to be 'both a good king and a mighty warrior'.

CHAPTER V

Sources of information, a rising in Greece and preparations for Persia

1. The sources of information for the Balkan campaign

We owe our knowledge mainly to four ancient writers, whose works were composed three and more centuries after the career of Alexander: Diodorus Siculus, author of a Universal History; Pompeius Trogus, whose work has survived in an epitome by Justin; Plutarch, the biographer and moraliser; and Arrian, the historian of *Alexander's Expedition*. It is obvious that these writers drew on the works of earlier authors who either had been contemporaries of the events or had composed standard works early in the Hellenistic period (which began after Alexander's death). When we assess the value of statements made by these four authors, we need to ascertain which of those earlier accounts was used by each author. For instance, we began this book with the handling of Bucephalus as described by Plutarch in his *Life of Alexander*. We inferred that Plutarch drew on the account of a contemporary eyewitness, namely Marsyas Macedon, who wrote for contemporaries, and that Plutarch's version was therefore soundly based. On the other hand, the accounts of a drunken scene at the wedding of Philip and Cleopatra which were provided by Plutarch and Justin have all the marks of scandalmongering. We inferred that the accounts were drawn from a common source, namely a *Life of Alexander* by Satyrus, a sensationalist and untrustworthy writer, who wrote in the mid-third century when anti-Macedonian feeling ran high and no contemporaries of the events survived. We therefore suspect that the accounts are not dependable in any respect.

It so happens that Arrian alone gave a detailed account of the Balkan campaign. Our other three authors merely alluded to it, because their interest and that of the authors upon whom they drew were in Greek affairs and in the crossing to Asia. Arrian and the author or authors upon whom Arrian drew realised the importance of the Balkan campaign in relation to the invasion of Asia: 'Alexander thought that, when he was going on an expedition far from the homeland, he ought not to leave his neighbours planning revolt unless they had been completely humbled.' As we have seen, Arrian's account was remarkably detailed, specific and consistent throughout, presumably because it all came from the same author or authors. Fortunately, and almost uniquely among ancient writers, Arrian told his readers that he was drawing on the accounts of Ptolemy and Aristobulus, that he recorded as 'completely true' whatever they said in agreement, and that where they differed he gave the version which he judged to be 'more credible and more worth reporting'. His words are certainly true; for his own contemporaries were familiar with the full accounts of Ptolemy and of Aristobulus and could have seen at once if he was not doing what he said he was doing.

It is thus certain that for the Balkan campaign Arrian gave an unadulterated version of the accounts of Ptolemy and Aristobulus, unadulterated because he believed those accounts to have been 'completely true' and because 'they had campaigned with Alexander'. The only occasion on which he noted a difference between them was that Ptolemy reported exact numbers of the Macedonian casualties in cavalry and in infantry (Arr. 1.2.7). From this we infer two things, that Aristobulus either did not report the casualties or gave less 'credible' figures, and that thereafter when exact numbers are stated by Arrian they will have been taken from Ptolemy's account. The question at once arises: how did Ptolemy know 'more credibly' than Aristobulus the numbers of the dead and also, as we shall see later, the numbers of the wounded in the actions of many years? Similar questions arise with regard to the citations of orders given by Alexander of which some were not enacted (e.g. two in the Balkan campaign at Arr. 1.6.5 and 1.6.10), the naming of officers, the specification of units in action, and the intervals of time in terms of days. When we realise that within books 1 to 6 Arrian reported 147 orders, 78 intervals by days, and some hundreds of officers' names, these questions become imperative. For one man to recall all these by memory alone is inconceivable. Ptolemy must have had access to a written record, which Arrian knew to be itself 'credible' in these respects.

That record can only have been the *Journal of Alexander*. It survived in Alexandria; a lengthy commentary on it was written by Strattis in the middle of the third century (a fragment of a commentary, presumably that of Strattis, survives for events of 335), paraphrases of passages from it were given by Plutarch and Arrian, and reference was made to it by Philinus, Aelian and Athenaeus. The nature of the *Journal* is known from these writings and from descriptions of contents in later Royal Journals. It was a record, made at the time, day by day, of the activities and statements of the king, and attached to it were some relevant documents, e.g. in matters of diplomacy and in official correspondence. The *Journal* was secret during the lifetime of a king and for the limited time thereafter during which his orders were relevant, and then it was deposited with the other possessions of the king at the place of his burial – in Alexander's case at Alexandria. There Ptolemy, the ruler of Egypt, had access to it. Aristobulus, however, did not, since he wrote his work in Macedonia. Thus Arrian was justified in giving the casualties of the Macedonians against the Triballi as 'eleven cavalrymen and about forty infantrymen, as Ptolemy says'. For he knew that Ptolemy's history was based on the bedrock of historical facts which had been recorded in the *Journal* at the time of their happening without bias or revision.

Arrian considered the question whether Ptolemy himself distorted the record. He noted that Ptolemy, writing after the death of Alexander, was not compelled, nor tempted by hope of gain, 'to set down anything otherwise than as it happened'; and that being in a public position as a king he would incur more disgrace if he was found to be lying. Arrian was here concerned with the facts as they happened. There is no doubt that Ptolemy selected and presented those facts in his own way, that is in a way which was generally but not always favourable to Alexander as his friend and patron; for Ptolemy rose to the highest rank, that of Bodyguard to Alexander. In addition to making use of the *Journal* Ptolemy drew on his own memory for many of the vivid details which were repeated by Arrian, gave his own interpretation of Alexander's aims and generalship, and was not averse to blowing his own trumpet. Like most ancient writers he saw himself as a literary artist. Accordingly he did not cite factual documents like the *Journal verbatim* or even in paraphrase, but he composed his own fine account. We see an example of this in Arrian's treatment of Alexander's last illness. He himself delivered his own paraphrase of the account in the *Journal*, and he added that Aristobulus and Ptolemy had written accounts which were 'not far from' that paraphrase. Here it is evident that Ptolemy had not paraphrased the *Journal* but had written his own independent account – not surprisingly when we remember that as a Bodyguard he will have watched over the king in his illness.

The next question is how far did Arrian misunderstand or change what he read in the accounts of Ptolemy and Aristobulus. He was far better placed than any historian of Alexander then and now to understand the conditions in which Alexander carried out his conquests and organised his kingdom of Asia; for he wrote treatises on tactics and hunting, conducted a successful campaign against the Alani of Georgia and Azerbaijan, and held the consulship and the governorship of Cappadocia in the heyday of the Roman Empire. That he did not make changes is apparent from his own assurance that he reported as 'completely true' what was stated in agreement by Ptolemy and Aristobulus, and he announced the principle on which he preferred one or other account where they differed. We know less about Aristobulus, a citizen of Phocis, who enjoyed the confidence of Alexander and was entrusted with the repair of the Tomb of Cyrus at Pasargadae. As his interests were scientific and geographical rather than military, he provided in his history of Alexander much less material than Ptolemy did, but he seems to have taken a greater interest in Alexander's personality. It is probable that Arrian derived from Aristobulus the idea that Alexander's actions were sometimes prompted by a strong desire or yearning (*pothos* in Greek and *cupido* in Latin).

'Some statements by other authors I have also recorded, because they seemed to me to be worth mentioning and to be not entirely incredible, but only as stories (*legomena*) about Alexander.' Some of these were different interpretations of events described by his main authors, and others conveyed additional matter, particularly about affairs in Greece and the Aegean area where Alexander was not personally present. That Arrian was critical of these other writers is clear from his comments, notably in variant versions of Alexander's end (Arr. 7.27). We shall discuss some of these *legomena* as they arise.

2. The revolt and capture of Thebes, and the sources of information

The fullest surviving account is that of Arrian, based on the longer accounts of Ptolemy and Aristobulus. We shall take it first.

Alexander had just returned from his pursuit of the Illyrians, when reports reached him of a revolutionary movement at Thebes. These were to the effect that exiles, returning to the city on the invitation of their partisans, had killed two unsuspecting Macedonians of the garrison; that they had reported Alexander as dead in Illyria; and they had persuaded the Thebans to rise in the cause of liberty and autonomy. Alexander realised the danger that the revolt would spread; for he had long been suspicious of Athens, Aetolia, Sparta and some other Peloponnesian states. Accordingly he marched his army at top speed over the high country of Mount Grammus, Mount Pindus and Mount Cambunia, where there was abundant pasture and where cheese, meat and transport animals could be requisitioned from the transhumant shepherds. Arriving unannounced at Pelinna in northern Thessaly after marching for six days at some 33 kilometres a day, he rested the army for a day. From there he reached Onchestus in Boeotia on the sixth day, having covered some 200 kilometres at an average of 40 kilometres a day. His march was so swift that the Thebans did not know of his approach. He had come unopposed through the Pass of Thermopylae and he could now draw supplies and troops from supporters in northern Boeotia and from Phocis.

The speed of Alexander's march enabled him to pin down Thebes on the next day and to deter any would-be helpers from Athens and other states. He waited in the hope that the Thebans would repent and send an embassy to him, but they made an attack on his camp and killed a few Macedonians. Even so Alexander waited. There was a division of opinion inside Thebes, but the ringleaders and especially the generals of the Boeotian League who had broken their oath of loyalty to the Greek Community persuaded the majority to fight. Alexander was now encamped close to the citadel of Thebes (the Cadmea) in which the Macedonian garrison was surrounded and likely to be overwhelmed. Even so Alexander was not intending to attack, but 'Ptolemy states' that Perdiccas, commanding the brigade on guard, did not await an order from the king but himself led an attack on the Theban field defences, which consisted of two palisades, one behind the other and both in front of the massive city-wall. When he broke through the first palisade, he was joined by another brigade. As they advanced to attack the second palisade, they were likely to be overwhelmed by Theban reinforcements. Alexander had no option but to move his army into action stations.

We learn from another account that the Thebans had received plenty of arms and equipment from Athens. They were famous for their field defences, their walls were almost impregnable by the standards of Greek warfare, and their hoplites had a high reputation. Since Alexander had come without his siege-train, everything seemed to be in favour of the defence. But the initiative of Perdiccas created a situation of which Alexander could take advantage. He ordered the Archers and the Agrianians to enter the space between the two palisades. There Perdiccas fell, seriously wounded. He was carried back to the camp. Alexander waited outside in command of the Infantry Guard of Macedonians and the Royal Hypaspist Brigade in phalanx formation, and behind the phalanx stood the two other brigades of Hypaspists. As Alexander foresaw, the attacking Macedonians were routed by a counter-attack, fled with the loss of seventy archers, and were hotly pursued through the gap in the first palisade by the Theban hoplites, who were no longer in phalanx formation but had scattered. The charge by Alexander's pikemen in formation was decisive, and the Macedonians in close pursuit followed the fugitives through the city-gates. One group liberated the garrison on the Cadmea, and another manned the walls and let the main army enter. Organised resistance soon broke down. The cavalry fled into the countryside. In the street-fighting which followed Alexander appeared now here, now there, but 'it was not so much the Macedonians as Phocians and Plataeans and the other Boeotians' who went on killing Thebans, even suppliants at the altars and women and children.

Arrian's narrative is a summary of the Macedonian view of the action as related by Ptolemy and Aristobulus. Other authors had reported a very different view, seen from the Greek side. According to Diodorus,

Alexander went from Thrace into Macedonia, mustered the full army of more than 3,000 cavalry and 30,000 infantry, and reached Thebes to find the garrison on the Cadmea hemmed in by field defences, such as palisades and trenches. Equipment had already been received from Athens thanks to Demosthenes, and the Assembly there had voted to help Thebes but then procrastinated. Arcadia, Argos and Elis responded to an appeal by despatching troops, but they stopped at the Isthmus on learning of Alexander's arrival. However, inspired by their leaders, the Thebans all decided to fight to the end in the cause of autonomy. They disregarded the divine warnings which the gods sent in the form of fantastic phenomena and oracular utterances. Alexander spent three days preparing for the attack. During those days he would have forgiven Thebes. For instance, he announced through a herald that any Theban might come over to him and enjoy the Common Peace of the Greeks. The Thebans countered by announcing that anyone should join them who wanted to take the side of the Great King of Persia and of Thebes, overthrow the dictator of Greece and liberate the Greeks. At these words Alexander flew into a towering rage, and in bestiality of spirit decided to destroy the city utterly.

An epic account was then given of the fighting which began with an exchange of missiles and went on to sword-play. The outnumbered Thebans, superior in physique, training and morale, outfought the Macedonians so that Alexander had to commit all his reserves to the battle. Even then the Thebans proved unshakable. They had high hopes of victory, but the king spotted an undefended postern-gate and sent Perdiccas with a large force into the city. The Thebans then retreated into the city in disorder, cavalry killing infantry under the feet of their horses, and there they fought heroically to the end. The Macedonians were merciless, and Thespians, Plataeans, Orchomenians and others joined in the massacre, which resulted in the death of more than 6,000 and the capture of 30,000. This account has much in common with later accounts of fighting by Diodorus. From a military point of view they are worthless; for they are fictions on the Homeric model in the style and mode of battle. The account is also blatantly pro-Theban.

There is no doubt that Diodorus derived this and later accounts from Cleitarchus, who was a citizen probably of Colophon in Asia Minor and ended up in Alexandria in Egypt. He did not serve in Asia, and as a young man he studied philosophy. Between 315 and 290 approximately he published a long, sensational account of Alexander's expedition which was widely read well into Roman times. In the judgement of Quintilian he was a talented writer, but as a historian he was 'notoriously untrustworthy'; in that of Cicero he was a rhetorical writer of rather puerile mentality, and as a historian he took the liberty 'to lie outright' in order to achieve a brilliant effect. Longinus scorned him as 'a superficial windbag'. The description of the fighting at Thebes and of the bestial rage of Alexander is itself an illustration of the qualities which were summarised by Cicero, Quintilian and Longinus. These capable critics knew the work of Cleitarchus in full. We have only paltry fragments, which afford no basis for modifying their judgements in any way. Cleitarchus' account was used also by Trogus (as epitomised by Justin) and by Plutarch, whose versions have much in common with that of Diodorus. One chapter in Plutarch's *Life* which described Alexander's chivalrous pardon of a Theban woman, Timoclea, was taken from the history of Aristobulus and reflects something of his fine style.

3. The judgement passed on Thebes by the Council of the Greeks

That Alexander treated the revolt of Thebes as a breach not of her treaty with Macedonia but of the charter of the Greek Community is clear from the accounts of Arrian, Diodorus and Plutarch. Thebes had indeed broken all the rules of the charter in recalling exiles, killing Macedonians of the garrison, denouncing the Greek Community as tyranny, and espousing the side of Persia against the Greek Community. It also suited Alexander as *Hegemon* of the Community to call up the troops of loyal members such as the Phocians and some of the Boeotian states, and on arrival outside Thebes to offer generous terms if Thebes would rejoin the Community. Had Perdiccas not acted, Alexander might have succeeded by diplomatic means; but as it was he had to save his own troops from destruction. Once Thebes was captured, he had to take into account the fact that Athens, Aetolia, Arcadia, Argos and Elis had been prepared to join in the revolt from the Greek Community.

How then should he handle the final verdict on the captured city? To take the decision himself would be to act as king of Macedonia and to disregard the very existence of the Greek Community. He could then be seen to be acting as a dictator in relation to the city-states. On the other hand, if he wished the Greek Community to continue and have any authority, he had no option but to refer the decision to the Council of that body. That was in fact what he chose to do. It was in line with his actions and proclamations at Thebes.

The clearest account is given by Diodorus, who was drawing on Cleitarchus. 'Convening the Councillors of the Greeks Alexander entrusted to the Common Council the question what should be done with the city of the Thebans.' Some light is shed on this meeting of the Council in the various accounts. 'The allies who took part in the action' – named as Phocians, Plataeans, Thespiaeans and Orchomenians – swayed the meeting by the violence of their hatred of the city which had massacred their citizens on more than one occasion. They and no doubt others who had reason to hate Thebes accused her of treason in joining Persia against the Greeks now as in the past. The majority of the Councillors present (we do not know how many were there) decided the fate of Thebes: 'to raze the city, sell the captives, outlaw any Theban escapees, forbid any of the Greeks to shelter a Theban, and rebuild and fortify Orchomenus and Plataea.' Then 'in compliance with the verdict of the Council the king [as *Hegemon* under the charter] razed the city and thereby instilled great fear in those who were revolting from the Greeks', i.e. in the leaders at Athens and in other states. It had a much wider deterrent effect thereafter, as Polybius, writing two centuries later, was to note.

That Alexander showed moderation in implementing the verdict was stated in more than one account. Those who had voted against the revolt, the descendants of Pindar, those who had diplomatic ties with Philip, Alexander and the Macedonians, the priests and priestesses, and Timoclea and her family were exempted and went free; and when he was in Asia, he treated Theban envoys and mercenaries in Persian service with generosity. He did not need to take the initiative against the states which had agreed to support Thebes. The Arcadians condemned to death those who had advocated that support. The Eleans reinstated those whom they had exiled as pro-Macedonian. The Aetolians, tribe by tribe, sent envoys to ask for forgiveness. The Athenians, after a debate in their Assembly, sent envoys to convey their decree in which they congratulated Alexander on his safe return from the Balkan campaign and on his punishment of Thebes. Alexander is said to have thrown it away in disgust. However, in reply he sent a *Letter* (a copy was no doubt kept with the *Journal*) in which he asked for the surrender of nine named Athenians whom he held to be as guilty as the Theban ringleaders for the revolt of Thebes and also responsible for the policy which had led to the Battle of Chaeronea, and for the offences at the time of Philip's death. They were to be tried 'in the Council of the Greeks'. Athens appealed against this demand and promised to try the men in her own court. The appeal was granted by Alexander with the exception of one man, the general Charidemus, who escaped to serve Persia. Thus Athens was treated very leniently.

Arrian's comment on the leniency of Alexander towards Athens is interesting: 'It may have been due to his respect for Athens, or it may have been due to his eagerness to embark on the expedition into Asia, he being unwilling to leave behind in the minds of the Greeks any suspicion of himself.' Philip and Alexander had always treated Athens with exceptional generosity for reasons which varied with the exigencies of the situation. But from the hour of victory at Chaeronea onwards they were anxious to form a genuine alliance and cooperation with Athens or at least to obtain her neutrality. Respect for her cultural leadership may have been an ingredient, but there is no doubt about the practical need to win over or at least place in baulk the Athenian fleet; for a combination of that fleet and the Persian fleet would dominate the Aegean Sea, the Hellespont, the Bosporus and the Black Sea, and it would put an end to Macedonian expansion.

Athens was only part of a wider problem for Alexander. The Greek Community was a form of political organisation which had three practical values for him: it kept the city-states at peace within Greece, it linked them to Macedonia in close alliance, and it committed itself to fight alongside Macedonia against Persia. Everyone knew that its existence and its policies were due to Macedonia's military power. Demosthenes and like-minded politicians saw it as the mask of dictatorship, the negation of city-state independence, and they urged their citizens to repudiate the Greek Community and to combine with Persia against Macedonia. To other politicians the Greek Community provided the best *modus vivendi* with Macedonia and the prospect of an actual Common Peace; moreover, a successful campaign in Asia would liberate the Greeks there and provide an outlet for the floating population of the mainland. In such a mixed climate of political opinion Alexander had to keep his military power in the public eye. His capture of Thebes in a matter of hours did so in an unforgettable manner. He had to maintain the authority and the principles of the Greek Community not only by entrusting to it the punishment of Thebes but also by finding peaceful means of bringing other malcontents to heel. Thus he showed respect for Athens as an independent state, outwitted Demosthenes' policy of collaboration with Persia, and in the crossing to Asia was accompanied by an Athenian squadron as part of the Greek Community's forces.

Alexander was eager to reach agreement quickly, not because his lion-like rage was exhausted by the savage destruction of Thebes, as Cleitarchus maintained, but because the vanguard of Macedonian and Greek forces in Asia was suffering reverses in the latter part of 335, and he had to go to its relief with all speed. It was also essential that the main force should be in Asia and in control of the harbours near the Hellespont, before the Persian fleet could enter the Aegean in the early summer of 334. He foresaw, no doubt, that once in the Aegean the Persians would try to promote risings by mainland states and thus break up the Greek Community. He could try to counter that attempt now only by convincing the city-states of his sincerity in respecting their political independence within the framework of the Greek Community. Hence in his settlement in autumn 335 'he was unwilling to leave behind in the minds of the Greeks any suspicion of himself'. For that reason he and his army did not enter the Peloponnese.

4. Alexander prepares for the campaign against Persia

After these dealings [with Athens] Alexander returned to Macedonia. He conducted the sacrifice to Zeus of Olympus at Dium in the form which Archelaus had initiated, and he celebrated the games in honour of Zeus of Olympus at Aegeae. Some say that he held a contest also in honour of the Muses.

The national festival was that which Philip had celebrated at Aegeae in 336. The sacrifice was a thanksgiving by the Macedonian State to Zeus the Saviour and Protector. Alexander had good reason to give thanks. In all warfare the time factor is important, sometimes all-important. In 335 Alexander had been able to crush the Illyrians a fortnight before he isolated Thebes. If the rising of Thebes had preceded the massing of the Illyrian forces at Pelium, the Macedonian army would have been in Boeotia and Macedonia would have been completely overrun by the Illyrians. We may say that the time factor was fortuitous; but Alexander and his Macedonians saw the hand of Zeus in the sequence of events. He had saved them from disaster. In Asia too the time factor had been important. Troubles arising from the succession at the Persian court and other distractions caused Darius III Codomannus not to deploy the Persian fleet or mount a major counter-attack on land during the time when Alexander was campaigning in the Balkans, capturing Thebes and reaffirming the authority of the Greek Community. For that blessing also Alexander had reason to thank Zeus of Olympus.

It had been a year of astonishing successes against Thracians, Getae, Triballians, Illyrians and Thebans, with minimal loss of Macedonian lives except at Thebes, where the figure of 500 Macedonian dead may be exaggerated, since it comes ultimately from Cleitarchus. Alexander had pardoned revolutionary moves by some city-states in 336, and he had taken military action in 335 only against Thebes, where his hand had been forced by the behaviour of Perdiccas. He would probably have preferred a less severe sentence for the Thebans; but their fate had been in the hands of the Greek Council and the recent history of Greece was full of conquered populations being sold into slavery. Indeed by Greek standards the Thebans had not suffered the worst; for the Thebans themselves had massacred the adult males and sold all others into slavery at Orchomenus in 363, and the Athenians had done the same at Sestus in 353. If the charter of the Greek Community was obeyed in the future, there would be no more cases of such destruction. In the Balkans too Alexander made arrangements which he hoped would promote peace and prosperity. When Glaucias acknowledged his defeat and made submission, Alexander left him on his throne as a client king; and Cleitus was probably treated in the same manner.

After his absence of eight months the festival at Aegeae gave Alexander the opportunity to organise a lavish entertainment, which lasted for the nine days consecrated to the nine Muses.

Constructing a marquee with one hundred couches, he invited to the banquet the Friends and the Commanders and in addition the envoys from the cities [of Macedonians] ... and by distributing animals for sacrifice and everything appropriate for feasting to the entire force of the King's Men he raised the spirits of the army.

Alexander had to make decisions on matters in Macedonia which had lain outside the scope of his deputy's powers. For instance, it was probably now that he heard an embassy from Philippi about the distribution of reclaimed land, and he initiated the setting up of a 'city of Macedonians' at Calindoea (above, p. 31). He convened a meeting of the Commanders and the leading Friends to discuss his plans for the crossing to Asia. According to Diyllus, a competent Hellenistic historian on whom Diodorus drew for this information, Antipater and Parmenio advised Alexander to beget an heir first and to cross to Asia later, but he replied that it would be disgraceful for the leader of the Greek and Macedonian forces to sit down and await the birth of children. With hindsight we see that they were right and that he made a serious misjudgement (for a wife could have accompanied him overseas). But his rejection of their advice is understandable. His father had married first at the age of twenty-four. Alexander was only twenty-one, and like most young men of that age he did not think of death as being near at hand.

The plans which Alexander put before his Commanders and Friends were extremely bold when we bear the situation in Europe in mind. He was to take to Asia one half of the remaining Macedonian phalangites (some were aleady active in the vanguard), some two-thirds of the Companion Cavalry and the light-armed cavalry, and a small number of light-armed infantry. If there should be a general rising of the Balkan tribes and/or of the city-states, Macedonia would be in a desperate situation; for her army would consist only of 1,000 Companion Cavalry, 500 light-armed cavalry, 12,000 phalangites, and some light-armed infantry reinforced by the militia of the cities. He planned also to take to Asia 22 triremes and 38 smaller warships, which was probably the full strength of the Macedonian fleet. Their crews, totalling some 6,000 men, were recruited mainly from Chalcidice. Arrangements had already been made for the Greek Community to contribute the following forces (in addition to those serving in the vanguard): 2,400 cavalry, 7,000 infantry, and 160 triremes with crews totalling 32,000. Some of

Alexander's officers may have argued that the Greek fleet was not to be trusted, and that it could easily turn on the small Macedonian fleet or desert *en bloc* to the Persian fleet. But Alexander persisted in the plan. The Balkan tribes were to provide 500 Agrianians and 7,000 other infantrymen from tribes which he had defeated in 335. Some officers may have doubted whether they would be dependable. We do not know what plans were made for the provision of auxiliary services in terms of merchant-ships, siege-train, baggage-train, wagons, draught-animals, engineers, grooms, cooks and so on.

A fragmentary inscription found on the Acropolis of Athens announced the regulations for payments in currency and in corn which were to be made to soldiers serving in the security forces at home. It seems that Macedonians served alongside men of the city-states, for a drachma a day was to be paid to a 'hypaspist'. Alexander was mentioned in his capacity presumably as the overall commander, and a copy of the regulations was to be set up in Macedonia, in the temple of Athena at Pydna. The officers responsible for publishing the regulations in this way were 'those in charge of the common defence', sometimes called 'guardians of the peace' (*eirenophylakes*, a term coined by Xenophon: above, p. 10). Their duties were 'to prevent massacre, banishment, confiscation of property, redistribution of land and cancellation of debts which were contrary to the existing laws of the member-states' of the Greek Community, and also 'to prevent the liberation of slaves for revolutionary purposes'. Thus Alexander and the Greek Council hoped to check any movement towards the party-strife (*stasis*) which would undermine the Common Peace and might invite intervention by Persia.

The financial strain on the Macedonian kingdom during recent years and now in prospect was very great. For the personnel of the army and the navy were well paid when on active service, not least because the loot from a successful campaign went not to the men but to the state. In addition Alexander planned to take to Asia 5,000 Greek mercenaries (over and above those already employed in the vanguard). Moreover, he had to pay his part in advance for the provisions which were needed to feed the entire force, until such time as it could overrun new territories. Aristobulus stated that Alexander had only 70 talents in hand for the final provisioning; Onesicritus – another contemporary but less dependable – said that he owed 200 talents; and a later writer claimed that he had taken supplies for 30 days only. Whatever truth there is in these statements, the personal credit of Alexander as king was almost inexhaustible, because he owned all mineral deposits in the kingdom and in the Balkan Empire, all stands of fine timber in the kingdom, and a large number of royal lands. Thus he was able on the eve of crossing to Asia to reward some of his Companions for outstanding service with the revenues of an estate, a village, a harbour or a hamlet (*synoikia*). Some refused to accept the rewards. One such was Perdiccas, who was so far from being punished for his initiative at Thebes that he continued to command a brigade and was soon promoted to be a Bodyguard of Alexander.

When Plutarch wrote of the distribution of rewards, he had Perdiccas ask Alexander what he had left for himself, and Alexander reply, 'My hopes.' This may come from Cleitarchus, but it has the ring of truth. Those hopes were confident hopes, partly because Alexander had calculated the risks which his country would run in Europe, but mainly because he believed that the gods were on his side. He sacrificed daily to them on behalf of the state; he believed that like his predecessors he was descended from Zeus and Heracles; and he was encouraged in his faith by omens and oracles. One such omen was reported by Plutarch and Arrian, who followed a common source, probably Aristobulus. A statue of Orpheus, made of cypress and revered at Leibethra in Pieria, was seen to be sweating profusely when Alexander was about to leave. Diviners gave various interpretations. Alexander accepted that of his favourite diviner, Aristander of Telmessus in Lycia, who prophesied that Alexander's deeds in Asia 'would cost poets and musicians much toil and sweat to celebrate'. To us this may seem childish. It was not so to Alexander. For he took Aristander to Asia, consulted him at critical moments, and accepted his prophecies except on one occasion, when Alexander was proved wrong and Aristander was proved right (Arr. 4.4.3 and 9). To say that Alexander believed in second sight is misleading. For it was an article of faith that the gods may reveal the future through physical phenomena and through the words of inspired individuals, men or women of whatever race.

5. Coinage and culture in 336-335

'Philip raised the Macedonian kingdom to a high pitch of greatness because he had an abundance of money.' All mineral deposits within the kingdom and the Balkan Empire were the personal possession of the king, and early in Philip's reign the techniques of mining were greatly improved. The gold and the silver of his coins were of a pure quality, which was important since coins were valued as bullion. Philip's most famous coins were his gold *Philippeioi* with the head of Apollo on one side and a two-horse chariot at the gallop on the reverse side. Being on the Attic standard of weight, they were intended primarily for large-scale transactions in the Mediterranean area. Hoards of *Philippeioi* have been found throughout Greece and the Greek West (especially in Sicily), Asia Minor, Syria, Cyprus and Egypt, and also in the Balkans and in South Russia. The largest silver coins were tetradrachms showing the head of Zeus wreathed with laurel and on the reverse side a racehorse ridden by a jockey. All the silver coins were on the Thracian standard, which favoured transactions in and beyond the Balkans.

Hoards of tetradrachms have been found there and in Greece and Sicily. The wide circulation of the *Philippeioi* and the tetradrachms gives us some idea of Macedonia's orbit of trade and transactions. Small denominations in silver and very large issues of bronze coins were used for internal exchange within the kingdom. Thus the economy of Macedonia became fully monetary, and Alexander inherited the strongest currency in Europe.

Philip was also a lavish spender, especially in financing the wars of 340-338 and in mounting the invasion of Asia in 336. In a speech which Arrian summarised, following Ptolemy's version, Alexander claimed that Philip left at the time of his death 'a few gold and silver drinking-vessels, a treasury of less than 60 talents and debts of some 500 talents'. The facts are no doubt true, but the picture is somewhat misleading, in that the king was not on the verge of bankruptcy but had enormous capital resources. Indeed it was those resources which enabled him to raise loans of such magnitude. Alexander spent money on an even grander scale in his opening years. No expense was spared in the funeral of Philip. Then within the span of twelve months he marched his army in full strength to Corinth, conducted campaigns in Thrace, Illyria and Central Greece, maintained his part of the forces in Asia, and celebrated his successes in a most extravagant manner during the nine-day festival at Aegeae. It was probably during these months, when Alexander surpassed his father in his commitments, that Alexander capped his father's debts by raising loans of 800 talents. In the winter of 335-334 he faced very great expenditure in the organisation of security forces at home, the payment of Greek mercenaries and Balkan troops, and the financing of the Macedonian forces and their infrastructure for the large-scale invasion of Asia.

During this period of financial stress and for some years thereafter Alexander issued his father's gold *Philippeioi* and silver tetradrachms with the lettering 'Philippou'. He used these for large transactions abroad, such as the hiring of companies of Greek mercenaries. It was wise to do so, because these coins were as acceptable everywhere as Victoria's gold sovereigns proved to be. In 335 he began to issue in his own name a silver coinage mainly in small denominations from a drachm downwards. Whereas his father's posthumous silver tetradrachms continued to be on the Thracian standard, Alexander's coinage now was on the Attic standard, probably for use by Alexander in his capacity as *Hegemon*, for instance for the payment of security forces. He made the change to the Attic standard for these and later silver coins because the interests of Macedonia were to be primarily in the Mediterranean area. It was also convenient to have his gold and silver coinages on the same standard, so that the ratio between the two precious metals could be fixed or modified more easily.

The first silver coinage in Alexander's name showed the head of a young Heracles and on the reverse an eagle standing on a thunderbolt, both being emblems of Zeus. He issued a large amount of bronze coinage in three denominations for exchange within the kingdom and the Balkan Empire. This had the head of a young Heracles and on the reverse the quiver and the club associated with Heracles. It is clear that Alexander wished his subjects to regard their new king as a young Heracles who enjoyed the favour of Zeus.

Coinage and culture are to some extent inter-related. The wealth of Athens in the Periclean period and to a lesser extent in the fourth century attracted men of all kinds of ability, many of whom became resident aliens and contributed to her prosperity. The wealth of Macedonia had the same effect. Among those who visited the court in the fifth century were Pindar, whose epithet for Alexander I, 'bold-scheming' (*thrasymedes*), might be taken as the motto for the kings of the Temenid dynasty; Euripides, who produced two plays in Macedonia and was made a Companion; Choerilus, an epic poet, who also settled and died in Macedonia; the leading historians Herodotus, Hellanicus and probably Thucydides; and the founder of scientific medicine, Hippocrates of Cos. The palace of Archelaus was decorated by the leading painter of fresco, Zeuxis, who came from Heraclea in Italy. Philip continued in the same tradition; for he attended the lectures of his philosopher-in-residence Euphraeus (he was to succeed Plato as head of the Academy), employed Aristotle and Theophrastus from 343 to 335, brought the historians Anaximenes, Callisthenes and Theopompus to his court, and hired leading actors to compete in the dramatic contests which were a part of the Festival in honour of the Muses. That Philip was a man of culture and a patron of the arts was admitted even by his critics. So too was at least one of his entourage; for Antipater was a pupil of Aristotle and wrote a history of the Illyrian Wars.

Archaeology came late to Macedonia. It has completely altered our perception of Macedonian culture. The statement of Alexander that Philip left a few gold and silver drinking-vessels did not prepare us for the discovery of almost fifty silver vessels in the unplundered tombs of Philip and Alexander IV. They are of unsurpassed beauty in their varied shapes and exquisite workmanship. The miniature heads at the base of the handles are most skilful. One (Plate 4(b)) represents a young Heracles with the features of Alexander. There was nothing comparable in the city-states, and the recently discovered cache of silver vessels at Rogozen in northwest Bulgaria has shown us that the Thracian versions, though imitating Macedonian forms, were inferior in workmanship. Nor were these silver vessels a monopoly of the royal court. Equally lovely specimens have been found, for instance, at Derveni (in Mygdonia), Sevaste (near Dium), and Nikisiani (near Kavala). Gold work was no less fine. The two gold coffers in which the cremated remains of Philip and his Queen were placed are of pure gold and beautifully decorated with the bursting star, rosettes and lotus flowers, which were associated with a belief in the after-life (see Plate 5(a)). Coloured glass-paste is used for the rosettes. Equally remarkable are the gold wreaths (see Plate 5(b)). Similar wreaths have been found in tombs of the period throughout Macedonia. Skill in working precious metals was of long standing in Macedonia, as we know from the finds of the archaic period at Sindos, Aegeae and Aeane and from discoveries of silver-gilt fittings and gilded iron at Katerini early in the fourth century. The gilded silver diadem in Philip's Tomb is decorated with the snake-skin pattern, suggestive of immortal life.

The miniature ivory heads, only an inch high, are realistic portraits of members of Philip's family and of his close Friends. Those representing Philip's parents, Philip, Olympias and Alexander lay together with their limbs of gold and ivory on the floor of his Tomb where they had fallen. They were miniatures of the gold-and-ivory statues of the same persons, which were dedicated in Philip's circular shrine at Olympia as a thanksgiving to Zeus. The artistry of the ivory heads is beyond compare. See Plate 1(b).

The frescoes on the walls of the Tombs of Amyntas and of Eurydice, and on the façade of Philip's Tomb are far superior in artistic skill, use of shading and understanding of perspective to any paintings elsewhere in the Greek world. Under the patronage of the kings the school of Zeuxis set a fashion in painting which was to inspire Hellenistic and Roman painting (as at Pompeii and Herculaneum). Alexander chose the subject of the fresco which was painted below the cornice in honour of his father (see Plate 2). The subject is a Royal Hunt with the royals on horseback and the Pages on foot. Philip is shown as a bearded man of mature age about to despatch a mountain-lion, on which the gaze of his left eye is fixed (for he was blind in the right eye). The conspicuous royal in the centre (Plate 15) is Alexander, laurel-wreathed, rushing with poised spear to help his father. He is young, clean-shaven, with slightly protruding eyes. The third royal, seen from behind and naked, is treated with less honour. He was probably Amyntas, the son of Perdiccas. The composition of the figures in motion and the trees in the background is masterly.

A related art was that of mosaic, not with flat tesserae but with rounded pebbles, which reflect the light in a more lively manner. The mosaic floors of the houses at Pella, which date from the last quarter of the fourth century, are highly sophisticated with representations, for instance, of Dionysus riding a panther and of a lion-hunt, in which the hunters were probably Alexander and Craterus as young men (Plate 6(a)).

'Pella, previously small, was enlarged by Philip who was brought up there. It has a fortified headland in Lake Loudias. The outlet of this lake is the river Loudias, and the lake is fed by an offshoot of the Axius.' Excavation has revealed a large city with rectangular building-plots

47 m square, bounded by streets 9 m wide and 6 m wide. There were two paved roads with sidewalks which led from the harbour to a central avenue 15 m wide. Most houses had one or two inner courtyards, surrounded by a colonnade. The harbour is of great interest, because it is the first riverine harbour to be mentioned in literature. The canal from the Axius to the lake basin and the outflow-channel must have been maintained by artificial banks and locks. Some remains of the Palace date to the reign of Philip; its area of 60,000 square metres was entered through a monumental Propylon. The city was fortified with a circuit-wall of brick on a stone base. Philip encouraged the Macedonian cities to build such walls. He planned many new cities in the enlarged kingdom and in Thrace. As we have seen (above, p. 6), Alexander founded one in the Strymon valley.

The building of temples was encouraged by Philip. At Pella there were small temples to Aphrodite-and-Cybele near the Agora and to Darron, a local god of healing with an attached sanatorium. A circular pit, like one in the sanctuary of the Cabiri in Samothrace, was associated with fertility cults and local deities, and there was worship of Artemis, Pluto and Athena as protectress of cattle. The people of Pella, as of Dium, worshipped not only the deities of the Greek pantheon but also many others which were native to the varied peoples of the enlarged kingdom. One form of architecture in which Macedonia led the way was that of built tombs. The line of development is clear from the cist-tomb of Amyntas III, *c.* 370, through a larger two-chambered cist-tomb near Katerini to the very large, vaulted, two-chambered Tomb of Eurydice, set within a framework of parallel walls, which were

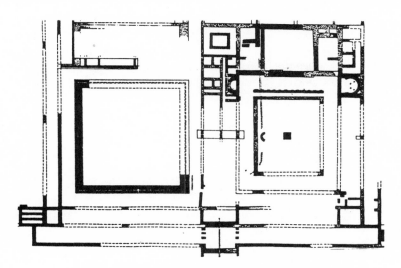

6. The Palace of Philip and Alexander at Pella

designed to help to carry the weight of a tumulus of soil. The vaulted Tomb of Philip dispensed with that framework, and it therefore developed the fine façade with the fresco of the Royal Hunt. The addition of a classical façade to a functional building of different shape, and the building of a vaulted crypt in honour of a deity, or a dead hero, have had a long and distinguished history in European architecture.

Finally we have learnt from excavation that Macedonian craftsmen excelled in the making of weapons and armour, whether of iron or bronze. Philip's cuirass and helmet were made of iron. They were such as Alexander put on before the Battle of Gaugamela – 'gleaming like polished silver' (evidently a form of mild steel). He and his Queen were equipped for the after-life with a variety of weapons (pike, spear, javelin, sword, bow, arrows and quiver-case of gold) and fine armour (greaves with gold engraving, and a gilded iron gorget). It was Macedonian armourers who equipped and maintained the army of Alexander in Asia with the weapons and the armour which played a major part in their victorious advance to the Hyphasis in Pakistan.

CHAPTER VI

The crossing of the Hellespont
and the first victory

1. Arrangements in Europe and
calculations for Asia

Alexander made the arrangements which he judged necessary for a long
absence in Asia. He appointed his senior Friend, Antipater, to be
'General with full powers' as his deputy 'in the affairs of Macedonia and
the Greeks'. Within Macedonia Antipater exercised the military command (*hegemonia*) over 12,000 phalangites and 1,000 Companion Cavalry of the king's men, 500 light-armed cavalry and some light-armed
infantry, and he was able to call up the militia of the cities in case of
need. He was the acting headmaster of the School of Pages, and he
handled the finances of the state for military and naval purposes. As
Macedonian commander he was in charge of 'Triballi, Agrianes, Illyrians' (including the Dardanians as 'Illyrians'), and 'Epirus up to the
Ceraunian mountains' (from the Macedonian point of view the northern
part only of Epirus). In regard to the Greek Community Antipater as
deputy *Hegemon* exercised the powers which had been laid down in the
agreement between the Common Council and Alexander. These powers
included command of the security forces and of any other forces, military and naval, which might be raised by the Greek Community within
its orbit of authority. Antipater had the right to appoint his own
deputies to positions of command.

There were other aspects of the monarchy. The most important was
the religious activity of the king both as head of state and as the
representative of the Temenid royal house, and this involved daily
sacrifice, leading processions, organising festivals, providing sacrificial
victims and so on. An acting head of the royal family in Macedonia had
to administer the royal estates and manage the finances of the royal
house, which included the receipt of taxes and much routine expenditure. In addition there were some departments of civic administration
which were directed by the king. The responsibility for all these matters
in the absence of the king was laid upon the holder of an office called
the 'Protectorship of the Monarchy' (*prostasia tes basileias*). This office
was held in the highest esteem among the Macedonians. Alexander

conferred it on Olympias, the Queen Mother. We know that during his absence she 'conducted sacrifices on his behalf' (*prothuetai*) and was expert in the traditional sacrifices of the Argeadae (the royal tribe) and in those paid to Dionysus.

In some matters Antipater and Olympias were to act together, for instance in dealing with Athens over the arrest of a deserter. But in general it seems that each had a clearly defined sphere of activity. Even so friction was likely to develop between these two strong characters, and in that event Alexander would have to make the decision between them. It seems unlikely that Antipater was authorised to hold an assembly of the 13,000 King's Men under his command and treat it as an assembly of state. The situation was rather that the Macedonian state operated wherever the king and the King's Men happened to be, and it was clear in spring 334 that for some years he and they would be in Asia. The arrangements which Alexander thus made for Macedonia were on the whole wise. It is important to notice that the military command of Thrace was entrusted not to Antipater but to a separate 'General of Thrace', answerable directly to Alexander and responsible for maintaining the vital line of communication from the Hellespont to the eastern frontier of the Macedonian kingdom at the river Nestus. To this responsible post Alexander appointed his namesake, Alexander Lyncestes, who had been the first to acclaim him as king.

The obvious criticism of Alexander's arrangements was that 13,000 King's Men was a tiny force in relation to its responsibilities. But at the same time one might equally well have claimed that to undertake the conquest of Asia with 13,800 King's Men under his own command was wellnigh absurd. Alexander must have assessed the risks in each case with extreme care. He evidently relied on the acceptance of the Macedonian system of control by the Balkan tribes and on the loyalty of the Balkan troops which he took to Asia in 334 and later. Similarly he must have reckoned that the majority of the city-states and Athens in particular would honour the charter of the Greek Community during his absence, and that the fleet and the soldiers with him in 334 would be eager to liberate the Greek city-states from Persian rule and to take revenge on Persia for past acts of sacrilege.

At the beginning of spring in 334 the Macedonian contingents (1,800 Companion Cavalry, 12,000 phalangite infantry and some light-armed troops, both cavalry and infantry) and the Balkan contingents (Illyrian, Triballian, Agrianian and Odrysian, totalling 7,500 men) mustered in Amphaxitis. From there they marched through the Kumli valley, past Lake Cercinitis to Amphipolis, where they met Parmenio in command of 2,300 cavalry and 7,000 hoplites of the Greek Community and of 5,000 Greek mercenaries. Thus the total of fighting troops was 5,100 cavalry and 32,000 infantry, of which those provided by the Macedonian kingdom were considerably less than a half. The army was accompa-

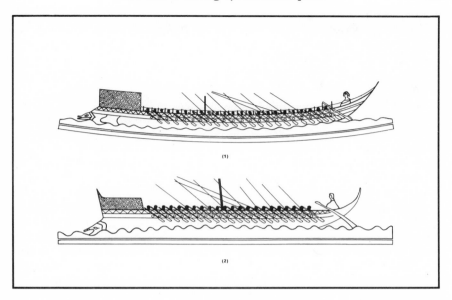

7. The penteconter

nied by various services and specialists. The march from Amphaxitis to Sestus on the Hellespont, a distance of some 350 miles, took 20 days, so that if we allow for some three days of rest the daily march was one of 20 miles more or less.

The fleets met at Amphipolis. The Macedonian fleet consisted of 22 triremes and 38 smaller warships (penteconters and triaconters), with crews totalling perhaps 6,000 men, and the Greek fleet, provided by the Greek Community, numbered 160 triremes with crews of some 32,000 men. In addition to the warships there were merchant ships which carried equipment and supplies, the latter sufficient for one month only. The entire force may be estimated at 90,000 men. At least half of these men came from the Greek Community and from centres of mercenary recruitment in Greece, and only a quarter at most came from within the Macedonian kingdom. They were all under the supreme command of Alexander as king and *Hegemon*, and he appointed the commanders of the various contingents and flotillas.

Of the financial commitments we know very little. The King's Men must have received pay during the lengthy campaigns of Philip, and they were to do so for the campaigns in prospect now. The rate of pay may have been a drachma a day for a first-line infantryman, as it seems to have been for one in the security forces (see Tod no. 183), and three drachmae a day for a cavalryman. The Greek hoplite was paid probably five obols (the drachma having six obols) and the Greek cavalryman two drachmae and three obols a day. The Greek mercenaries were paid by the month, both cavalry and infantry, but we do not know their rates of pay. In addition basic rations were provided for the soldiers and the crews, and these could often be supplemented by personal purchase wherever a market was available. The financial responsibility was divided between Macedonia and the Greek Community. The king provided wages and maintenance for the Macedonian and Balkan soldiers and for the crews of the Macedonian fleet. He equipped and armed the Macedonians, but the Companion Cavalrymen brought their own horses and presumably their own grooms. The member states of the Greek Community which sent a flotilla of ships manned them with crews at their own expense (Tod no. 192), and those which provided soldiers must have seen to it that they were properly equipped, for instance with cavalry mounts and remounts. When the expeditionary forces were in the field, it is evident that Alexander was the paymaster with funds sent initially from Macedonia and from Greece. According to Aristobulus he had only 70 talents in hand for supplies when he marched towards Sestus, and by the summer the shortage of funds was one reason for his decision to disband the Greek fleet. In this department too we can see that Alexander's calculations were finely drawn.

2. The crossing of the Hellespont

The crossing of the Hellespont was fraught with religious associations. The ancestors of Alexander, Heracles on his father's side and Achilles on his mother's side, had fought against Troy on different campaigns. 'The Achaeans', the ancestors of the Greeks in Alexander's army, had conducted the siege and capture of Troy, celebrated by Homer. When the army reached Sestus, Alexander was 'fired with incredible exaltation of spirit' by the sight of Asia. There, at Sestus, he set up twelve altars, which were dedicated to the twelve Olympian gods for the impending war, and he made sacrifices for victory in that war, for which he had been appointed commander as avenger of Persian wrongdoing in Greece. The Persians had ruled for long enough, and better rulers would take their place. This account comes ultimately from Cleitarchus, whose interest was primarily in the Greek part in the expedition. After the sacrifices Parmenio was ordered to oversee the transportation of all non-Macedonian trooops from Sestus to Abydus on the Greek fleet and a number of merchant ships.

Alexander marched with his Macedonians to Elaeus at the tip of the peninsula. He sacrificed there at the tomb of Protesilaus, who had been 'far the first to leap ashore' but had been killed by a Trojan; for Alexander hoped his landing would be more successful. He and his men then embarked on the Macedonian fleet of 60 warships and sailed for

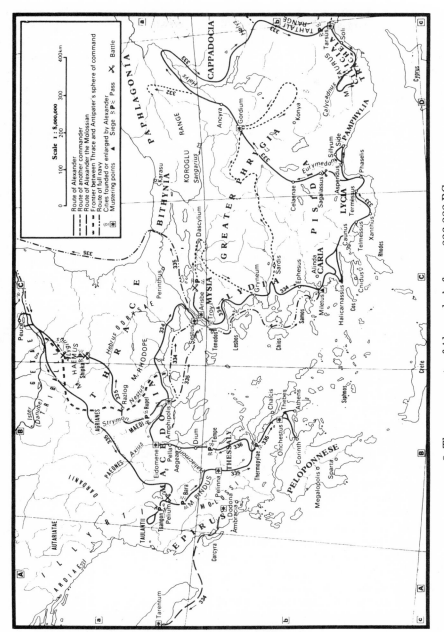

8. The movements of Alexander's forces, 336-333 BC

'the harbour of the Achaeans'. Halfway across the Hellespont Alexander sacrificed a bull and poured libations from a golden goblet to Poseidon and the Nereids. On arrival Alexander, fully armed, was the first of the Macedonians to cast his spear into the ground and to leap ashore with the declaration: 'I accept from the gods Asia won by the spear.' He sacrificed there and then with the prayer that 'those lands would accept him as their king not unwillingly'. For his safe landing he set up altars both at Elaeus and at the harbour of the Achaeans in honour of Zeus of Landings, Athena and Heracles. These accounts came from Ptolemy, Aristobulus and others such as Callisthenes and Onesicritus, who had been with Alexander at the time.

The ceremonies at Sestus on the one hand, and those accompanying the crossing from Elaeus on the other hand reveal the aims which Alexander had for the war. As *Hegemon* of the Greeks he would take vengeance for Persian wrongdoing, liberate the Greeks in Asia from Persian rule and establish a better regime. These limited aims, of vengeance on Persia and liberation from Persia, were those which had been stated by the Greek Community from the time of Philip. There had been no mention of the Greek Community acquiring land in Asia or incorporating the liberated Greeks in its own organisation. As an individual Alexander had his own additional aims: to become King of Asia, which he accepted from the gods and which he intended to win by the spear. Thus his purpose was not merely to overthrow the Persian rule and provide a better regime for Persia's subjects; it was to accept 'Asia' as his own kingdom, namely the continent bounded in the east by Ocean. From that moment 'Asia' was his, and he prayed that the Asians would accept him willingly as their king. That was the will of the gods. Once again we see the extraordinary confidence of the young king.

Alexander loved the *Iliad* beyond any other literary work. To him it was a record of historical persons and actions. He laid a wreath on the tomb of Achilles, and Hephaestion laid one on the tomb of Patroclus; for Hephaestion was Alexander's 'trusted friend', just as Patroclus had been Achilles' trusted friend. They and the other Companions then ran a race naked, in the customary manner, in honour of Achilles. Proceeding inland from the tomb of Achilles to Troy, Alexander sacrificed to the Trojan Athena, dedicated his armour in her temple, and took from it some of the shields which survived from the Trojan War. He atoned for the sacrilege committed by his ancestor, Neoptolemus, the son of Achilles, who had killed Priam, the king of Troy, at the very altar of Zeus Herkeios (Zeus of the Household). For he sacrificed there to Priam, and he prayed that Priam would not vent his wrath on Neoptolemus' descendants. It was evidently important to Alexander that the Trojan Athena as goddess of war and the potent spirit of Priam should be won over to his side. He was said to emphasise his connection through Olympias with Andromache, a granddaughter of Priam; for she bore to

Neoptolemus a son Molossus, after whom the Molossian royal house was named. We see here the depth of Alexander's belief in his own descent, in the power of the gods wherever their shrines might be, and in the power of a king centuries after his death.

An unknown artist portrayed the moment when Alexander fixed his long pike (*sarissa*) into the soil of Asia. The painting, a copy of a Hellenistic original (Plate 7), survived under the lava of Mount Vesuvius at Boscoreale. Alexander is shown as a young man, wearing the traditional cap (*kausia*), and beside him there is a Macedonian shield with a star at its centre. He is on one side of the blue water of the Hellespont, and the personified figure of Asia on the other side returns his intent gaze with a look of acceptance. To the spectator's left, the philosopher Aristotle watches from a distance.

3. The battle of the river Granicus

From Troy Alexander rejoined the main army. He paraded and numbered the forces which had crossed with him to Asia. A record was made in the *Journal*, but different figures were released to deceive the enemy. Most of the record has come down through Diodorus from Ptolemy (above, p. 64). Alexander had been able to make the crossing in peace, because the vanguard which Philip had sent was in control of the Asiatic coast of the Hellespont, and because the Persian fleet had not yet entered the Aegean. During the last eighteen months Alexander and the Greek Community had not reinforced the vanguard, which had been driven back by the Persian commander-in-chief, Memnon (above, p. 25). In the Greek cities there were partisans for each side. Parmenio enslaved the population of Gryneum, a city in the south which had evidently joined Memnon, but he failed to take Pitane by siege. On this front the Persian forces reached Rhoeteum in the Troad. To the north Memnon and his officers, wearing the Macedonian cap (*kausia*), nearly tricked the people of Cyzicus into opening their gates, but he then ravaged their land with a force of 5,000 Greek mercenaries. Alexander arrived just in time to save the holding force of Macedonians, Greek mercenaries and probably Greek troops from the Greek Community, whose commander-in-chief then was Calas.

As we have seen, Alexander needed a speedy victory to obtain supplies. Memnon probably realised this, for he advised a strategy of retreat leaving scorched earth; but the Persian satraps refused to sacrifice their lands and concentrated their forces near Zelea, inland to the east of Abydus. Their intention was to attack Alexander's base at Abydus, if he should advance southwards; or to draw him eastwards and block his advance there. They adopted a strong defensive position on the east bank of the river Granicus, placing their excellent cavalry 20,000 strong on the level ground facing the river and their 20,000

Greek mercenary infantry on the hillside above the level ground. It was a position which could not be turned on either flank, and it blocked the approach to the 'Asian Gates', a narrow pass through which a Persian road ran eastwards.

Alexander acted with characteristic speed and confidence. Three days after completion of the landing he advanced into the Granicus plain not with his full army but with the Macedonian forces, the Agrianians and the Greek cavalry. They numbered some 13,000 infantry and 5,100 cavalry. Alexander will have learnt from Calas the strength of the Persian army, and he was sure that his élite forces could defeat the superior numbers of the enemy. It was after midday when his scouts galloped back to tell him of the Persian position on the far side of the river. Alexander halted to consult his commanders. Some record of the discussion was preserved in the *Journal* which Ptolemy was able to consult, and we probably owe to him a summary of what Parmenio advised. He was opposed to a frontal attack (presumably proposed by Alexander), because the river was deep in places and the far bank was steep and high, and because if some troops did force their way onto the level ground they would be swamped by the enemy cavalry. He proposed camping where they were and deciding next day how to make a crossing. Alexander's comment in reply included the remark: 'I am ashamed if, after crossing the Hellespont easily, this little stream will stop us from crossing as we are.' He then issued his detailed orders. These had to envisage the development of the action and provide for tactical moves, because he himself as 'a mighty fighter' would be immersed in combat.

Alexander formed his line for a frontal attack as follows. On the left, which Parmenio commanded, the units were from the left the Greek cavalry (1,800 Thessalians and 600 from other states), a squadron of Thracian cavalry (150) and three brigades of phalangites (4,500). On the right, which Alexander commanded, the units were from the right the Agrianians (500), the Archers (500), the Companion Cavalry (1,800), a squadron of Paeonian cavalry (150), the Lancers (600), the Hypaspists (3,000) and three brigades of phalangites (4,500). The numbers of cavalry were the same in each part of the line, but the infantry were more numerous in the right part and the Archers and the Agrianians formed an extension on the extreme right. If the cavalrymen were ten horses deep and the infantry eight men deep, as was normal, the length of the line was some two and a half kilometres. It matched the length of the Persian line of cavalry with a depth of some sixteen horses, of which the rear ranks had plenty of room to manoeuvre on level ground.

The Persian commanders stayed in the position which they had initially adopted and which had been reported to Alexander. If the Macedonian infantrymen had been armed like Greek mercenaries with seven-foot spears, they would have had no chance of fighting their way up and over the bank in the face of the Persian cavalrymen's missiles and against the weight of the horses. But the twelve-foot range of the Macedonian pike was another matter; for a pikeman could strike a horse or its rider from below with deadly effect, and once engaged he was no longer an easy target for missiles. Alexander, on the other hand, counted on his infantry pinning down and gradually defeating the opposing cavalry, and he planned in the meantime to make a breakthrough with massed cavalry at one point and by extending his line to the right to outflank the enemy. He attacked at once, in order to exploit the folly of the Persian commanders in immobilising their Greek mercenaries.

Alexander, wearing white plumes on his helmet, was a conspicuous figure at the front of the Royal Cavalry Guard. The Persian commanders moved to face him with their finest cavalry. At Alexander's order the trumpets blew and the army went down into the wide, shingly riverbed. The initial assault was delivered to the left of Alexander's position by one Companion Cavalry squadron, the Paeonian cavalry, the Lancers and the Royal Brigade of Hypaspists. While the attack pinned down the opposing cavalry, Alexander did not engage but was extending his line on his side of the riverbed to his right, so that the Archers and the Agrianians outflanked the opposition. By then the Companion Cavalry squadron which had led the assault and inflicted casualties was being driven back. At that moment Alexander ordered the general attack. At the head of the Royal Cavalry Squadron he charged into the enemy group which had repulsed the weakened squadron.

In ferocious hand-to-hand fighting Alexander and his entourage prevailed thanks to their 'strength, experience and lances of cornelwood against javelins'. Alexander's lance had broken; so too had that of his groom. But Demaratus gave him his own lance. Alexander and those with him were on top of the bank but not in formation, when a wedge of enemy cavalry, led by Mithridates, began to charge. Alexander rode out ahead, struck Mithridates in the face and unseated him, just as Rhoesaces charged Alexander and smashed part of his helmet with his scimitar. As Alexander struck Rhoesaces in the chest with his lance, Spithridates was raising his scimitar to kill Alexander when his right arm was hacked off by Cleitus. The Persians were now losing ground all along the line. On the right the Archers and the Agrianians, attacking the cavalry in the flank and mingling with their own cavalry, were rolling up the enemy's left wing, and the squadrons of the Companion Cavalry fought their way onto the top of the bank. To the left of Alexander the Hypaspists and the phalangites used their pikes to good effect. 'When the Persian centre had given way, the cavalry on each wing broke and fled precipitately.'

Alexander regrouped his men and surrounded the phalanx of the 20,000 Greek mercenary infantry, which had stood still 'more in astonishment at the unexpected turn of events than from tactical considerations'. They were a formidable force, because they outnumbered Alexander's phalangites by a large margin and were experienced fighters. But when they stayed still and were surrounded, they had little chance of survival; for the Macedonian phalanx would deliver a frontal charge and the cavalry and the light-armed infantry would attack their exposed flanks and rear. According to Plutarch, who was probably following Aristobulus, the commander of the mercenaries asked for terms of withdrawal under oath, but Alexander refused; for he knew they would then fight again in Persian service. He himself on horseback led the attack 'more in passion than in reason', and his horse was killed under him by a sword-thrust. But the outcome was as it had been with the Sacred Band at Chaeronea; for the pikemen in formation shattered the Greek phalanx. The surrender of 2,000 was accepted.

The total defeat of the enemy was due to the military genius of Alexander. His immediate grasp of the tactical situation, his coordination of all arms in a coordinated attack, and his ingenuity in combining the initial assault with the extension of his line upstream to the right were all brilliant. His speed in deliberation and in action left the Persian commanders no chance of reorganising their forces and enabled him to defeat the cavalry and then the infantry separately. The cavalry battle caught the public eye. For the Persian cavalry was an élite force recruited from as far afield as Bactria and commanded by members of Darius' family and entourage, known as 'The Kinsmen' (*syngeneis*). 'The meed of valour' (*aristeia*) went to Alexander in person; and 'the mighty warrior' must have felt that he bore a charmed life, as any young man is apt to do in battle.

The 2,000 Greek mercenaries were sent to Macedonia to labour in chains for life (corpses so chained have been found recently in Chalcidice), because 'being Greeks they had fought against Greece in violation of the decisions of the Greeks'. The Greek mercenaries who had fallen in battle and the Persian officers were given an honourable burial. The loss of the Persian cavalry was put at 1,000 men; for there had been no pursuit. Of the Macedonians the twenty-five dead of the Companion Cavalry squadron which had led the assault were treated as heroes. Alexander commissioned Lysippus to make bronze statues of them, which were to be set up at Dium, alongside the statues of the Temenid kings. Of the other cavalry sixty and of the infantry some thirty had fallen. All were buried with their arms and equipment, and 'remission of taxes on land and property, and of personal services' was granted to their parents and their children. The wounded were visited by Alexander, who listened to the accounts of their exploits and examined their wounds. The spoils were collected for Alexander. He sent 300 sets of Persian armour to be dedicated to Athena on the Acropolis of Athens with the inscription: 'Alexander son of Philip and the Greeks except the Lacedaemonians from the barbarians living in Asia.' Similar dedications may have been made in other states; for Alexander 'wished to make the Greeks partners in the victory', rightly since the Greek cavalry had won on the left wing and the Greek fleet had mounted the invasion of Asia. The bulk of the spoil, notably drinking vessels and purple robes, was sent to Olympias.

We owe our information mainly to Arrian, using Ptolemy, who was himself a combatant and had access to the *Journal* in which Alexander's orders and acts were recorded. A less accurate account, that of Aristobulus, was used by Plutarch who reported the fallen as twenty-five cavalrymen and nine infantrymen; and it was evidently Aristobulus who criticised Alexander for acting 'in passion' and understood his wish to make the Greeks partners in the victory. An entirely different account has survived in Diodorus, who used Cleitarchus. It is complete with omens in advance, huge figures (100,000 Persian infantry, 20,000 prisoners), a crossing next day at dawn, separate battles of cavalry against cavalry and then of infantry against infantry, and 'chance' pitting Alexander against 'The Kinsmen'. This account is as worthless as that of the capture of Thebes in Diodorus (above, p. 46). One deduction of interest is that Aristobulus must have published his account of the Macedonian casualties before that of Ptolemy, which rested on the *Journal* and was clearly correct.

CHAPTER VII

The winning of Asia Minor

1. Alexander's policy and advance to Ephesus

The morale of the satraps was shattered. Their leader, Arsites, committed suicide, the others fled each to his satrapy, the large force of Persian cavalry disintegrated, and Parmenio occupied Dascylium, the capital of Hellespontine Phrygia, without opposition; for its garrison had fled. The weakness of the Persian imperial system in this western area was apparent. Each satrap governed his own satrapy (analogous to a Roman province) with full powers, and he recruited his own armed forces, which consisted primarily of the native aristocrats as cavalrymen and of Greek mercenary soldiers as infantrymen. When infantry was recruited from the indigenous peoples, it was of poor quality and reluctant to fight in support of Persia's oppressive rule. So far from recruiting Greeks the satraps often had to supply garrisons to buttress the rule of dictators or juntas imposed on the Greek cities by Persia. Moreover, the satraps were often at odds with one another. The Great King, living at Susa in Iran, exercised a remote control in that he appointed and deposed members of his own family or of his entourage as satraps, and he was informed of the situation in each satrapy by his agents, known as the King's Eyes. But that control was loose; and when he appointed Memnon to be commander-in-chief of the resistance to the Macedonians, Memnon was unable to impose his will on the satraps. After the defeat at the Granicus Memnon received little or no support from the satraps and relied on the garrisons in the Greek cities to slow down the advance of the Macedonians.

Alexander was able to publicise his own policy in these early days. It was not that which Isocrates and Aristotle had advised, namely the subjection of the barbarians as slaves to their Greek and Macedonian masters. The self-declared King of Asia, he regarded the land as his possession and the peoples of Asia, whether Greek or native, as his subjects. His aim was to overthrow the oppressive Persian rule and to introduce his own rule, under which the native peoples would be respected and fairly treated. Thus when he reviewed his army after the landing, he placed a ban on looting and ravaging, because 'his own property was to be spared'; and when hillsmen came to make their submission, expecting slavery, he told them 'to return each to his own property'. The Greek city Zelea had served as the Persian base. On capturing it Alexander did not punish the people by enslaving them as Parmenio had done at Gryneum (above, p. 65). He pardoned them on the grounds that 'they had been forced to fight on the side of the barbarians'. He showed respect for the Persian officers who had so nearly killed him; for he gave honourable burial to those who had fallen, and he took into his service any Persian cavalrymen who wished to join him. Immediately after the battle he made dedications to the Trojan Athena and he declared Troy a free city, i.e. exempt from paying tribute; for this Asian goddess had accepted and supported him. It was indeed said that one of the shields which he had taken from her temple saved his life during the hand-to-hand fighting at the Granicus.

The wisdom of Alexander's policy appeared as he approached Sardis, the satrapal centre of Lydia. 'He was met by the chief citizens of Sardis (Lydians) and by Mithrenes (the Persian commander), who surrendered the city and the treasury ... he kept Mithrenes by his side, according him honourable rank, and he granted to the Lydians the use of their ancestral laws and he left them to be free' – 'free' in the sense that they were to govern themselves in their own way. He retained the satrapal system and the payment of tribute to which the Asians were accustomed, and he appointed Calas, a Macedonian, as satrap of Hellespontine Phrygia. He made an important reform in the case of Lydia and elsewhere thereafter: for Pausanias was put in charge of a garrison of Argive troops at Sardis, Nicias in charge of assessing and collecting tribute, and Asander in charge of civil affairs with some troops 'for the time being'. Each officer was responsible directly to Alexander. Their names are known to us from Arrian, whose source, Ptolemy, drew on the *Journal* in which their appointment and their responsibility to Alexander were recorded. The separation of military, financial and civil duties was a measure which Rome was not to take in Asia until the time of Augustus. Another innovation was made now or soon afterwards in Lydia, namely the training of young Lydians for service in the king's forces; some four years later Lydian troops joined his field army (below, p. 123).

The liberation of the Greek cities was undertaken by a number of task forces which Alexander sent out under Macedonian commanders. He marched with the rest of the army from Sardis to Ephesus, which he reached on the fourth day. He overthrew the pro-Persian oligarchy, brought back the exiles and set up a democracy. He himself was fortunate in having no political ideology. So when the democrats began to kill their political opponents, Alexander put a stop to 'further interrogation and reprisal, realising that if permission was given the people would kill the innocent as well as the guilty, from personal hatred or in order to seize their property'. His prevention of the excesses of party-strife (*stasis*) was highly praised at the time. It was to be characteristic of all his dealings with Greek city-states.

After his action at Ephesus he passed a general order that all liberated Greek cities were to replace oligarchies with democracies, again with an insistence on amnesty, and to re-establish their own legal procedures. He dealt with the Greek cities in person, not through the local satrap, and he exempted them from the payment of tribute. Thus they were granted a favoured status within the kingdom of Asia. But they were still subject to the orders of the king, and for the prosecution of the war he required payment for the time being of a financial contribution (*syntaxis*). At Ephesus he asked not for a contribution but for the payment of the assessed Persian tribute to the authorities of the temple of Artemis, perhaps in gratitude for their action in setting up a statue of Philip in the temple. His concern to win the favour of the Greek deities was apparent also at Sardis, where he planned to build a temple to Zeus and was guided by a violent thunderstorm to the divinely revealed site. While political changes were being made in many of the liberated cities, Alexander stayed in Ephesus, offered a state sacrifice to Artemis, and mounted a grand procession in which the army under arms was drawn up as for battle. He had good reason to thank the deities. For his anxiety over finance and supplies was a thing of the past, he now ruled over two-thirds of the western coast of Asia Minor, and he had publicised his policy as King of Asia towards his new subjects.

2. The war at sea and the siege of Halicarnassus

While he was still at Ephesus, Alexander must have known that a Persian fleet was about to enter Aegean waters. When it did so, he would face the problem which Agesilaus, king of Sparta, had faced in 396. He had already avoided the mistakes of Agesilaus which Xenophon had revealed in his *Hellenica*. For Agesilaus had made excessive demands on the 'liberated' Greek cities, had treated the indigenous peoples as enemies, and had ravaged far inland in pursuit of booty. In the Greek mainland and in the islands the oppressive rule of Sparta had led to a rising by states which hoped for Persian aid in gold and in troops. Sparta had recalled the bulk of Agesilaus' army and left the Greek navy under Spartan command to face the Persian fleet. The result had been the defeat of the Greek navy, Persian support of the Greek rising against Sparta, and the Peace of Antalcidas in 386, under which Persia took over the Greek cities in Asia and guaranteed the autonomy of the Greek states elsewhere. In 334 Alexander knew that the Persian fleet would be formidable; for Persia was in control of Egypt, Cyprus, Phoenicia and all the coast up to Ephesus, and it was from these areas that Persia now conscripted triremes with their native crews of trained oarsmen.

On the day after the procession at Ephesus Alexander marched towards Miletus. He invested the inner city and brought the Greek fleet of 160 triremes to the offshore island of Lade, where they were beached and protected by a large force of his Balkan troops. A Persian fleet of 400 triremes appeared three days later and sailed northwards for some fifteen kilometres to establish a base on Cape Mycale. Should the Greek fleet offer battle? Alexander consulted his staff. According to Arrian Parmenio wished to engage the enemy and offered to go on board himself. He thought a Greek victory probable, particularly because an eagle had been seen on the beach astern of the Greek fleet and its appearance there was, he thought, a presage of victory sponsored by Zeus. Alexander was not willing to engage. He judged the Phoenician and Cyprian crews to be better trained than those of the various Greek contingents, and in the event of defeat by such superior numbers he would lose the lives of the Macedonians acting as marines and increase the danger of a rising by some Greek states of the mainland. The omen he interpreted differently. The fact that the eagle was on the land meant that 'he would master the Persian fleet from the land'.

A leading Milesian offered to open the city to both sides. Alexander told him to expect an attack at dawn. During the siege the entry to the harbour was blocked by a line of Greek triremes, so that the Persians were unable to intervene. The city fell with considerable losses among the Greek mercenaries and the Milesians. Alexander pardoned the other Milesians and declared them to be 'free', in the sense that they would govern themselves. He took into his own service 300 Greek mercenaries who had been prepared to fight to the death. During the siege the Persians were prevented from landing at Mycale by a detachment of Macedonian cavalry and infantry, and they ran so short of supplies and water that they withdrew to Samos. They returned only to see the fall of Miletus, the strongest city of the west coast.

Alexander now sent the bulk of the Greek fleet to home waters. There the crews were not demobilised but were to be ready for recall. He knew that his Greek fleet was no match at sea for the Persian fleet, and he was able to shift the payment of its wages from his own funds in Asia to those of the Greek Community. His plan now was to follow the indication given by the eagle, the bird of Zeus, namely to capture all the bases of the Persian fleet on the Mediterranean coast, prevent it from obtaining replacements of crews and equipment, and so force it to surrender. The plan was extraordinarily bold. For its success was dependent on a number of factors: the ability of his army to capture the bases, the ability of the Macedonian fleet to hold the Hellespont, and the unwillingness of most city-states and especially of Athens to desert the Greek Community and join forces with Persia. To many that boldness may have seemed a gamble. To Alexander it was a matter of precise calculation and of faith in the divine will as it was revealed in the omen of the eagle.

For the rest of the sailing season Darius appointed Memnon to take command of 'lower Asia (southern Asia Minor) and the entire fleet'. It might have been expected that he would sail unopposed across the Aegean in the hope of raising a revolt in Greece. However, he decided to hold Halicarnassus (Bodrum) with the pick of his Persian troops, many Greek mercenaries and a part of the fleet, stationed inside the harbour. The defences of the city were exceptionally strong: a deep, wide moat to make approach difficult, a masonry wall six feet thick, high masonry towers, battlements and sally-ports, and two inner cita- dels. There was a large stock of missiles for catapults, and supplies of every kind could be brought in by sea. If the city should hold out, the Persian fleet would have an impregnable base within the Aegean basin and the advance of Alexander might be halted.

During the march from Miletus Alexander won over the cities 'by his kind treatment' and granted self-government and freedom from tribute to the Greeks. The deposed ruler of the Carians, Ada, came as a suppliant to meet him and to surrender her stronghold, Alinda; for his part Alexander accepted adoption as her son and entrusted Alinda to her. His chivalry won the approval of the Carian cities, which sent missions to crown him with golden crowns and promised to cooperate with him. This welcome was of great importance, since the Carians were a warlike people and had fought for their freedom in the past. He was now able to concentrate all his forces outside Halicarnassus. Dur- ing the inactivity of the Persian fleet his small Greek fleet, led by the Athenian flotilla of twenty triremes, brought from Miletus the scaling ladders and the siege-engines (battering-rams, wheeled towers, man- tlets and catapults), many of which had been made in sections and were re-assembled on arrival. Some ships carried supplies of food for the army, and these were supplemented by contributions from friendly cities. After an abortive attempt to capture Myndus nearby Alexander settled down to what was certain to be a long and difficult siege.

Two accounts of the siege have survived, each in an abbreviated version. That of Diodorus, drawing on Cleitarchus, was written from the point of view of the defenders and magnified their successes in an epic manner; it is of little worth. That of Arrian, drawing on Ptolemy and Aristobulus, who had written for participants, portrayed actions mainly from the Macedonian standpoint and derived some details from the *Journal* (e.g. the numbers of Macedonians killed and of Macedoni- ans wounded when the defenders made a sortie at night). It did not omit successes by the defence; but it named only Memnon, Orontobates (satrap of Caria) and a Macedonian deserter on the Persian side, whereas a number of Macedonian officers were named as commanders and as casualties, no doubt as in the *Journal*.

It is enough here to describe the final stage of the siege. The attackers had brought down two high towers and the intervening wall, but the defenders had built a crescent-shaped brick wall behind the gap and manned high towers, one at either end, so that the missiles from their catapults enfiladed those who attacked the brick wall. When Alexander in person led a second attack on this wall, the entire force of the defenders made two coordinated sorties and came near to success. But in the end they were driven back with great loss, and the Macedonians might have forced an entry, had not Alexander halted his forces in order to spare the Greeks of Halicarnassus from the horrors of street-fighting. During this operation we have the first mention of engines firing 'great stones' and of more powerful bolt-shooting catapults, which relied on the torsion of twisted horse-hair. These were invented by Diades and Charias, pupils of Philip's Thessalian expert, Polyidus. The stone-throwers could smash a doorway or a masonry face, and the improved catapults could drive defenders from towers and parapets.

Orontobates and Memnon now decided that they could not withstand another assault. They therefore set fire to their own equipment and to the houses near the walls that night, and they withdrew their troops into the two citadels. Entering the city, Alexander ordered that Halicarnassian citizens should be spared and the fires extinguished. Next day he decided not to lay siege to the citadels. He moved the population elsewhere, since he could not protect them, and he razed the buildings of the city. He appointed Ada to be satrap of Caria, confident that she would be loyal to him, and a Macedonian officer to command 200 cavalry and 3,000 Greek mercenaries. They were to keep the Persians at Halicarnassus under observation, but they were a small force for such a task. For the Persians held the harbour and could bring in reinforcements. Alexander must have known that he was leaving a dangerous centre of resistance and a base for the Persian fleet in 333 (for the sailing season was ending). But he decided to go ahead with his plans elsewhere.

3. The division of forces and the advance of Alexander to Pamphylia

In the autumn of 334 Alexander had a fair idea of what Persia intended to do the following year. The decision of Orontobates and Memnon to keep control of the citadels and the harbour of Halicarnassus was a clear indication that the Persian fleet hoped in the spring to use Halicarnassus as a base and to advance through the Aegean either to raise revolt in the Peloponnese and/or to wrest the Hellespont from the Macedonians – things which it had failed utterly even to attempt in 334 because Memnon had concentrated all his forces on the defence of Halicarnassus. Then on land it was surprising that after the defeat at the Granicus Darius had not sent a part of his imperial army from Persia into Asia Minor to attack Alexander's lines of communication or to face him in battle. The explanation could only be that Darius intended to do so with a very large army in the spring or summer of 333. He was planning presumably to advance along the Royal Road through the centre of Asia Minor towards the coast, or to engage Alexander in a set battle in Cilicia or in Syria. In either case he would be in a very strong position if he was able to meet his fleet and conduct a coordinated offensive.

Alexander knew from the experience of Philip in Macedonia and Thrace that possession of a coastal strip alone was precarious and that it was essential to control the hinterland. This was particularly true in Asia Minor; for the valleys of the great rivers (Caïcus, Hermus, Caÿster and Maeander) provided easy routes to the coast, and Alexander did not have sufficient forces to block those valleys. The best defence therefore was to take possession of the very extensive Anatolian plateau from which these rivers flowed. That plateau was very suitable for cavalry, and its enormous resources of grain and fodder would supply his army throughout the winter. Concurrently he intended to continue his policy of 'mastering the Persian fleet from the land' by gaining control of the harbours on the southern coast of Asia Minor – a major undertaking because the mountainous terrain was suitable only for infantry and the native peoples were warlike. If he was to pursue both policies, he would need to divide his army and increase, if possible, the number of his troops.

After burying those who had been killed during the final night at Halicarnassus Alexander sent those of the Macedonians who were recently married to Macedonia, so that they could spend the winter with their wives – an act of compassion which won him much popularity. The officers in charge of them were ordered to 'enlist as many as possible from the countryside, both cavalry and infantry' and to bring them on their return. Another officer was sent to the Peloponnese to hire mercenaries with money which Alexander was now able to spare from his winnings in Asia. The Thessalian and other Greek cavalry, 'a hipparchy of the Companions' (perhaps half of the squadrons with the exception of the Royal Squadron), the Greek infantry, the siege-train and the baggage-train were sent under Parmenio via Sardis to capture the northern part of the Anatolian plateau, known as 'Greater Phrygia'. This task was completed during several months. We know nothing of how it was done, because the actions of Parmenio were not recorded in the *Journal* and so were not known to Ptolemy, on whose account Arrian was largely drawing. Alexander set off with the rest of the army 'towards Lycia and Pamphylia to gain control of the coastal region'.

The Lycians were a warlike people both on land and at sea. They had become partly Hellenised, as we know from a bilingual inscription of 337/6 at Xanthus, and they had been ruled by the satrap of Caria. Alexander's army captured at the first attack the city of Hyparna, and Alexander let the mercenary garrison of its acropolis depart under terms. All the cities of southwest Lycia joined Alexander 'by agreement' or 'by surrender'. He attacked the mountaineers of the interior, probably to benefit the coastal cities, and envoys came to him from the coastal cities of southeast Lycia to offer 'friendship'. Alexander ordered them to put themselves in the hands of his representatives. This they did. Alexander benefited them and in particular the Greek city Phaselis by joining forces with them and destroying a garrisoned strongpoint inland, from which the Pisidians had launched raids on the coastal peoples. Arrangements were made for the training of young Lycians in the Macedonian manner. The first draft of them reached Alexander in 329 (below, p. 123).

As Alexander advanced into Pamphylia, one part of his army used a mountain road, which had been made by his Thracian infantry, and the other part followed the seashore, which was passable when a north wind was blowing. Alexander was with the latter group. When he drew near, a southerly wind fell and a strong north wind blew, so that the passage became 'easy and swift', 'not without divine aid, as Alexander and his retinue used to explain'. The belief that the gods were on his side suited Alexander. He himself did not make any such claim in his *Letters*. But he allowed Callisthenes as his official historian to suggest that the sea 'bowed down' to Alexander. In Pamphylia he made Perge, a Greek city, his base. Envoys from another Greek city, Aspendus, came to surrender the city but asked that it should not be garrisoned. Alexander agreed, but he required Aspendus to contribute 50 talents to the expeditionary force and send him the horses they were breeding for the Great King as a form of tribute. The envoys accepted these conditions. Alexander continued along the coast to Side, a city Greek in origin but of mixed population, as bilingual inscriptions reveal. He garrisoned Side and went on to Syllium, a strongly fortified city which had a garrison of mercenaries and Pamphylians. But he turned back on a report that Aspendus had refused entry to his envoys and was preparing to withstand a siege.

Aspendus, beside which the river Eurymedon entered the sea, was an ideal base for a Persian fleet, as it had been in c. 467. Alexander found the population concentrated on the naturally strong, well fortified acropolis, and he did not have the equipment to mount what was likely to be a long siege. Negotiations therefore followed, during which the Aspendians offered to accept the same terms as before. These would have left their city ungarrisoned. Alexander made his own demands, which were accepted: the payment of 100 talents, the provision of the horses, the surrender of the leading men as hostages, payment annually of tribute to 'Macedonians', acceptance of an adjudication about some disputed territory, and obedience to the orders of a satrap appointed by Alexander. These terms were no doubt recorded in the *Journal*, from which Arrian obtained them through the medium of Ptolemy's history. When we consider the original terms and those now imposed on Aspendus, we can see that a liberated Greek city-state in Asia was required to make an *ad hoc* contribution to help the army, exempted from payment of annual tribute, not garrisoned normally, not subject to the orders of a satrap but dealing directly with Alexander. Aspendus was now penalised in that its contribution was doubled, it had to pay annual tribute to 'Macedonians', it was made subject to the orders of the satrap, it had to accept an adjudication by an outside body, and it had to give hostages as a guarantee of future conduct. There is no doubt that Alexander garrisoned the city in order to keep control of the harbour.

The payment of tribute to 'Macedonians' is of particular interest. Alexander did not ask that the money be paid to himself either as King of Macedonia or as King of Asia; for he did not wish the conquest to be regarded as a personal one – similarly Philip had made the Thracians pay a tithe to the Macedonians –, and he did not wish as King of Asia to make a departure from his practice in dealing with the Greek city-states in Asia. Aspendus was thus placed in a separate category, being subject to the Macedonian Assembly in financial matters and subject to Alexander's satrap in local matters.

From Aspendus and Perge Alexander went inland. Before we follow him, we must mention a plot, of which he heard when he was near Phaselis. A Persian agent, called Sisines, was arrested by Parmenio (then invading Phrygia) and forwarded to Alexander. His story ran thus. He had been sent by Darius nominally to meet the Persian satrap of Phrygia but actually to make contact with Alexander Lyncestes, who was then in command of the Thessalian cavalry with Parmenio (above, p. 77). For this Alexander had sent a letter to Darius by the hand of a Macedonian deserter, Amyntas, and in response to that letter Sisines was to say that, if Alexander Lyncestes would assassinate Alexander, Darius would make him king of Macedonia and add a bounty of 1,000 gold talents. Sisines had been arrested before he could reach Alexander Lyncestes.

Alexander convened his Friends and sought their advice. They judged Alexander Lyncestes to be guilty of treason on the evidence of Sisines' report. They were influenced also by an omen. During the siege of Halicarnassus, when Alexander was enjoying a siesta, a chattering swallow flew over his head, landed here and there on his bed, persisted even when it was brushed aside, perched on his head, and so woke him up. At the time Alexander had consulted his diviner, Aristander, who had said that it portended a plot by one of Alexander's Friends and that the plotter would be revealed. Alexander now reported this matter to his Friends in council. They advised Alexander to 'put Alexander Lyncestes out of the way speedily' in case he made himself more popular with the Thessalian cavalry and rebelled with them. A Macedonian officer, wearing local dress and accompanied by guides from Perge, reached Parmenio and delivered a verbal order for him to arrest Alexander Lyncestes. This was done successfully. Alexander kept Alexander Lyncestes under guard for some four years (below, p. 134).

Arrian's account, which we have summarised was based on the versions of Ptolemy and Aristobulus, and Ptolemy could have consulted accounts of the swallow's behaviour and the discussion by Alexander and his Friends which were recorded in the *Journal*. Scholars have generally inferred from the epithet 'Lyncestes' that this Alexander was a member of the disestablished royal house of Lyncus. But the epithet was simply the indication of his residence and so of his citizenship in Lyncus. Everything indicates that he was a member of the Temenid royal house; for he was the first to declare in favour of Alexander in 336, he was said to have succeeded to the command on the supposed death of Alexander in 335, he was given top-ranking appointments by Alexander, and he was a suitable person for Darius to put on the Macedonian throne. His father Aëropus was probably the grandson of Aëropus II, who had been king *c.* 398-395. Why did Alexander not bring the prisoner before the Macedonian Assembly on a charge of treason? The evidence which had convinced the Friends would certainly have convinced the King's Men. It may be that Alexander had an affection for his cousin. There may have been a public reason. Alexander risked his life frequently. If he were to be killed, who was competent to succeed? Arrhidaeus was half-witted. As a gifted and popular commander Alexander Lyncestes might be a suitable successor.

4. Anatolia and Gordium

Winter was well advanced when Alexander turned inland from Perge to force his way through the land of the Pisidians, renowned fighters, and to reach the Anatolian plateau. The first city to resist was Termessus. On approaching a precipitous defile which was held by the Termessians, Alexander encamped to give the impression that he would not attack. As he anticipated, most of the enemy went home, leaving a few guards in position. Alexander then made a rapid attack with a light-armed force, captured the defile, and encamped near the city. A rival of Termessus, Selge, sought and obtained Alexander's friendship with instructions to keep Termessus in check. He was thus able to pass on and attack Sagalassus, reputedly the most formidable of the Pisidian cities. The Sagalassians and some Termessians manned a steep hill in front of the city. Alexander led a frontal assault with 7,500 phalangites,

whose flanks were protected by light-armed troops, Archers and Agrianians on the right and Thracian javelin-men on the left. Since the
light-armed went ahead, the Archers in particular suffered some casualties but by then the phalangites began to engage the enemy who had
no defensive armour and were felled by the pikes. In the battle some
500 were killed and the rest fled, so that Alexander was able to take the
city by storm. His own losses were some twenty men. He quelled the
rest of the Pisidians by capturing some forts and accepting the surrender of others. He could claim that he had imposed his rule; but he made
no appointments and pressed on into Phrygia. 'On the fourth day' he
reached Celaenae (now Dinar), a central point in the communications
within Anatolia.

The satrap of Phrygia had been defeated and driven south by Parmenio. He had fled from the satrapy, but he had left 100 Greek mercenaries and 1,000 Carian soldiers under orders to hold the impregnable
citadel of Celaenae. They were to be reinforced on a specified date. On
the arrival of Alexander they offered to surrender the citadel on that
date, if no reinforcements should reach them. Alexander accepted the
offer, left 1,500 troops to guard the approaches, and in due course the
citadel was surrendered to him. He spent ten days in southern Phrygia,
during which the army had a well-earned rest and he made his administrative arrangements. He appointed Antigonus Monophthalmus
('One-eye') satrap of Phrygia, and led his army to Gordium (near
Ankara), where he was joined by the forces under the command of
Parmenio and by the reinforcements and the Macedonians who had
wintered at home. These reinforcements were 300 Macedonian cavalry,
3,000 Macedonian infantry, 200 Thessalian cavalry and 150 Elean
cavalry. It is probable that they more than made good the losses
incurred in action and through illness during the last twelve months.
For it was now late in April 333.

The achievements of Alexander's army in the one year of unremitting
action since it set out from Macedonia in April 334 almost exceed belief.
It had added to its control an area larger in extent and richer in
resources than the whole of Thrace. It had rendered the Persian fleet
ineffective through its own ability and daring in siegecraft. It had
anticipated any movement of Persia's imperial army into Anatolia by
the rapidity of its own movement. The greatest credit was due to the
King's Men and the Greek cavalry in battle. But their advance was
made possible only by the support system of the Greek fleet until its
departure from Asia, the Greek and Balkan infantry, the engineers of
the siege-train, and the organisers of the baggage-train. Because Alexander banned ravaging and looting, it was only rarely that he 'lived off
the enemy land', as he did for instance in Pisidia, when the baggage-
train was with Parmenio. Otherwise he relied on capturing enemy
dumps and on contribution or purchase of supplies. It was his mastery

of logistics which enabled the spearhead of the army to move with such speed.

His genius as a commander was apparent in his ability to inspire his men by his own bravery in every action and to obtain a heroic response to his commands. His bold strategy was justified by its success. His policy of liberation and favoured treatment for the Greek cities won their cooperation. As King of Asia he freed native peoples from Persian oppression and obtained the support, for instance, of Lydia, Caria and Lycia. Where he met opposition, as in Pisidia, he proved his superiority in war but did not impose garrisons or exact reprisals. There was no period of 'military government' of the modern kind. For he took over the existing form of satrapal government, made important improvements in it, and began the training of some young men in the Macedonian manner.

CHAPTER VIII

The battle of Issus and the capture of the Mediterranean coast

1. War at sea and the advance to Tarsus

On the acropolis of Gordium there was a wagon which, it was believed, had been dedicated to Zeus the King by Midas, a Phrygian king. Alexander was told of the local belief that anyone who untied the elaborate knot binding the yoke to the pole 'must rule over Asia'. He tried in vain; but then he took out the yoke-pin and so separated the yoke from the pole. That night thunder and lightning showed the approval of Zeus, and Alexander sacrificed next day to 'the gods who made the signs manifest and revealed the way to undo the binding'. Such was the account of Aristobulus, who saw that Alexander was actuated by a 'yearning' (*pothos*) in tackling the knot. Other authors said that Alexander lost his temper and cut the knot with his sword. Since Aristobulus may well have been present and wrote for contemporaries, his version is to be preferred. The incident was important in that Alexander's words at the Hellespont 'I accept Asia from the gods' were now confirmed by the deities. He knew beyond a doubt that he would be the ruler of Asia.

Between April and August Alexander consolidated his authority and extended it towards the Black Sea. Paphlagonia accepted his rule, provided hostages, and was added to the satrapy of Hellespontine Phrygia. It was exempted from paying tribute. The Greek cities on its coast were ordered to install democracies, as we know in the case of Amisus, east of Sinope. Alexander then led the recruits from Macedonia into Cappadocia, east of Paphlagonia, brought much of the region to his side, and appointed a Macedonian to be satrap of Cappadocia, which controlled the entry from Armenia into Asia Minor. He prolonged his stay in Anatolia for strategic reasons. From it he could move readily to the Hellespont, to the west coast or southeastwards into Cilicia, and his choice would depend on the outcome of the war at sea.

In March 333 Memnon sailed unopposed into the Aegean with 300 triremes and an abundance of money. He had a strong force of Greek mercenaries, which overpowered Alexander's supporters in Chios and in Lesbos except at Mytilene, where Greek mercenaries sent by Alexan-

9. Cilicia

der strengthened resistance. From late April until June Memnon maintained a blockade of Mytilene, thus losing the initiative at sea. Meanwhile Alexander had ordered the Macedonian fleet in the Hellespont to take the offensive, Antipater to recruit naval forces and hold the western Aegean, and the Greek Community to call up the Greek fleet 'in accordance with their treaty obligations as his allies' and hold the Hellespont. He sent 1,100 talents to the Macedonian commanders and to Antipater, and a letter to Athens, which with her stock of some 350 triremes (she could man half herself) held the balance at sea. The Greek Community stayed loyal. At Athens 'the orators' proposed refusal but the good sense of Phocion and others prevailed. Alexander's earlier confidence in 'The Greeks' was justified. The fleets were at sea when Memnon died in June. Thereafter the Persians stayed at Mytilene under the command of a Persian Pharnabazus, whose appointment was not confirmed by Darius for a month or so.

In July Alexander learnt of Memnon's death, and soon afterwards of the departure of Memnon's force of Greek mercenaries, who had been summoned to Syria by Darius. It was Alexander's belief that the Greek and Macedonian fleets would hold the Hellespont and the western Aegean. He therefore chose now to invade Cilicia and to encounter Darius' large army, which was evidently on the way to the Syrian coast. The Cilician Gates, a narrow cliff-bound pass, was held by Persian forces. Alexander encamped far off, and in person led a force of Hypaspists, Archers and Agrianians on a night march, hoping to surprise the enemy at dawn. In fact the Persians were on the alert, but when they saw that Alexander was leading the attack, they fled and the pass was open. When cavalry and other light-armed infantry came up, Alexander led them so fast that they covered the fifty-seven miles to Tarsus before dark. The Persian satrap had planned to plunder the city, but he fled, leaving it intact.

Alexander collapsed, either from sheer exhaustion or after a plunge into the icy waters of the Cydnus at Tarsus, and the doctors despaired of his life, except one, Philip, an Acarnanian. He was preparing a potion when Alexander was informed by a despatch from Parmenio that Philip was in the pay of Darius. Alexander handed the despatch to Philip and drank the potion, 'demonstrating his trust to Philip and his complete confidence to his friends – and also his strength of will in the face of death'. Such is Arrian's account, derived from Aristobulus. Other versions were even more sensational. The illness persisted from July into October. During that time Pharnabazus reinforced the Persians at Halicarnassus, and he captured Mytilene, Tenedos and Samothrace, from which he threatened the Macedonian hold on the Hellespont. Other Persian ships sailed to the Cyclades and an advance force of ten triremes reached Siphnos. There they were surprised at dawn by a Macedonian commander with fifteen warships, and only two escaped.

The defence of the Hellespont and the western Aegean was still holding when Alexander recovered his health.

By early October Alexander knew that Darius was on his way towards the coast. He sent Parmenio in command of the Thessalian cavalry, Greek and Balkan infantry, and some Greek mercenaries with the task of expelling the satrapal forces from the coast as far south as the Pillar of Jonah, where a narrow pass divided Cilicia from Syria. He himself led the rest of his army westwards into Cilicia Tracheia ('Rough'), where there was some support for Persia. He fined Soli, a Greek city, for that reason and placed a garrison in it, and he took a flying column into the mountains, where he won over some communities and expelled others, all in a week. Alexander's aim in sending Parmenio so far and himself reducing Cilicia Tracheia was to prevent the fleet of Pharnabazus and the army of Darius operating together on the Mediterranean coast; for if they should do so, they would be able to land troops in his rear and cut his line of communications and supply. As it was, after his and Parmenio's success, no port of call was available for Persian warships south of Halicarnassus and Caunus. On his return to Soli the news arrived that the satraps of Lydia and Caria had won a victory over the Persian forces of Orontobates near Halicarnassus. Alexander now celebrated the Macedonian state festival in honour of Olympian Zeus and the Muses, as he had done in 335, with a procession by the whole army, a torch-race and competitions. He made a sacrifice to Asclepius who had restored him to health.

Alexander then began the march to join Parmenio. He halted at Mallus, a Greek city, where he put a stop to a *stasis* among the citizens, and he was still there when news came that Darius was encamped at Sochi in Syria, a march of some two days inland from the Pillar of Jonah, which was held by Parmenio's force. It seemed that Alexander's strategy was succeeding. For he expected to engage the army of Darius, when it was inland and out of reach of the Persian fleet. See Plate 10.

2. The campaign of Issus

Alexander consulted his close Companions. They urged him to lead them into action forthwith. He thanked them, met Parmenio en route, placed his baggage-train and his sick at Issus, passed the Pillar of Jonah and encamped by Myriandrus on the coast (near Iskenderun). A night of storm and rain caused him to stay in camp and rest his army all day. A report came early on the following day that Darius was behind him on the far side of the Pillar of Jonah. Incredulous, Alexander embarked some Companions on a triaconter. They sailed back, entered the bay by the mouth of the river Pinarus (Payas), and came back with some information about Darius' position. It was only too true. Darius had cut Alexander's line of supply; and if he could stand firm, he would starve Alexander's army into surrender. How had it happened? Darius had waited for many days at Sochi, where a wide plain suited his superior numbers and his fine cavalry. He knew that Alexander's army was split, and he assumed from Alexander's delay that Alexander would stay at Tarsus. He therefore marched his army north, crossed the Amanus range by the Bahce pass, and reached the coast at Issus. Had his assumption been correct, he would have camped between the two enemy forces, dealt with each separately and probably been helped by his fleet. By sheer chance Alexander had marched from Tarsus to Myriandrus during the very days when Darius was on his way to and from the Bahce Pass. On reaching Issus Darius mutilated and then killed the Macedonian sick. He then moved his huge army – several times as numerous as that of Alexander – to a defensive position on the right bank of the river Payas.

When the triaconter returned, Alexander convened his commanders, exhorted them and received their enthusiastic support. He sent some cavalry and archers to ascertain if the pass at the Pillar of Jonah, six kilometres away, was occupied by the enemy. It was not, to Alexander's relief, for the route was along a narrow beach which was flooded when winds were adverse and which was flanked by cliffs on the landward side. The army was told to take its evening meal. It then marched to the pass, which it reached about midnight. Sentries were posted on the cliff-tops, and the men had a few hours of sleep. Alexander sacrificed in thanksgiving to the deities of the sea (Poseidon, Thetis, Nereus and the Nereids), because the beach was not flooded. At dawn the march began towards the Payas river, six kilometres away, and as the army, deploying from column into line of battle, began to descend slowly towards the low ground, Alexander was issuing his orders to his commanders.

The army numbered 5,300 cavalry and 26,000 infantry. Parmenio was to command the left-hand part of the line, which consisted from left to right of the squadrons of Greek cavalry but not the Thessalians, then the Cretan Archers and the Thracian javelin-men, and then three brigades of phalangites, the last under the command of Craterus. Parmenio was told to keep close to the coast, in order not to be outflanked. Alexander commanded the right-hand part, of which the units from right to left were Lancers and Paeonian cavalry, then Macedonian Archers and Agrianians, then Thessalian cavalry, Companion Cavalry, Royal Infantry Guard, Hypaspists and three brigades of the phalanx, which was eight men deep. There was a second line behind and shorter than the phalanx; it consisted of Balkan, Greek and Greek mercenary infantry. He changed some of these dispositions during the slow descent. The Thessalian cavalry was transferred to the left wing. Because his right was outflanked by a Persian force on a spur of the mountain (see Fig. 10), he detached 300 cavalry to keep it at bay and extended his own line to the right by bringing up Greek mercenaries from the second

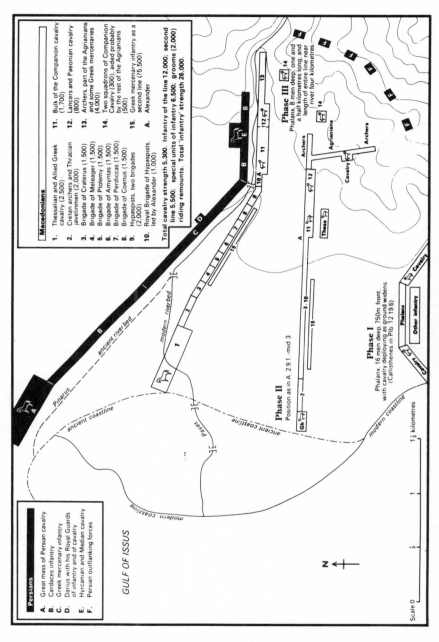

Persians

A. Great mass of Persian cavalry
B. Cardaces infantry
C. Greek mercenary infantry
D. Darius with his Royal Guards of infantry and of cavalry
E. Hyrcanian and Median cavalry
F. Persian outflanking forces

Macedonians

1. Thessalian and Allied Greek cavalry (2,500).
2. Cretan archers and Thracian javelinmen (2,000).
3. Brigade of Craterus (1,500).
4. Brigade of Meleager (1,500).
5. Brigade of Ptolemy (1,500).
6. Brigade of Amyntas (1,500).
7. Brigade of Perdiccas (1,500).
8. Brigade of Coenus (1,500).
9. Hypaspists, two brigades (2,000).
10. Royal Brigade of Hypaspists, led by Alexander (1,000).
11. Bulk of the Companion cavalry (1,700).
12. Lancers and Paeonian cavalry (800).
13. Archers, part of the Agrianians and some Greek mercenaries (4,000).
14. Two squadrons of Companion Cavalry (300), aided probably by the rest of the Agrianians (500).
15. Greek mercenary infantry as a second line (75,500).
A. Alexander

Total cavalry strength 5,300. Infantry of the line 12,000; second line 5,500; special units of infantry 6,500; grooms (2,000) riding remounts. Total 'infantry' strength 26,000.

GULF OF ISSUS

Phase II

Position as in A 2.9.1.-mid 3.

Phase I

Phalanx, 16 men deep, 750m front, with cavalry deploying as ground widens (Callisthenes in Plb 12.19.6)

Cavalry
Phalanx
Other infantry
Cavalry

Phase III

Phalanx, 8 men deep, one and a half kilometres long, and length of entire line near river four kilometres.

Archers
Cavalry
Agrianians
Archers
Archers

ancient river bed
modern river bed
ancient coastline
modern coastline
ancient coastline
modern coastline
Pinarus
Payas

Scale 0   ½   1   1½ kilometres

N

10. The Battle of Issus

line. When these dispositions were completed, he halted the four-kilometres-long line. He rode along it, exhorting his men, returned to his position at the head of the Royal Infantry Guard, and ordered the final advance in perfect line 'step by step'.

Although the army of Darius was much larger, there were no more men in his front line than in Alexander's front line, so that his superiority in numbers was of little value. The position he had chosen was exceptionally strong. On emerging from the steep mountainside the Payas today has a boulder-strewn bed some 35 metres wide, and shelving banks, sometimes eaten into by flood water. A little below the first bridge (Fig. 10) the river enters a channel, cut long ago through the conglomerate rock, with a cliff-like right bank some three to seven metres high but with occasional breaks. Below the second bridge the river flows through gravel and sand and has low banks. Its course was different here in antiquity, but the terrain was the same. Darius placed his best infantry on the top of the bank between the positions of the two modern bridges and strengthened any gaps with stockades. The infantry were Greek mercenaries, flanked on each side by Persian 'Cardaces', equipped like the mercenaries but having also bow and arrows. They were in an unusually deep phalanx. Behind them was Darius and his Royal Cavalry Guard, 3,000 strong. This part of the line was designed solely for defence. Between the second bridge and the coast Darius placed beyond the Cardaces a great mass of cavalry, which, he hoped, would break through the enemy and attack their flank and rear. Above the first bridge there were Cardaces and a relatively small force of cavalry, and in advance of them on a spur of the mountain a mixed force, which Alexander managed to isolate during his advance, as we have mentioned. The plan was sound, if the defensive position down to the second bridge should hold firm and the cavalry could break through.

As his line advanced from higher ground, Alexander could see the enemy's dispositions in increasing detail. When the righthand part of his line was some eighty metres from the enemy, Alexander led the Royal Infantry Guard 'at the double' through the riverbed just above the first bridge, charged the Cardaces and broke through their formation. On his left the Hypaspists and the phalanx-brigades entered the channel and engaged the enemy. On his right the Companion Cavalry and beyond them the infantry crossed the riverbed, outflanked and broke the enemy position. Alexander now joined the Royal Cavalry Guard and attacked the flank and rear of the Cardaces and then of the Greek mercenaries, for he was followed by the victorious troops of his right wing (Plate 3(b)). Meanwhile the phalangites, trying to storm the defensive position of the mercenaries and the Cardaces, suffered considerable casualties but maintained the pressure with extraordinary courage. On the left the Persian cavalry charged time and again. However, the Thessalian and other Greek cavalry managed to hold their ground.

The impetuous advance of Alexander towards Darius decided the issue (Plate 12). As the infantry of the right wing attacked the flank of the Greek mercenaries, and behind them Alexander and the Cavalry Guard forced their way towards Darius, the king turned his chariot around and fled, followed by his Cavalry Guard. Alexander pressed on towards his left wing, where the Persian cavalry joined the general rout. Only then did Alexander order the pursuit by his cavalry, which covered a distance of 37 kilometres until nightfall and inflicted very heavy losses on the Persian cavalry. The surviving Greek mercenaries escaped into the hills and some of them later rejoined Darius. Alexander's losses were 150 cavalry and 300 infantry, and he was one of 4,500 wounded. The victory and the small number of killed were due to Alexander's planning, to superior weapons and armour, and to fighting in formation. The defeat of the imperial army was total. Its numbers were no doubt inflated in the official reports by Callisthenes, and so also its losses (110,000 being the standard figure). Whatever the true numbers were, the full strength of the Persian Empire failed utterly on the banks of the Payas. Alexander expressed his thanksgiving by erecting altars there to Zeus, Heracles and Athena.

There was a considerable fall-out of the defeated forces. One large group, led by Persian officers, escaped to Asia Minor where they recruited some Cappadocian and Paphlagonian troops and then invaded Lydia. Alexander did not pursue them. He relied on the capable satrap of Phrygia, Antigonus Monophthalmus – justifiably, for Antigonus defeated the Persians in three battles. Another group, which included 4,000 Greek mercenaries and was commanded by the Macedonian deserter Amyntas, son of Antiochus, fled southwards to Tripolis, from which they sailed to Cyprus and then to Egypt. There Amyntas claimed to be the new satrap appointed by Darius. His mercenaries defeated the Persian garrison of Memphis but were then annihilated when they scattered on a spree of looting. A third group of 8,000 Greek mercenaries made their way eventually to Taenarum in the Peloponnese.

3. The winning of the coast and the siege of Tyre

To capture Susa and to pursue Darius before he had a chance of recruiting another imperial army may have been a tempting prospect after the total victory at Issus. But Alexander persisted in the strategy of mastering the Persian fleet from the land, and of controlling the Mediterranean coast, although he would thereby give Darius the opportunity to recruit an even larger imperial army. His decision was to be epoch-making.

Darius fled so precipitately that he abandoned his mother, wife and children and some ladies-in-waiting who were in his advanced camp. When Alexander heard of their capture and their mourning for Darius, whom they supposed to be dead, he sent Leonnatus to tell them that Darius was alive, and that they were accorded by Alexander the status and the title of their royal rank; for 'the war was not one of enmity towards Darius but had been conducted lawfully for the rule over Asia'. Such was the account of Ptolemy and Aristobulus, said Arrian, and it is without doubt correct. There was also a statement, derived not from these two Macedonians but probably from Cleitarchus, that next day, when Alexander and Hephaestion paid them a visit, the mother of Darius mistakenly made obeisance to Hephaestion and in her embarrassment was consoled by Alexander who said 'Hephaestion too is Alexander'. True or not, this statement inspired a splendid painting by Paolo Veronese (Plate 11). Some weeks later a request for the restitution of the royal family was made by Darius. The substance of his letter and the reply of Alexander, both as reported by Ptolemy from the *Journal* and then transmitted by Arrian, help us to understand why Alexander was treating the family of Darius as royalty.

After accusing Philip and Alexander of unprovoked aggression Darius offered 'friendship and alliance' on terms which would be arranged by negotiation. In reply Alexander accused Persia of aggression in the past 'against Macedonia and the rest of Greece' – citing the Persian Wars, interference at Perinthus, and invasion of Thrace by Artaxerxes Ochus; of organising the murder of Philip; and of urging 'the Greeks' to attack Macedonia and destroy the (Common) Peace, 'which I organised'. Alexander certainly had the stronger case. He evidently felt it important to justify his action in the sight of men and of the gods. In his letter he represented himself as legitimate king of Macedonia, ruler of Thrace and *Hegemon* of the Greeks, whereas he accused Darius of being responsible for the murder of his predecessor Arses and of having seized the throne 'unjustly and not in accordance with the law of the Persians'.

'Now it is I who possess the land, since the gods gave it to me; and I take care of those of your soldiers who have joined me of their own will. Come then to me as I am the Lord of all Asia ... You shall have your family and anything which you persuade me as King of Asia to grant to you.' He here repeated the claim he had made on landing in Asia, that he accepted Asia as the gift of the gods, and he now required Darius to recognise him as Lord of all Asia. The suggestion which was implicit in his treating the family as royalty and in offering whatever Darius could persuade him to give was surely that this family would continue as the royal family of the Medes and Persians and Darius would continue as their king, provided that they and he recognised Alexander as their overlord, the King of all Asia. 'But if you refuse in the matter of the Kingship, stand and fight for it.' At the time Darius made no reply.

Meanwhile Alexander had overcome any financial difficulties. For he had acquired 3,000 talents in the advanced camp of Darius and a much greater quantity of gold in the Persian base at Damascus. He began to issue a prolific coinage in silver and in gold on the Attic standard for circulation primarily in Asia. The silver tetradrachm portrayed the head of a youthful Heracles and on the reverse Zeus seated on a throne, holding an eagle on his right hand and a sceptre with his left hand. For the Macedonians Heracles was the ancestor of the royal house, and his youthful aspect might be associated with the youthfulness of Alexander himself; and for the Asiatics Heracles was a familiar deity under other names. Zeus the King ruled far and wide, and his eagle had guided Alexander in the decision to defeat the Persian fleet on land. For the Asiatics the seated figure was Ba'al, even as he had appeared on the Persian coins minted at Tarsus. Now Ba'al was represented as the sponsor of Alexander. The victory at Issus was commemorated on the gold coinage with the head of Athena and on the reverse Nike, holding a wreath and a *stylis* (used for the outlook-post on a warship). The Athena here was the goddess of war, both Alcidemus for the Macedonians and Trojan for the Asians, and the *stylis* recalled the daring of the Companions who sailed to the mouth of the Pinarus in order to observe the dispositions of Darius.

The success of Alexander's propaganda was apparent as he advanced along the coast. Those in power at Aradus, Byblus and Sidon accepted the rule of Alexander over themselves and their dominions. Thereafter they and their successors issued only the coinage of the King of Asia with a monogram of the ruler or of the city in Aramaic. Envoys from Tyre met him on his march and reported the decision of the Tyrians 'to do whatever Alexander may order'. Alexander expressed his commendation and said that he wished to enter Tyre and to sacrifice to Heracles (worshipped as 'Melkart' by the Tyrians). The Tyrians replied that they would obey Alexander's other commands but would not admit any Persians or any Macedonians into their city. Alexander's request had been the acid test of Tyre's submission, deliberately made because Tyre was the leading sea power in Phoenicia and her flotilla the strongest in the fleet of Pharnabazus. The Tyrians thought of their strongly fortified city on its island as impregnable; their fleet could bring in supplies; and they hoped for help from Carthage. Alexander convened a meeting of Companions and Commanders and made a speech of which Arrian gave his own version, derived from Ptolemy, who had read a report of the speech in the *Journal*.

Alexander's arguments were concerned with strategy. To advance into Mesopotamia in pursuit of Darius and to leave the Persian fleet at sea with Tyre, Cyprus and Egypt as its bases would be an act of folly; for that fleet with reinforcements, with Sparta's collaboration and with Athens wavering would 'transfer the war into Greece', quite apart from recapturing harbours on the Mediterranean coast. Nor would it be reasonable to advance towards Egypt with the fleet and Tyre endanger-

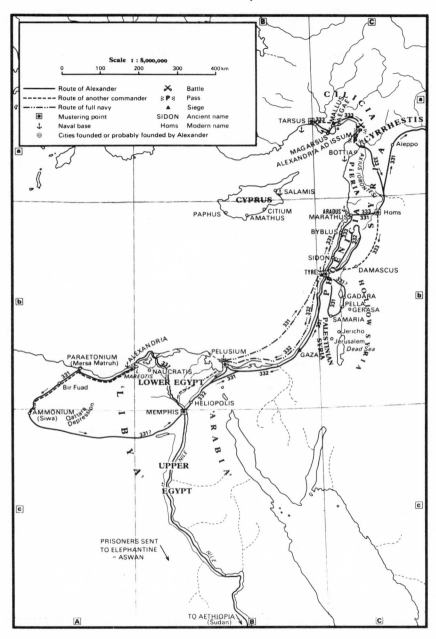

Scale 1 : 8,000,000

0	100	200	300	400 km

——— Route of Alexander   ✗   Battle
- - - - Route of another commander   ᴾ   Pass
-·-·- Route of full navy   ▲   Siege
⊞   Mustering point   SIDON   Ancient name
↓   Naval base   Homs   Modern name
◎   Cities founded or probably founded by Alexander

CILICIA
CYRRHESTIS
TARSUS
MAGARSUS
MALLUS
AEGAE
ALEXANDRIA AD ISSUM
BOTTIA
PIERIA
AXIUS (ORONTES)
Aleppo

CYPRUS
SALAMIS
PAPHUS
CITIUM
AMATHUS
ARADUS
MARATHUS
Homs
BYBLUS
SIDON
TYRE
DAMASCUS
GADARA
PELLA
GERASA
SAMARIA
Jericho
Jerusalem
Dead Sea
HOLLOW SYRIA
PALESTINIAN SYRIA

PARAETONIUM
(Mersa Matruh)
ALEXANDRIA
NAUCRATIS
MAREOTIS
LOWER EGYPT
PELUSIUM
GAZA
Bir Fuad
AMMONIUM
(Siwa)
Qattara Depression
'LIBYA'
MEMPHIS
HELIOPOLIS
NILE
'ARABIA'
UPPER
EGYPT

PRISONERS SENT
TO ELEPHANTINE
= ASWAN

TO AETHIOPIA
(Sudan)

11. The movements of Alexander's forces, 333–331 BC

ing the lines of communication. It was essential, therefore, to capture Tyre first. The results would then be the disintegration of the Persian fleet through Phoenician disaffection and through Cyprus changing sides willingly or perforce; a relatively easy invasion of Egypt; and a complete thalassocracy of the Eastern Mediterranean with the Macedonian fleet commanding the support of the Phoenician, Cyprian and Egyptian navies.

The Companions and Commanders were persuaded. Alexander was all the more confident because he dreamed that night of Heracles leading him into Tyre. Aristander's interpretation of the dream was that Alexander would succeed but only after a Herculean effort. The siege began in January 332 and ended in July. Immense heroism and ingenuity were shown on both sides. During the first phase Alexander worked with his men and rewarded their best efforts with gifts as they constructed a causeway about half a mile long into the bay. When the end of the causeway came within range of the city-wall which was 150 feet high, Tyrian catapults and archers operating from the parapet and from triremes inflicted casualties and stopped the work. Alexander then built two-wheeled towers, 150 feet high, moved them to the end of the causeway, and attacked the enemy on the city-wall and on the triremes with catapult fire, while work continued on extending the causeway. But the Tyrians countered with a huge fire-ship, which was towed to the causeway-end, where it was set alight with a favourable wind and burnt both towers, while supporting troops landed and burned all the siege-equipment. Alexander ordered his men to make the entire causeway wider and his engineers, led by a Thessalian Diades, to build more siege-equipment and towers. He went off to collect as many triremes as possible, 'since the conduct of the siege appeared more impracticable with the Tyrians in control of the sea'.

The situation at sea was altering radically. In autumn 333 the Persian fleet had dominated the Aegean with bases at Halicarnassus, Cos and Chios, held advanced positions at Siphnos and Andros, and even established a base at Callipolis within the Hellespont. The time seemed ripe for any dissident states on the Greek mainland to join Persia. Pharnabazus brought his finest flotilla of a hundred triremes to Siphnos. But he was joined only by Agis, king of Sparta, with a single trireme, who asked for men, money and ships to promote a rising in the Peloponnese. During their discussion the news arrived that Darius had been utterly defeated at Issus (in November). Pharnabazus turned back to deal with a possible rising in Chios. Agis was given thirty talents of silver and ten triremes, but he chose now to operate not in the Peloponnese but in Crete. In the Hellespont a Macedonian fleet and a flotilla of the Greek fleet captured Callipolis and destroyed the Persian force there, probably in December. Operations lapsed for the rest of the winter, but news reached the Phoenician and Cyprian crews that their cities apart from Tyre were in Alexander's hands and were being treated liberally. With the start of the sailing season the Persian fleet began to disintegrate. By midsummer 332 some eighty Phoenician warships and one hundred and twenty Cyprian warships made their submission to Alexander, who 'let bygones be bygones'.

Thus Alexander was able to muster at Sidon a large fleet, which included also ten triremes each from Rhodes and Lycia. While it was being equipped for action, he campaigned inland to the Antilebanon, in order to safeguard the supply of timber from Mount Lebanon. He then opened the second phase of the siege of Tyre by bringing up his fleet and confining the Tyrian ships to their harbours; for the Cyprians and the Phoenicians, who had suffered at the hands of Tyre, were eager for revenge. Great efforts were made to breach the wall facing the new causeway, but the Tyrians had dropped rocks into the sea by the foot of the wall and Alexander's ships were unable to reach the wall. These rocks were eventually dragged away and ships carrying siege-engines attacked the wall. The Tyrians made a successful sortie against the Cyprian fleet off one of the harbours, but Alexander intercepted the Tyrian ships and destroyed most of them. Having complete control by sea, Alexander now tested various parts of the circuit-wall and planned the assault for a day of calm weather.

Three attacks were delivered at the same moment. The Phoenicians broke the booms blocking one harbour and destroyed the Tyrian ships. The Cyprians captured another harbour and forced their way into the city. The Macedonians brought up ships carrying siege-engines and towers and breached the wall. These ships were replaced by ships carrying the Hypaspists and a phalanx brigade, gangways were lowered onto the fallen wall, and the assault began. The first man to land, Admetus, was killed, and after him Alexander and his Companions drove back the enemy and secured the landing-place, from which they led the way into the city itself. There those Tyrians who had retired under the attack of the Cyprians joined the other troops and faced the Macedonians, but to no avail; for they were surrounded on all sides. 'The Macedonians went to all lengths in their anger; for they were enraged by the length of the siege and by the Tyrian slaughter of Macedonians taken prisoner and the throwing of the corpses into the sea in front of the Macedonian camp.' It was estimated that 8,000 Tyrians were killed during the siege, and of the survivors 30,000 were sold into slavery, while others were smuggled out by Phoenicians. The Tyrian king, his nobles and some Carthaginian envoys on a sacred mission were pardoned as suppliants at the altar of Heracles. The Macedonian dead were reported as some 400 by Arrian, and the wounded probably exceeded 3,000 (see above, p. 90, for the proportion of dead to wounded).

Alexander now paid honour to Heracles. The army paraded under arms, the fleet mustered for review, and games and a torch-race followed within the precinct of Heracles. The successful siege-engine and the Tyrian sacred ship were dedicated by Alexander to Heracles. Thus the interpretation by Aristander of Alexander's dream was confirmed, and Alexander's faith in that interpretation and in the favour of Heracles was justified.

4. The advance to Egypt and the estabishment of thalassocracy

The way to Egypt was blocked by Gaza. Alexander's engineers said that it was impossible to take by assault the fortified city; for it stood on a mound 250 feet high and had a strong circuit-wall. But Alexander was not to be deflected. He set the entire army and the local people to build an equally high mound around the city, and when it reached the height of the point in the circuit-wall which seemed weakest, Alexander brought up his siege-engines and made sacrifice. As he did so, 'a carnivorous bird flying over the altar dropped a stone onto his head'. Aristander gave his interpretation: 'O king, you will capture the city but you must take care for yourself today.' At first Alexander stayed out of range. But when the first wave of the assault failed he led the Hypaspists into action and was hit by a catapult-bolt which went through his shield and cuirass into his shoulder. He lost much blood and was healed with difficulty; but he rejoiced in his belief that the first part of the interpretation was also to prove true.

The ruler of Gaza, called Batis, had hired a force of Arab mercenaries who fought with fanatical courage. Alexander's siege-engines were brought by sea from Tyre, moved with difficulty through sand and erected on the mound. The wall was pounded by stone-hurling catapults and battering rams and undermined by sapping, until it collapsed at several places. Three assaults failed. Then as a great stretch of wall came down the phalanx-troops crossed on gangways with much rivalry in courage. The prize of valour went to Neoptolemus, a member of the Molossian royal house. 'The men in Gaza all died, each fighting at his post.' Women and children were sold into slavery, and the city was repopulated with people of the locality. This is the account of Arrian, based on Ptolemy and Aristobulus. On the other hand Curtius had Batis taken prisoner, taunted by a furious Alexander and dragged round the walls by Alexander in his chariot, in imitation of Achilles dragging Hector round the walls of Troy – a finale probably drawn from the account of Cleitarchus. It is to be rejected; for Alexander always honoured the brave.

In December 332 fleet and army proceeded together from Gaza to Egypt in seven days, averaging some twenty miles a day – a fine example of planned logistics. The fleet entered Pelusium (Port Said) unopposed, the army was welcomed by the priests and the people, and the Persian commander surrendered to Alexander at Memphis. The fleet sailed on the waters of the Nile, and a naval base was soon established at Alexandria. By now the Persian fleet was indeed 'conquered on land'. For reports were reaching Alexander that the Macedonian fleet and the Greek fleet, helped by risings in the islands, had driven the remnants of the Persian forces and their supporters at sea, 'the pirates', from the Aegean islands, and that fighting continued only within Crete.

At Tyre Alexander had envisaged a Macedonian thalassocracy. It was rapidly achieved. The Phoenician cities and the Cyprian kings placed their navies under Alexander's command, and they were treated with due honour by him. In the summer of 331, when trouble was brewing in the Peloponnese, a Macedonian fleet was reinforced there by 100 Phoenician and Cyprian ships. The fleet of 'The Greeks', numbering 160 triremes, operated mainly within the Aegean. The constituent parts of the multiracial fleet under the control of Alexander as King of Macedonia, *Hegemon* of 'The Greeks' and King of Asia were all commanded by Macedonian officers, and their orders for 331 were to free Crete and 'above all to clear the seas of the pirate fleets'. In 331 a thalassocracy extending from the Black Sea to the shores of Egypt was established for the first time in history. Alexander intended that thalassocracy to be the basis of a maritime intercontinental trade which would bring an unparalleled prosperity to all the coastal peoples of the area. That intention was indeed fulfilled despite the later division of the Macedonian world into warring kingdoms. This achievement by Alexander ranks with his organisation of the Kingdom of Asia in the East. Its effects were to be even more longlasting; for they underlay the prosperity of the Roman Empire and its successor, the Byzantine Empire.

CHAPTER IX

Advance to the East and the battle of Gaugamela

1. Events in Egypt in early 331

With the opening of communication by sea between Greece and the southeastern Mediterranean fifteen envoys from the Council of the Greeks came to greet Alexander. As they sailed up the Nile, some may have recalled the attempt of Athens and her Allies to control Egypt which had ended in the disaster of 454. Now they bestowed on Alexander a golden crown in recognition of his services as Hegemon 'for the safety and freedom of Greece'. In the Aegean islands the supporters of Alexander and the Greeks were now in power. They arrested some pro-Persian leaders and sent them to Alexander in Egypt. He sent them back for trial by their fellow-countrymen, except for those of Chios, a member of 'The Greeks', who were to be tried by the Council of that body. He rewarded Mytilene for its stalwart resistance to Persia with a gift of territory on the Asian coast, which he had won 'by the spear'. He granted the requests of embassies from mainland Greece, one being the release of Athenians captured in the Battle of the Granicus. His purpose was to encourage loyalty to the Common Peace and resistance to Sparta, which was at war on the side of Persia.

To the Egyptians Alexander was 'Pharaoh'. Hieroglyphic inscriptions reveal that they gave him the traditional titles: 'Son of Ra' (the supreme god) and 'King of Upper Egypt and King of Lower Egypt, beloved of Ammon and selected of Ra'. As Pharaoh he sacrificed 'to the gods (of Egypt) and especially to Apis'; for Apis was the god against whom Cambyses and Artaxerxes Ochus had committed gross sacrilege. Thus Alexander showed his respect for the Egyptians and his acceptance of their religious beliefs. At the same time he sacrificed and held athletic and musical competitions in the Macedonian manner, for which athletes and artists came from the Greek mainland. There was no inconsistency; for in the belief of the polytheist there were innumerable gods. From Memphis he and a select force sailed down the western branch of the Nile. There he decided to build a city on an isthmus between the sea and Lake Mareotis which could be connected by a canal to the Nile, so that the city would have two harbours. He was seized by a longing (*pothos*) to start work at once. So he marked out the circuit-wall fifteen kilometres long, the city-centre, and the sites of temples to Isis (analogous to Demeter) and to Greek gods. The deities smiled on the enterprise; for a sacrifice proved favourable, and the barley with which Alexander marked the ground was devoured by flocks of birds. Aristander said this portended 'prosperity especially in fruits of the earth'. The date was probably 20 January 331, and the city was to be named Alexandria.

From the start of his campaign Alexander had foreseen the importance in his Kingdom of Asia of cities, whether native, Greek or mixed. After the first battle he declared Troy, then a native village, to be a city 'free and exempt from paying tribute', and he left instructions for its buildings to be erected. He gave the same status to the liberated Greek cities, and he played an important part in the building of Priene near the mouth of the Maeander. The most southerly of the Greek cities were Magarsus, where he sacrificed to its goddess Athena, and Mallus, founded by Amphilochus, to whom he sacrificed as a hero. He put a stop to faction (*stasis*) at Mallus, as he had done at Ephesus (above, p. 72). Thereafter he founded mixed cities: Aegae and Alexandria on the coast of the Gulf of Issus, Bottia on the Orontes, and inland Arethusa in Syria, and Gadara, Pella and Gerasa in eastern Palestine and in Jordania. In these cities he placed Macedonians no longer fit for his very active service, Greeks and native peoples; and it was the Macedonians who gave the cities and the districts their Macedonian names. Alexandria was his only foundation in Egypt.

These cities were of economic importance, those on the coast as terminals of trade from inland and as exporters of goods in the Eastern Mediterranean, and those inland as key-points on caravan routes from the interior. For instance, Alexandria was to be the outlet for the produce of Egypt, of the coasts of the Red Sea and of Aethiopia (Sudan), and a centre of exchange with Cyrene (Libya) and the countries of the East Mediterranean; and Gerasa was to be a market for the spices and unguents of Arabia. If Alexander had stayed west of the Euphrates, as Parmenio was said to have advised, he would already in 331 have ensured a rapidly growing prosperity within the area of his conquests in Asia, the Balkan peninsula, the Black Sea and the Aegean basin. That was the result of three years of forward planning, and it was now guaranteed by the establishment of the thalassocracy which he had foreseen at Miletus in 334. The cities spread Greek skills in agriculture, land reclamation and capitalism, and a knowledge of the Greek language, which was the official medium in all cities. That language, known as the *koine*, was based on the Attic dialect and modified by Alexander and his staff.

The cities were centres of culture and education. Each had its theatre and its Odeum for the production of plays and music of the traditional kind; for Alexander studied the writings of Homer, Pindar and the tragedians, and he was deeply interested in 'philosophy', which covered ideas in the arts and the sciences. The form of education in the mixed cities was Macedonian. The curriculum seems to have resembled that of the Royal School of Pages (above, p. 5), lasting from the age of fourteen to the end of the seventeenth year. It was an early form of state-education, organised and paid for by Alexander as King of Asia, and the lessons in Greek and the military training were given in a standard form of building, known as the 'Gymnasion' (excavated for instance at Priene). Manuals for the teaching of Greek as a foreign language and for the study of Greek literature and philosophy have been found in Egypt. Thus Alexander was laying the foundations of what has been called 'Hellenisation'. But it was in a Macedonian form; for training in hunting, horsemanship and the pikeman-phalanx was included, and the graduates were sufficiently skilled to enter the King's Forces. We gain some idea of the numbers from a statement that '6,000 King's Boys on the order of Alexander the Macedonian were practising thoroughly the arts of war in Egypt'. The intake was at least 1,500 a year. 'The order of Alexander' was no doubt given by him in Egypt early in 331, and the place of education was to be Alexandria.

Politically the model for the cities in Asia was the Macedonian city and not the Greek city-state. For although the liberated Greek cities passed decrees as if they were free democracies with their own magistrates, council and assembly, and although they dealt directly with the king and not with his satrap, they had to accept the foreign policy and the orders of the King of Asia. This loss of sovereignty was offset by certain advantages: they were exempt from tribute, had no expenses for defence, provided no troops to the King's Forces, and devoted their energies to economic progress. Violent party-strife (*stasis*) was banned. Respect had to be shown for the law, as in the rules governing the Common Peace. The cities south of Magarsus and Mallus were like those founded by Philip in Thrace, in that they had a mixed population and were in direct contact with the king.

The organisation of a mixed city is best known to us at Alexandria. The city was divided into wards, called 'demes'. The citizens were the Greek-speakers of two origins: soldiers drafted by Alexander, and Greek settlers. The former alone carried arms, maintained law and order, and had a deme-membership. The citizens of both grades conducted the administration with an Assembly, Council and Magistrates. The Egyptians were subject to the laws of the city; but they retained their own customs, practised their own religion and were subject to Egyptian law, administered by Egyptian judges. They had no say in the administration of the city. But if they should learn Greek and become 'Hellenised', as the 6,000 King's Boys were to do, they could be admitted to the citizen class. Thus the boundary between citizen and non-citizen was not as rigid as it was in a Greek city-state.

Alexander's arrangements for the administration of Egypt were as follows. A Macedonian admiral with a fleet of thirty triremes, two Macedonian generals in command of 4,000 troops, and commanders of garrisons at Pelusium and Memphis were each answerable directly to Alexander. Their soldiers, mainly Greek mercenaries, were under strict control and regular inspection. Alexander appointed two Egyptians to conduct the administration, including the taxation, of Upper Egypt and Lower Egypt according to the traditional system. All revenues were sent to Alexander's finance officer, a Greek called Cleomenes. The frontier areas – 'Arabia' (Suez) and 'Libya' (adjoining the western desert) – were administered each by a Greek with civil powers. These administrators were all answerable directly to Alexander. Throughout the country the daily life of the Egyptians was regulated only by their own civil governors, and they were free to live in accordance with their own traditions.

Although Alexander was not affected by Egyptian religion, he led his select force from Alexandria via Mersa Matruh to the shrine of Zeus Ammon in the oasis of Siwah. The gods favoured the journey by sending rain and then two crows to guide them, when they lost the way in dust-storms. Alexander wished to emulate his ancestors Perseus and Heracles, who had visited the shrine. He was greeted by the priest as 'Son of Ra', that is as the reigning Pharaoh (this was translated as 'Son of Zeus'). Alexander entered the shrine alone. The utterances of the god were not divulged. Such was the gist of the official account, written by Callisthenes and approved by Alexander. Moreover, in a *Letter* to Olympias Alexander wrote that he had received 'secret prophecies' from the god, which he would tell her, and her only, on his return to Macedonia. There was of course speculation by others. Ptolemy and Aristobulus thought 'he was trying to some extent to trace his birth to Ammon', and they reported Alexander as saying that he had heard 'what was to his liking'. Other writers, led by Cleitarchus, invented questions and answers to delight their readers.

To Alexander Zeus Ammon was a Greek god, who had a shrine at Aphytis in Chalcidice and was revered at Dodona. Alexander's faith was such that he believed those 'secret prophecies' would come true. One of them had probably proved correct on the occasion when on beginning the voyage down the Hydaspes Alexander sacrificed to Ammon. Later, in the estuary of the Indus, Alexander sacrificed to the gods, to whom, he said, he had been ordered by Ammon to sacrifice. It seems likely that one of Ammon's prophecies was concerned with Alexander reaching the bounds of Asia. Whatever the priest of Ammon really said, the belief which developed in the rank and file of the Macedonians was that Alexander had been encouraged to regard Ammon as his father and that in the end Alexander came to think so. While he was still in Egypt, it was reported that Apollo of Didyma, whose oracle had been silent since the conquest by Persia, had declared Alexander to be 'born of Zeus', and that the Sibyl at Erythrae had spoken of 'his exalted birth' (*eugeneia*). These reports were published by Callisthenes with the approval of Alexander. It is not a necessary conclusion that Alexander believed himself to be 'born of Zeus'. For he may have encouraged the idea for propaganda purposes.

For some four months in Egypt the army enjoyed a respite from combat. It was not idle but engaged in building the city of Alexandria, undertaking expeditions and regular training. One expedition was up the Nile. Alexander himself had a 'longing' (*cupido*) to go into Aethiopia 'almost beyond the limits of the sun', but he was represented by Callisthenes, who reported that the flooding of the Nile was due to enormous rainfall. This satisfied Aristotle. The expedition was halted by 'the blazing zone of parched sky'. The strength of the King's Forces had been maintained by reinforcements of 300 cavalry and 3,000 infantry from Macedonia which had arrived in 333. From Gaza Alexander sent an officer in late 332 to Macedonia 'to enlist young men suitable for campaigning'. A year was to pass before these young men reached Alexander near Susa. He had received 350 Greek cavalry in 333, but he relied mainly on recruiting Greek mercenaries, 3,300 who had been in Persian service and 4,400 from Greece. He was joined at Memphis by 500 Thracian cavalry.

As spring approached, Alexander held a festival in honour of Zeus the King, which corresponded to the Xandica at home. The army under arms paraded in the procession, contests in athletics and in the arts were held, and sacrifices were made on a lavish scale. The Nile at Memphis and the canals had been bridged for the departure of the army. The fleet and the army set out at the beginning of spring and they met again at Tyre.

2. The campaign and the battle of Gaugamela

Tyre had been refounded with a Phoenician population, and it was securely held by a Macedonian commander who was in charge of the region. Alexander had planned in advance a splendid festival with sacrifices to Heracles, athletic contests and competitions in the arts. It was an occasion to celebrate the winning of the sea by Alexander and the Greeks. The kings of Cyprus equipped and trained the choruses for the plays, actors came from Athens, and the judges of the dramatic competition were the leading Macedonian generals. When an actor to whom Alexander was devoted did not obtain first prize, Alexander said he would have given up part of his kingdom to have it otherwise, but nevertheless he accepted the verdict. He was deeply moved by the music

12. The central satrapies

CASPIAN OR HYRCANIAN SEA

ARMENIA

ASSYRIA

MESOPOTAMIA

CADUSIA

MEDIA

HYRCANIA

MARDI

DESERT OF KAVIR

PARAETACENE

SUSIANA

GABIENE

PERSIS

BABYLONIA

MARDI

UXII

COSSAEI

CARMANIA

RED SEA (PERSIAN GULF)

330 Gorgan

ERIGYIUS Shahrud
?Hecatompylus

Sari (Zadracarta)

CRATERUS Damghan

Caspian Gates

Rhagae

Heraclea

Ecbatana (Hamadan)

Bagistane

PARMENIO 330

PERDICCAS

Celones

Opis

324

331 Tigris

Babylon

Euphrates

Euphrates

Pallacopas Canal

Tigris

323

331

326

Al-Charax

Pasitigris

Eulaeus

Susa

324

Choaspes

Pasitigris

Ispahan

330

Araxes

Ardakan

Persian Gates

Shiraz

Gyndis

Pasargadae

Persepolis

334

330

323

Buhtan

CUDI DAG

Khabur

Mosul

Al-Mygdoniae

Arbela

Great Zab

Lesser Zab

Lycus

Ashur

Tigris

THAPSACUS (Jerablus)

?Nicephorium

Euphrates

KARACALI DAG

2561 m
Sarrekishan

A 2561

Scale 1 : 9,000,000
0   100   200   300 km

■ Place of Darius' death
✗ Battle of Gaugamela
● City founded by Alexander
○ Al. Alexandria, founded by Alexander
        Ancient course of river or of coastline
P ·: Pass
MARDI Tribe
ARMENIA District
→ Harbour
        Route of Alexander
----- Route of a subordinate commander
- · - Voyage of Nearchus

RED SEA

Hierats

Gogana

Apostana

Ira

Oracta

C. Maceta

HEPHAESTION

Siraces

(PERSIAN GULF)

of the lyre; when a favourite player was killed in battle beside him, he dedicated at Delphi a bronze statue of the player with a lyre and a spear in his hands. The state-ship of Athens and probably those of other mainland states came to the festival, both to congratulate the *Hegemon* and to make their requests.

Alexander stayed in Phoenicia and Syria for at least three months. During them the harvests were garnered, and supplies were dumped on the route to two bridges which he was having built at the Euphrates. He made some changes in his administrative service. The satrap of Syria, for instance, was replaced, because he had failed to collect the necessary supplies. The Jews of Samaria rebelled and burnt the Macedonian satrap of that area alive. Alexander executed those responsible, expelled the population and made Samaria a mixed city, like Gerasa. He may have hoped that Darius would bring his army to the far side of the Euphrates for a decisive battle, in which case Alexander's supplies were close at hand. When it became apparent that Darius would fight in Mesopotamia, Alexander decided to advance in late July 331. At about that time Antipater sent off from Macedonia the reinforcements which had been demanded, and Alexander ordered a fleet of Macedonian, Greek, Cyprian and Phoenician warships to sail towards the Peloponnese, where a danger of risings in support of Sparta was reported.

On the far side of the Euphrates a Persian commander, Mazaeus, with 3,000 cavalry, 2,000 Greek mercenaries and other infantry held a defensive position. But on the advance of Alexander he withdrew on the main Persian road down the Euphrates, probably in the hope that Alexander would pursue and run short of supplies. Alexander completed his two bridges, brought his troops and supply-train across, and waited for some days, perhaps misleading Mazaeus about his intentions. Then he marched northeastwards along the Armenian foothills to obtain pasture for his horses, use local supplies and avoid the great heat; for he had to feed some 47,000 men and perhaps 20,000 horses and mules. The two armies were completely out of touch with one another for some six weeks, during which the Macedonians made incursions into Armenia. Alexander was the first to capture some opponents, who revealed that Darius' plan was to hold the Tigris. 'Alexander went in haste towards the Tigris'; he crossed its fast-flowing waters with difficulty at an undefended point, for he was higher up river than Darius had expected. While the army waited for the supply-train, the moon was eclipsed on the evening of 20 September 331. Alexander restored confidence by sacrificing to the deities who caused the eclipse – Moon, Sun and Earth – and Aristander announced that the eclipse portended victory over Persia in the present month. Moving south through fertile country Alexander captured some Persian cavalrymen and learned that Darius was in a prepared position not far off. He halted for four days 'to rest his men', fortified a base camp with a ditch and a palisade, and placed in it his sick and the supply-train.

Alexander's scouts reported that the army of Darius was eleven kilometres away, on the far side of low hills. In order to avoid the heat Alexander set off during the night with his army ready for action, crossed over the hills, and at dawn halted his army on seeing the enemy drawn up for battle some five kilometres away on the plain. He had already discussed his advance with some commanders. Now he consulted all his commanders. The majority advised him to engage at once, but 'Parmenio's advice prevailed': to carry out a thorough reconnaissance. When this was done, Alexander reconvened his commanders, exhorted them to fight 'for the rule of all Asia', and insisted on the importance of obeying orders immediately, precisely and in silence. A camp was made for the baggage-animals which carried such essential supplies as barley for the cavalry mounts. The army took its evening meal, and the units slept in the positions which they would take for battle. Towards midday Alexander started the march into the plain.

Darius had mustered in their ethnic units the finest cavalry of the empire from Cappadocia to Pakistan, and the Sacae from beyond its border. He had armed some units with lances and swords, but most were to fight in their traditional manner with archery, javelins and scimitars. They 'were said', wrote Arrian, to total 40,000. He had fifteen Indian elephants, but he left them in his camp, probably because the Indian horses alone had been trained to act with elephants. His élite infantry consisted of some 6,000 Greek mercenaries and 1,000 Persian Guards. Other infantry supported their cavalry units or formed a general reserve. The lowest estimate of the infantry was 400,000, no doubt an inflated figure. Darius had also a new weapon, 'the scythed chariot' with razor-sharp blades attached to the turning wheels, the chassis and the yoke-pole. He reckoned that a charge by 200 such two-horse and four-horse chariots would break up the phalanx-formation and expose the pikemen to close combat, in which the pike would be more of a hindrance than a help.

Darius was the first to reach his desired battle-ground, a stretch of flat pastureland and ploughland. He cleared three fairways for the scythed chariots, and he laid caltrops (spikes) in some places to maim the enemy's horses. On learning that Alexander had set off from his base camp at night (on 29 September), Darius deployed his army and kept it under arms, in case Alexander should attack at or soon after dawn. The huge army stayed in battle-positions throughout 30 September and the next night and on into 1 October towards midday, whereas the Macedonian army had rested one day and slept one night in camp.

On 1 October Darius was pinned to his prepared ground. The centre of his line consisted from front to rear of 50 scythed chariots; four ethnic units (two of cavalry, two probably of infantry); the Royal Cavalry

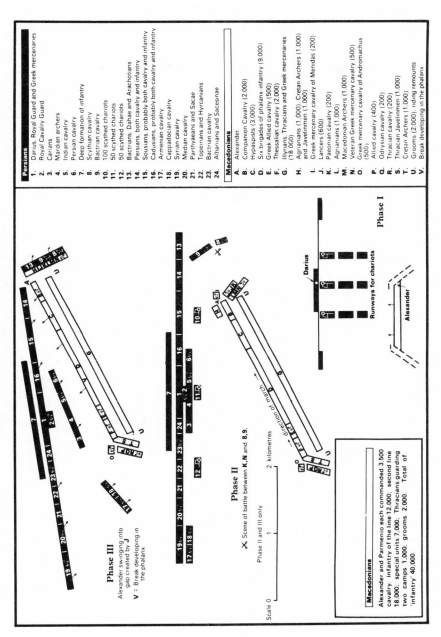

Persians

1. Darius, Royal Guard and Greek mercenaries
2. Royal Cavalry Guard
3. Carians
4. Mardian archers
5. Indian cavalry
6. Persian cavalry
7. Deep formation of infantry
8. Scythian cavalry
9. Bactrian cavalry
10. 100 scythed chariots
11. 50 scythed chariots
12. 50 scythed chariots
13. Bactrians, Dahae and Arachotians
14. Persians, both cavalry and infantry
15. Sousians, probably both cavalry and infantry
16. Cadusians, probably both cavalry and infantry
17. Armenian cavalry
18. Cappadocian cavalry
19. Syrian cavalry
20. Median cavalry
21. Parthyaeans and Sacae
22. Topeirians and Hyrcanians
23. Bactrian cavalry
24. Albanians and Sacesinae

Macedonians

A. Alexander
B. Companion Cavalry (2,000)
C. Hypaspists (3,000)
D. Six brigades of phalanx-infantry (9,000)
E. Greek Allied cavalry (500)
F. Thessalian cavalry (2,000)
G. Illyrians, Thracians and Greek mercenaries (18,000)
H. Agrianians (1,000), Cretan Archers (1,000) and Javelinmen (1,000)
I. Greek mercenary cavalry of Menidas (200)
J. Lancers (600)
K. Paeonian cavalry (200)
L. Agrianians (1,000)
M. Macedonian Archers (1,000)
N. Veteran Greek mercenary cavalry (500)
O. Greek mercenary cavalry of Andromachus (500)
P. Allied cavalry (400)
Q. Odrysian cavalry (200)
R. Thracian cavalry (200)
S. Thracian Javelinmen (1,000)
T. Cretan Archers (1,000)
U. Grooms (2,000), riding remounts
V. Break developing in the phalanx

Phase III

Alexander swinging into gap created by **J**

V = Break developing in the phalanx

Phase II

✗ Scene of battle between **K,N** and **8,9**.

Phase II and III only

Scale 0   1   2 kilometres

direction of march

Darius

Runways for chariots

Alexander

Phase I

Macedonians

Alexander and Parmenio each commanded 3,500 cavalry. Infantry of the line 12,000; second line 18,000; special units 7,000; Thracians guarding two camps 1,000; grooms 2,000. Total of 'infantry' 40,000.

13. The phases of the Battle of Gaugamela

Guard; Darius in his chariot flanked by all the élite infantry; and finally a second line of infantry. The right part of his line in the same order started with 50 scythed chariots, followed by nine ethnic units of cavalry, some supported by infantry of their race, and in the background a part of the second line of infantry. On the extreme right there was an advanced group of two ethnic units of cavalry. The left part of the line had 100 scythed chariots; five ethnic units of cavalry with supporting infantry of their own race; and on the extreme left an advanced group of two ethnic units of cavalry (Bactrians and Scythians). The second line of infantry in the background was in support of only one ethnic unit of cavalry. Darius hoped that Alexander would make a frontal attack with a line parallel to his own, as at Issus; that the charging chariots would break up the infantry phalanx; and that the greatly superior number of his fine cavalry would not only outflank Alexander's shorter line but also charge through the gaps created by the scythed chariots. It was a good plan, but only if Alexander made his attack in accordance with Darius' hopes.

The army of Alexander moved into the plain with perfect precision, as on a parade ground. At first the line was parallel to that of Darius and advanced facing the Persian right and part of the centre, but at a predetermined moment the line made a right incline and advanced towards its right front in an oblique formation, the right wing in advance and the left wing retarded (see Fig. 13). Darius saw that Alexander's army was now moving away from the prepared fairways of the chariots. He therefore ordered the Bactrians and the Scythians to attack Alexander's right flank and halt the movement. But Alexander counter-attacked with squadron after squadron, each in wedge formation, and meanwhile kept advancing to his right front. Darius sent his scythed chariots into the charge before it was too late. But they proved ineffective; for in accordance with their orders the Macedonians opened ranks to let them pass through, the Agrianian and the Thracian 'javelin-men' struck drivers and horses with their javelins, and the troops made a tremendous din which frightened the chariot-horses off their course.

At this point the disposition of Alexander's forces becomes important. In front of and to the flank of his advanced right he had the Agrianians, the Thracian javelin-men, Macedonian archers and 'old-timer Greek mercenary infantry' – some of these dealt with the scythed chariots – and squadrons of cavalry, being the Greek mercenary cavalry, the Paeonians and the Lancers – these delivered the counter-attacks as we have seen. The continuous line consisted from right to left of Alexander at the head of the Companion Cavalry squadrons, the Hypaspist Guard, the other Hypaspists, the six brigades of the phalangites, and the Greek cavalry of which the Thessalians held the wing. On the left there was a flank-guard consisting of Greek mercenary cavalry in front; then some Greek cavalry, the Odrysian cavalry, and the Thracian cavalry; and in support of them Thracian javelin-men and Cretan archers. Behind the main phalanx there marched a second phalanx of the same length, consisting of Greek mercenary infantry, Illyrian infantry and Thracian infantry. This second phalanx was to face about if Persian cavalry should come at it from the rear.

While the scythed chariots were making their attack, Darius ordered a general advance and at the same time sent some Persian cavalry to support the defeated Bactrians and Scythians. Alexander ordered the last unit of his flank-guard, the 600 Lancers, to charge into the Persian cavalry at the point where it was leaving the Persian main line. When the Lancers broke through and created a gap, Alexander turned his line ninety degrees to his left, formed 'a wedge of the Companion Cavalry and the infantry there' (Hypaspists), charged with a resounding battle-cry through the gap, and swung left 'in the direction of Darius himself'. In fierce fighting the long lances of the Companion Cavalry and the bristling pikes of the Hypaspists prevailed, and as they drew near Darius panicked and fled. The impetuous charge of Alexander's wedge had been delivered at the moment when the attacking cavalry of the Persian right was bringing the left part of the Macedonian phalanx to a halt. A gap inevitably arose between that part of the phalanx and the brigades which were advancing in line with Alexander's wedge.

The gap was exploited by Indian and Persian cavalry. But instead of wheeling and attacking, they rode to the camp which was guarded only by a small force of Thracians. Part of the second line of the halted phalanx turned about 'as they had been ordered to do' and defeated the enemy in the camp. But the whole of the left wing, which was under the command of Parmenio, was hard pressed by attacks from all sides. A request for help reached Alexander. Although he must have been tempted to pursue Darius, now in flight, Alexander turned the squadrons of Companion Cavalry to his left and fought his way through the cavalry of the Persian right centre which met him head on in formation. Sixty Companions fell. 'But Alexander overcame these enemies also.' He was about to attack the cavalry of the extreme right, when it broke and fled under the brilliant charges of the Thessalian squadrons. The whole of the huge army was now in flight.

Alexander and the Companions led the pursuit, and they were followed by the troops of Parmenio. The aim was to break the morale of the enemy cavalry. When light failed, Alexander camped until midnight. Meanwhile Parmenio captured the Persian camp. Thereafter Alexander carried the pursuit to Arbela, where he captured the treasure and the possessions of Darius. The pursuit over 110 kilometres cost the lives of 100 men and 1,000 horses, but the casualties of the enemy ensured that Darius would never again raise an imperial army. At Arbela Alexander made sacrifices of thanksgiving to the gods and distributed rewards. He was acclaimed 'King of Asia' by the Macedonians, who in the flush of victory undertook to win all Asia for their king. He himself proclaimed his triumph in a dedication to Athena of Lindus in Rhodes in his own words: 'King Alexander, having mastered Darius in battle and having become Lord of Asia, made sacrifice to Athena of Lindus in accordance with an oracle.' He saw the defeat of Persia as a preliminary to the winning of all Asia.

CHAPTER X

The advance to Persepolis and the situation in Greece

1. Babylon, Susa and military reorganisation

It is important to realise that Gaugamela was the victory of the Greeks as well as of the Macedonians. During the slow advance into the plain Alexander addressed the Greeks on his left wing. Raising his right hand in appeal to the gods he prayed, as Callisthenes says: 'If in truth I am descended from Zeus (*Diothen gegonos*), guard and strengthen the Greeks.' He was referring to the oracles which Callisthenes had made known from two Greek cities that he was 'a son of Zeus' and 'of exalted birth' (above, p. 103). He was addressing Greeks, not Macedonians, and he was also addressing his own faith – which must have seemed later to be justified by the victory. He now reported to 'The Greeks' (of the Common Peace) that liberation (from Persia) was complete and the liberated cities were autonomous; and he paid special tributes to Plataea and Croton for their part in the Great Persian Wars. His attention to the Greeks was timely, because he knew that there was a danger of a rising in the Peloponnese (above, p. 105). But communication was slow. It took perhaps two months for a courier, and three months or more for troops to proceed from Pella to Susa. Thus the first news of a double rising, in Thrace and in the Peloponnese, was not to reach Alexander until late November or early December 331.

The firstfruit of victory was Babylonia, the wealthiest satrapy in the Persian empire. The satrap, Mazaeus, who had commanded the Persian right wing at Gaugamela and had fought with distinction, came to meet Alexander and surrendered the city of Babylon to him. As Alexander approached at the head of the army, the priests and the people welcomed him, bearing gifts and covering his path with flowers. For the Babylonians it was the end of two hundred years of Persian occupation, during which their temples had been violated for instance by Xerxes. Alexander acted as he had done in Egypt. He sacrificed under the direction of the priests to their supreme god, Belus (Ba'al), carried out their recommendations in regard to the temples in Babylon, and ordered the people to repair the damage done by Xerxes. He was accepted by the Babylonians as a liberator and as a king approved by Belus.

In his arrangements for the administration of Babylonia Alexander made different officers responsible for military, financial and civil duties. At the outset Apollodorus commanded 700 Macedonians and perhaps 1,300 Greek mercenaries, and Asclepiodorus was in charge of the collection of tribute. As civil governor, 'satrap', Alexander appointed the Persian holder of the office, Mazaeus. This must have astounded the Macedonians; for they were at war with Persia. It was as if King George VI had appointed Rommel after the Battle of El Alamein to be his Viceroy in India. What was the motive of Alexander? He had always honoured any Persians who of their own volition joined his service – and he had made a point of this in correspondence with Darius – and he had treated them 'in a manner worthy of their rank', which implied that they were Persians of some distinction. A case in point was Mithrenes, who had surrendered Sardis (above, p. 72). Now Alexander appointed him satrap of Armenia, thus indicating that Mazaeus was not exceptional. This policy led to the peaceful taking of Susa; for on his march towards Susa, he was met by a son of the Persian satrap of Susiane, Abulites, offering surrender. That was no small gain; for at Susa Alexander took over treasure worth 50,000 talents of silver. Alexander continued Abulites in his position as satrap. For their part Mazaeus, Mithrenes and Abulites must have accepted the rule of Alexander as King of Asia. At this time too the captured women of the Persian royal family were still being treated as royalty. We shall consider the significance of this later (below, p. 116).

While the army was recuperating for a month in winter quarters near Babylon, Alexander distributed a bounty of 600 drachmae a head to Macedonian cavalrymen, 500 to Greek cavalrymen, 200 to Macedonian infantrymen, two months' pay to Greek mercenaries, and analogous payments to Balkan cavalrymen and to Greek and Balkan infantrymen. When he led the army on the long march towards Susa, he met Amyntas with the reinforcements which he expected (above, p. 105). These numbered 500 Macedonian cavalry, 6,000 Macedonian infantry, 600 Thracian cavalry, 3,500 Thracian infantry, and 'from the Peloponnese' 380 Greek mercenary cavalry and 4,000 Greek mercenary infantry. The total of some 15,000 men may be compared with those who crossed the Hellespont in 334, some 37,000 men.

The number of Macedonian infantry is of particular interest. Philip's vanguard in Asia included at the most 3,000 such infantry in two brigades; Alexander entered Asia with 12,000; and he received 3,000 at Gordium. With the new 6,000 he was able to fill his complement of 12,000 (in three Hypaspist brigades and six phalanx-brigades) and add a new phalanx brigade of 1,500 men. Thus the loss from front-line service was 4,500. Those killed in battle were in hundreds rather than thousands. A large part of the 4,500 were stationed in the new cities from Aegae to Alexandria. Occasionally active Macedonians were

1. (a) Gold medallions of Olympias and Philip

1. (b) Ivory heads of Olympias (left) and Alexander

2. Fresco of a Royal Hunt

3. (a) Phalanx of pikemen

3. (b) Alexander in action

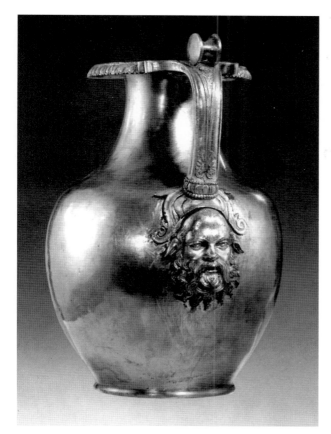

4. (a) Silver oenochoe with the head of a Silenus

4. (b) Head of a young Heracles on a silver amphora

5. (a) Gold larnax

5. (b) Gold wreath

6. (a) Mosaic of a lion hunt

6. (b) Mosaic of Dionysus riding on a panther

7. The right-hand half of the Boscoreale fresco

8. (a) Satellite photograph of the Pelium area

8. (b) The plain beside Pelium

9. Alexander in action

10. Satellite photograph of Cilicia

11. The family of Darius before Alexander

12. The Alexander Mosaic

13. The Porus medallion (left) and the Indian archer

14. The Derveni crater

15. A young Alexander riding Bucephalus

16. A mature Alexander, somewhat idealised

placed in a garrison, but when danger passed they were recalled to active service. On receiving his last reinforcement Alexander was able to place 1,000 over-age Macedonians (*aetate graves*) as a garrison of the citadel of Susa. The corresponding figures for Companion Cavalrymen, if we assume that there was one squadron in Philip's vanguard, are 200, 1,800, 300 and 500, totalling 2,800. Here the loss from front-line service was 1,000 or so.

Had Alexander taken too many men from Macedonia? He must have asked himself that question when news reached him at Susa that Agis, king of Sparta, with his own army and some 10,000 mercenaries hired with Persian gold, had defeated a Macedonian force in the Peloponnese and had then gained the support of Elis and of most of Arcadia and Achaea. There had also been a rising in Thrace, for which the General in Thrace, Memnon, was held responsible, but Antipater, mustering all his forces, had overawed him and made an agreement. All Alexander could do at Susa in December 331 was to send off 3,000 talents which would not reach Antipater until late February at the earliest; and to let the Athenians know that he was sending them the statues of Harmodius and Aristogeiton which Xerxes had removed. Antipater had probably been able to maintain the army of 12,000 phalangites and 1,500 cavalry which Alexander had left him in 334. For Alexander had taken for reinforcements not any of Antipater's troops but specifically 'young men', i.e. from the militia.

At Susa Alexander held a traditional festival with a sacrifice, a torch-race and athletic events for his Macedonians. He left the mother of Darius, his daughters and his son at Susa and appointed teachers to instruct them in the Greek language. They were still being treated as royalty in the Persian capital. The fighting which lay ahead in Persis and Media would take the form of mountain warfare rather than of set battle. With this in mind, and with the transfer of 1,000 older Macedonians to garrison duty, Alexander made promotions of men who distinguished themselves in tests of courage, and he formed new units which were alternatives, not substitutes for the traditional units: namely Companion Cavalry companies of 75 to 100 troopers, and eight Infantry Commandoes of 1,000 men each (but not taken from the Royal Guard and the Hypaspists). They were trained in the use of the appropriate weapons and tactics for mountain warfare. The Commandoes were first deployed against the Uxii, to the southeast of Susa, with such devastating effect that the Persian commander, Medates, capitulated and was pardoned, and the Uxii submitted and thereafter paid as tribute 600 horses and mules and 30,000 cattle, goats and sheep a year. In the reorganisation of the cavalry it seems that the Paeonian and the Thracian squadrons, originally of 150 men each, were disbanded, and the men were allocated to the Lancers; for these light-armed units must have had heavy losses in the Battle of Gaugamela.

Together with the reinforcements Antipater sent to Alexander 'fifty grown-up sons of Alexander's Friends to act as his bodyguards'. These were one intake of Royal Pages (above, p. 5). They were now to spend their last year under instruction from Callisthenes and other philosophers at court and were to be in close attendance on the king; and Alexander probably let it be known that their successors each year would come likewise to his court. To Macedonians this made an important issue more acute. Where was the centre of their society to be? At Pella or at a moving court in Asia? There was already a dichotomy, in that Alexander was 'King of Macedonians' and 'King of Asia'; and in addition his position as King of Macedonians was fragmented in that his deputy acted in Macedonia as Head of State and he acted as Head of State wherever he happened to be in Asia. The transfer of Royal Pages to Asia must have seemed to tip the balance; for on graduation these ex-Pages and their successors each year were to start their career not in Macedonia but in Asia. Why did Alexander make the transfer? Presumably he felt the need to strengthen his constitutional position in Asia as King of Macedonians and to exert his influence on those who would be leading men later in his reign. But he endangered the close relations he had at the time with the Macedonians in Asia and especially with the Friends and Companions.

2. Persepolis and the future of Persia

The direct route to Persepolis was blocked by a very large Persian force, which held 'the Persian Gates', a narrow defile ten kilometres long between high mountains. A frontal attack failed with some casualties. Alexander withdrew his force which consisted of the Companion Cavalry, the Lancers, the majority of the Macedonian infantry, the Agrianians and the Archers – in fact the élite of the army – and mounted a most daring night operation. Craterus held the camp with a small force and bluffed the enemy by keeping many camp-fires alight. Alexander took the main body through forested country on a circuitous route. Around midnight he divided it into two parts: one consisting of most of the cavalry and part of the infantry was to bridge the river Araxes (Pulvar) between the Persian position and Persepolis, and the rest under Alexander's command was to reach the Persian position before dawn. Everything depended on surprise. Alexander captured or dispersed three Persian guardposts, fell unobserved on the Persian camp, and summoned by bugle the force under Craterus which, as prearranged, delivered a frontal attack. The Persian force in complete disarray was shattered between the hammer and the anvil. A race to Persepolis between Alexander's Companion Cavalry and the survivors of the Persian force was won by Alexander, who entered the city at the head of his men and took over the citadel and the treasury intact. The whole operation was brilliant, and the prize was the heart of the Persian Empire, the capital of Darius I and Xerxes.

On arriving at Persepolis in January 330 with his Macedonians (for the main army and the baggage-train, using a slower route, were still on the way) Alexander sent a force to capture the treasury at Pasargadae, the early capital; appointed a Persian to be satrap of Persis; and convened a group of Friends and Commanders to discuss what course he should pursue at Persepolis. Arrian, following the accounts of Ptolemy and Aristobulus, reported a difference of opinion between Alexander and his leading Friend, Parmenio. Alexander proposed to burn the Palace of Darius and Xerxes in retaliation for their acts of sacrilege against the Greek gods (the same motive was mentioned by Strabo). It is obvious that such a burning would be a striking demonstration that 'The Greeks' had triumphed. When the news would reach Greece, in March 330, it would encourage the loyal Greek states to hold firm against Sparta and the rebels in the Peloponnese. Parmenio opposed the proposal. He thought it would alienate the Persians, who would regard the Macedonians merely as conquerors and ravagers.

Alexander put his proposal into effect. Having removed the treasure, he rewarded the Macedonians for their hard fighting by letting them loot the Palace, the Throne Room and the Treasury, and he then fired the Palace which was reduced to a heap of burnt mud-brick and debris. Excavation has revealed two facts: the looting was so hurried that many small objects of gold and of precious stone were left on the floors, and the firing was so immediate that these objects were not retrieved but buried under the burnt debris. When the Greek troops arrived, the deed had been done. But Cleitarchus invented a sensational story to delight the Greeks, that at a drunken party an Athenian prostitute, called Thaïs, proposed the burning and applied the torch, followed by an inebriated Alexander. The excavation has shown beyond doubt that the burning was not a random, unpremeditated act.

The main army rested for some four months at Persepolis (the city not being affected by the burning of the Palace), but in March Alexander led a select force into the mountains south of Persepolis, where he subjugated the Mardi and other tribes in Arctic conditions. The campaign lasted for a month, with Alexander often in the lead. He continued in office the Persian strap of Carmania, who accepted his authority after the expedition against the Mardi.

In May, when he led his army northwards, he left a garrison of only 3,000 Macedonians at Persepolis. He was evidently confident that the Persians would not rise and create a second front, while Darius had an army in Media which Alexander was now entering. The reasons for that confidence deserve consideration. From the fall of Sardis onwards Alexander had welcomed into his entourage any Persian satraps and governors who surrendered and accepted his regime. They and their retinue were given the status they had had under Persian rule, whether as cavalrymen or courtiers or administrators. In 332, when the wife of Darius died, Alexander gave her a lavish funeral with Persian rites, which were conducted by the leading Persians of his court. Alexander's relations with Darius' mother, Sisigambis, were particularly respectful – indeed he was said to have treated the Uxii leniently at her request. When he accorded royal status to Darius' family, whether on the campaign or at Susa, he was treating it as the royal house of Persia; and in arranging for the education of Darius' eight-year-old son, Ochus, at Susa he was regarding him as the heir presumptive to the throne of Persia. And the tomb of Persia's national hero, Cyrus the Great, at Pasargadae was restored on the order of Alexander.

These actions showed that Alexander did not intend to disestablish the royal family and the leading statesmen of Persia. His appointment of Persians as satraps of the defeated areas, Susiane and Persis, showed that Persia was to be a self-governing state within Alexander's Kingdom of Asia, no less than Egypt and Babylon. More remarkable still was his appointment of Persians as satraps of Babylonia, Armenia and Carmania on their liberation from Persian rule. For this could only mean that he intended that Persians should participate in the administration of his Kingdom. Moreover, he chose to implement this policy when Darius was still at war and in command of an army in Media.

Alexander's policy is to be contrasted with that of Rome after the defeat of Macedonia at the Battle of Pydna, which may be summarised as ruthless plundering, partition and impoverishment, the parading of the royal family in chains in Rome, and the lingering death of Perseus in prison. The only precedent in past history for an enlightened policy towards a defeated state or states was that of Philip after the Battle of Chaeronea. Subsequent history, whether in Europe or Asia, provides no analogy.

3. The situation in Greece

While Alexander wintered at Persepolis, he learned that only Arcadia and Elis had defected from the Greek Community, and that their forces under Sparta's command had not advanced into Central Greece but were laying siege to Megalopolis in Arcadia. In the attitude of the Greek Community the decision of Athens was of crucial importance. If she stayed loyal to the Common Peace, she would be able with her fleet to reinforce the thalassocracy of Macedonia in the Aegean Sea, and with her army to enfilade any army advancing from the Isthmus into Central Greece, where Sparta could rely on support from some states. On the other hand, if she joined Sparta, by manning 200 warships and providing vessels for any naval allies she could challenge the Macedonian fleet, as she was to do after the death of Alexander, and her army could join the Spartan coalition and invade Macedonia. In the Assembly Aeschines and Demades advocated loyalty. Demosthenes wished to join Sparta and bring out the fleet. Had he had his way, Alexander might have been compelled to halt his advance in Persia and send reinforcements from his army to Macedonia. However, the Assembly decided to take no action, as Alexander had foreseen; for 'he had favoured Athens beyond all other Greek states'. Once Athens' decision was known to Antipater, he could assure Alexander that, in view of the huge subsidy which had reached him, it was only a matter of collecting sufficient forces to crush Sparta and her allies. That assurance may have reached Alexander at Persepolis and encouraged him to advance into Media in May.

Although it was not known to Alexander at the time, Antipater marched unopposed into the Peloponnese in late April or in May. His army, reported as 40,000 strong, consisted of at least 1,500 Macedonian cavalry and 12,000 Macedonian infantry, the contingents of those states which actively supported the Common Peace (but none from Athens), Balkan troops and perhaps some mercenaries. Agis, king of Sparta, commanded 2,000 cavalry, 20,000 citizen hoplites and 10,000 Greek mercenaries, hired with Persian gold. The decisive battle was fought near Megalopolis. In one account the losses of Sparta and her allies were 5,300 and of Antipater more than 1,000 with very many wounded. Macedonia's losses were said to have excited the comment of Alexander that it had been 'a battle of rats'; for his battles had cost few Macedonian lives. But Antipater had calculated well. His enemies capitulated without terms. Would they be enslaved as Thebes had been enslaved in 335? Having commanded the joint forces as the deputy-*Hegemon* of 'The Greeks', Antipater asked 'the Common Council of the Greeks' to decide on the terms. He was acting as Alexander had done in 335. The Council imposed on Arcadia and Elis an indemnity of 120 talents, which was to be paid to Megalopolis, and arrested their leaders for violating the charter of the Common Peace. No doubt they were put on trial later. It is a sign of the Council's independence that it granted such moderate terms without waiting for the opinion of the *Hegemon*.

Sparta had not been a member of the Common Peace. She had consistently opposed Macedonia, and on this occasion she had tried to create a coalition under her own leadership on the lines of what we call the Peloponnesian League. The Council of the Common Peace was therefore correct in referring the decision on Sparta's fate to Macedonia. Antipater had already taken fifty leading Spartans as hostages, and now in summer 330 he sent them and a Spartan delegation to Alexander. It would be a matter of four months before Alexander's decision would be known in Greece. Meanwhile at Athens the Assembly elected Phocion general and passed proposals by Demades, which both implied acceptance of the Common Peace and of the alliance with Macedonia.

But two verdicts in the Law Courts showed that the People hankered after the days of unlimited sovereignty, which entailed withdrawal from the Greek Community. When Lycurgus prosecuted Leocrates for having left Athens after the defeat at Chaeronea and demanded the death sentence, the votes of the jury were equally divided. Probably in August Aeschines revived the prosecution of Ctesiphon, who had proposed early in 336 to crown Demosthenes for his services to Athens but had been accused of illegal procedure. Aeschines tried now to take advantage of the current situation. 'In a few days,' he said, 'the Council of the Greeks will meet ... and if you crown Demosthenes it will be seen that you are of the same mind as those who are violating the Common Peace.' But Demosthenes in his speech 'On the Crown' defended his entire political career. Aeschines failed to obtain even a fifth of the jury's votes and left Athens, never to return.

It was probably soon after the trial that the forces of the Greek Community which had defeated Persia came home and boasted of their victories and of the generous pay and bounty which they had received from Alexander. They also publicised the opportunities for Greeks to develop trade and to settle in the cities founded by Alexander. The gulf which had existed between the homeland and what Aeschines called 'the ends of the world' was closed. The returning warriors are likely to have strengthened support for the Greek Community in their individual states. Alexander could be confident that the Council of the Greek Community would control the situation on the mainland of Greece in the coming years.

CHAPTER XI

The death of Darius and the decision to advance to the east

1. The advance to Ecbatana and the pursuit of Darius

For seven months Darius had been undisturbed in Media, which was a considerable part of the Persian homeland, and he had been in contact with his subjects from eastern Armenia to Bactria. Yet he failed to raise an army comparable to that which had fought at Gaugamela, partly because defeat had undermined his authority, and partly because Alexander's liberal policy, for instance in Babylonia and in Persis, offered an acceptable alternative to Persian domination. Alexander, however, was unaware of that failure, when he advanced in May from Persis with his entire army. Opposition in Paraetacene was overcome, and a Persian was installed as satrap. When he was twelve days' march from the border of Media, a report reached him that Darius had decided to stand and fight, his army being reinforced by Scythian and Cadusian allies. Alexander advanced in readiness for battle, while the wagons of the baggage and supply trains were to follow with their guards. But the report proved false. Darius' allies had not arrived, and he was withdrawing from Media. 'Alexander advanced all the more rapidly' towards the capital city, Ecbatana (Hamadan). He was met on the way by Bisthanes, a son of Artaxerxes Ochus (the predecessor of Darius on the Persian throne). His submission was an indication that the Persian aristocrats were accepting the rule of Alexander as King of Asia. Moreover, he reported that Darius had fled with 7,000 talents and an army of only 3,000 cavalry and 6,000 infantry.

Alexander knew now that he did not need his entire army for a set battle in the near future. On entering Ecbatana, the last of the three Persian capitals, Alexander as *Hegemon* brought to an end the war of the Greek Community against Persia; for the Greek forces had attained their objectives – the liberation of the Greek cities in Asia and the taking of revenge on Persia (above, p. 64) – and had no interest in winning the Kingdom of Asia for Alexander. In addition to full pay until they should reach Euboea in Greece, being conveyed from Cilicia by trireme, each cavalryman received a bounty of one talent and each infantryman one sixth of a talent. Alexander gave presents to all of them, and they were escorted on their way to the coast. Cavalrymen who volunteered to serve in the Macedonian forces received a donative. The total outlay was said to be 12,000 talents. The gap in his forces may have been partly met by the hiring of 6,000 mercenaries, who had come from the Aegean area via Cilicia under the command of an Athenian mercenary general.

Alexander moved his base of operations from Persepolis to Ecbatana. The palace there was not destroyed, but much of the silver tiles and of the gold and silver plating of the woodwork was looted by 'Alexander and his Macedonians'. Harpalus was to be the financial officer in charge of the accumulated treasure, which was said to amount to 180,000 talents and would be stored in the citadel. The garrison was to be 6,000 Macedonians (3,000 of these coming on from Persepolis), and at first Parmenio was to be in command. Alexander planned three operations. A force of Thracians, mercenaries and light-armed cavalry under Parmenio's command was to campaign in Cadusia and Hyrcania. At a later date the 6,000 Macedonians were to follow the Persian road into Parthyaea, where they were to meet Alexander. This force was to be under the command of Cleitus, who had been left sick at Susa and was to come to Ecbatana. Alexander set off at once in pursuit of Darius. He took the Companion Cavalry, the Scouts, the mercenary cavalry, the Hypaspists, the rest of the phalangites, the Archers and the Agrianians.

Alexander set off at such a pace that infantrymen collapsed and horses died of exhaustion during the first ten days. He had hoped to catch Darius west of the Caspian Gates (the defiles of Sialek and Sardar), but Darius kept ahead and entered the Gates. Alexander stopped short at Rhagae (near Teheran), where his troops rested for five days. He appointed as satrap of Media a Persian, Oxydates, who had been imprisoned at Susa by Darius and liberated by the Macedonians. From Rhagae he passed through the Gates and paused in Choarene at the edge of the desert. There Bagistanes, a distinguished Babylonian, and Antibelus, a son of Mazaeus, came from the camp of Darius to report that Darius had been arrested – in other words deposed – by three leading Persians (Nabarzanes, Bessus and Barsaentes). It might have been thought that Darius was no longer of any significance and that the three Persians were the enemy and could be pursued at leisure (as was the case months later). But Alexander made a superhuman effort to get possession of Darius.

Taking the Companion Cavalry, the Scouts and the fittest infantrymen, lightly armed, and rations for two days, he travelled at speed all night and next day till noon, and again that evening until next day, when he came to an abandoned camp and learnt that the enemy had split into two groups – Artabazus with his sons and the Greek mercenaries taking to the hills, and Bessus in command of the remainder, including Darius under arrest. 'Already his men and his horses were exhausted by the continuous hardship, but he led them on, covering a great distance that night and next day till noon.' He was now in the camp which Bessus had occupied the preceding night, and he learned from the villagers that there was a short cut ahead through waterless country. He selected the 500 fittest men, mounted them on cavalry horses, and had them take their infantry weapons. The rest were to follow the route taken by Bessus. At the head of his select force Alexander covered 74 kilometres that night, and at dawn he came upon the enemy marching without weapons. Only a few resisted his attack. Bessus and his party tried to escape with Darius in a closed wagon, but when Alexander was in pursuit Satibarzanes and Barsaentes drove their spears into Darius and fled with 600 cavalry. Darius was dead when Alexander reached the wagon, on a July day in 330.

This account by Arrian, following Aristobulus and Ptolemy, is far preferable to those of other writers; for Ptolemy drew on the day-to-day record of Alexander's doings in the *Journal*. Why did Alexander make this supreme effort to capture Darius alive? The probable answer is that he wished Darius and his family to continue as the royal house ruling over the Medes and the Persians but within the authority of Alexander as King of Asia. Darius was said to have had great personal charm, and he could have been accepted by the Persian nobles of Alexander's entourage. No other explanation has been put forward. As it was, Alexander did everything possible to conciliate Persian opinion. Darius was accorded a royal burial at Persepolis. The obsequies were conducted by Sisigambis, and Alexander mourned his death. Moreover, Sisigambis and her family continued to be treated by Alexander as the royal house of the Medes and the Persians. For Alexander never laid claim to their throne: 'He did not proclaim himself King of Kings.' His Kingdom was 'the whole of Asia'.

2. Alexander's concept of 'Asia' and the preliminaries to the advance eastwards

Alexander derived his concept of 'Asia' from the teaching of Aristotle, for whom 'the inhabited earth' was surrounded by 'the Great Sea', Ocean, and was divided into three areas – 'Europe, Libya and Asia'. Thus the earth was not round but flat, and 'Asia' was limited on the west by the Tanais (Don), the inland sea and the Nile, and on the east by 'India' and 'the Great Sea' (see Fig. 15). The basis of Aristotle's knowledge and his idea of scale are apparent from the following passage:

> To judge from what is known from journeys by sea and land, the length [of the inhabited earth] is much greater than the width; indeed the

distance from the pillars of Heracles [at Cadiz] to India exceeds that from Aethiopia [Sudan] to Lake Maeotis [Sea of Azov] and the farthest part of Scythia in the proportion of more than five to three (Aristotle, *Meteorologica* 362b19-23).

When Aristotle wrote this passage, he may have benefited from Alexander's early journeys by land, especially from the expedition to Aethiopia (above, p. 103); for the surveyors (*bematistai*) and scientists whom Alexander took into Asia sent reports on distance, climate, flora, fauna and human and animal oecology to the School of Aristotle in Athens. However, Aristotle did not yet know that he was mistaken in supposing that from the ridge of the Parapamisus (Hindu Kush) one would see 'the outer sea' and that 'India' was a small peninsula running east into that sea. We may therefore date the passage which I have quoted to a time before Alexander's invasion of the Indus valley. Thus it gives a fair picture of Alexander's beliefs in July 330, when he had to decide whether to accept Parthyaea as his eastern frontier or to conquer the rest of 'Asia'.

By July 330 Alexander knew that Antipater had defeated Sparta and confirmed the authority of the Council of the Greek Community on the Greek mainland, and that the Macedonian thalassocracy in the Eastern Mediterranean and the Black Sea was unchallenged. His rule as King of Asia had been accepted in Egypt and western Asia, and his policy of cooperation with the ruling class in Persis and Media seemed to be succeeding. His Macedonian forces were available for further conquest; for they were not required to serve as 'armies of occupation' or as garrisons in support of imposed governments, either in Europe or in Asia. Thus as Alexander looked back at what had been achieved in four years in Asia, there was nothing to deter him from the feeling that his hands were free for further adventure.

Practical considerations were not the only factors in Alexander's thinking. At the outset he had accepted the gods' gift of Asia to be won by the spear (above, p. 64), and his advance had been marked by expressions of the gods' favour at Sardis, Gordium, Erythrae, Didyma, Siwah and Gaugamela. Thus his faith required him to become 'Lord of Asia', as he had foretold in the dedication which he had made at Lindus in Rhodes (above, p. 110), and he had no doubt that with the continuing favour of the gods he would succeed in whatever lay ahead in 'Asia'. It was this conviction which was to carry him through several crises in the years ahead.

The willing cooperation of the Macedonians was the first requirement for his plans to succeed. In the flush of victory at Gaugamela they had elected him 'King of Asia', and he intended to keep them to their word. When the Greek troops returned home from near Ecbatana, the Macedonians may have entertained hopes of homecoming for themselves. Certainly those hopes came to a head when the pursuit of Darius ended and the Macedonians with Alexander – 2,000 Companion Cavalrymen, 3,000 Hypaspists and 2,000 phalangites – rested near Hecatompylus in Parthyaea. But Alexander addressed them in an Assembly. A summary of his arguments was given in a *Letter* to Antipater which was read by Plutarch (*Alex.* 47.1-3). To go home would be to abandon Asia to confusion, and to expose themselves to counter-attack by the Asians. Let any who wished desert their king now, when he was winning the inhabited world for his country, and he would go ahead with his friends and a force of volunteers. The response was immediate: let him lead them to anywhere in the inhabited earth that he desired.

The replacement of the troops of the Greek Community was another requirement. The 2,000 or more cavalry and in particular the Thessalians had a superb record. Alexander could not have won his three set battles without them. The 7,000 infantry, together with the cavalry, had carried out important operations under the command of Parmenio, for instance in the Anatolian plateau and on the coast from Tarsus to the Pillar of Jonah. Because they had served as garrison-troops and support-troops, all the Macedonians had been able to fight in the first line. As usual, Alexander had foreseen the need to provide replacements for these Greek troops by training young Asians in Lydia, Lycia, Syria and Egypt. In autumn 330 he was joined by 300 Lydian cavalry and 2,600 Lydian infantry, and in the winter of 329-328 by 1,000 cavalry and 8,000 infantry from Lycia and Syria, all fully trained in Macedonian weaponry. The cavalry lacked any experience of battle, but Alexander had been bringing into his entourage and so into his cavalry a steady flow of Asiatic aristocrats, mainly Persian, who had been the élite cavalrymen of the Persian army. It was probably now or soon afterwards that he formed a Cavalry Guard of Persians, called 'the Euacae', which was of the highest quality.

Advance to the east was possible only if the Medes and the Persians accepted his regime and cooperated in matters of supply and communication. There had been no disarmament after victory and no dislocation of the internal administration, so that a concerted rising might be organised without difficulty and cut Alexander off from the west. He continued with his policy of partnership in the top level of civil administration; for he appointed Persians as satraps of Parthyaea and of Mardia-Tapuria, and a Parthyaean as satrap of Hyrcania. At his court he now had a large number of distinguished Asiatics who were accorded the high honours they had enjoyed in the past. Among them were a brother of Darius, a son of Artaxerxes Ochus, Darius' second-in-command, a leading statesman (Artabazus) and commander (Mazaeus). Alexander decided to adopt a version of Persian ceremonial in his audiences with the Asiatic courtiers. Whereas he called his leading Macedonians 'Friends', he called the Asiatics 'Kinsmen' and let them

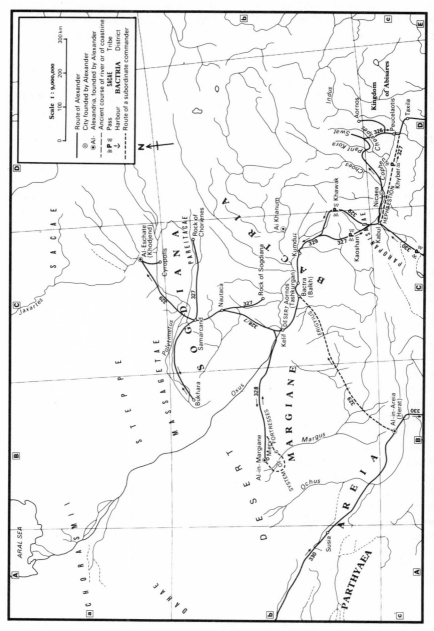

14. The northeastern satrapies

kiss him in the Persian manner, and they did obeisance to him (*proskynesis*). In these audiences he wore an idiosyncratic form of dress which combined Median and Persian features and did not include the attributes of a Persian king, and he was attended by mace-bearers in the Asiatic style. He instituted this form of ceremonial first in Parthyaea in mid-August 330. No doubt he consulted his Friends at this preliminary stage and was aware of opposition.

In preparation for the advance to the east Alexander divided his forces into three after the death of Darius, led that which followed the most dangerous route and subdued the Tapurians in the high country of Mount Elburz (18,550 feet). Further operations reduced the Mardi. Alexander made his base at Zadracarta (probably Sari) on the edge of the fertile plain betwen Mt Elburz and 'the Great Sea' (Arrian. 3.23.1); for at this time Alexander accepted the belief of Aristotle that the Hyrcanian (Caspian) Sea was an inlet of Ocean. The 1,500 Greek mercenaries who had served with Darius put themselves in Alexander's hands. He let those go free who had entered Darius' service before 'the peace and alliance (of the Greeks) with Macedonia' in 337. The others were required to serve under Alexander. Some Greek envoys also gave themselves up. Those from Sparta and Athens were arrested, but he let the envoy from Sinope (on the south coast of the Black Sea) go free, because Sinope was not a member of 'the Community of the Greeks' (Arrian 3.24.4). At Zadracarta he celebrated a traditional Macedonian festival with the customary sacrifices and with a competition in athletic events for fifteen days. He then returned to Parthyaea in mid-August. He was now in full control of the corridor between the Caspian Sea and the Kasht-i-Kavir desert.

It was at this point that the crucial choice between two policies had to be made in practice. One policy was to adopt a defensible frontier, running from the southeast corner of the Caspian Sea through the Elburz Mountains, across the corridor, along the west side of the two great deserts of Kavir and Lut, and through Kerman to the mouth of the Persian Gulf. Since Alexander could count on the support of Egypt and Babylon and on the cooperation of the Medes and the Persians, he would be in control of a huge and prosperous area of which the centre woud be Cilicia with its ports giving access to the Aegean Sea and to Macedonia. He would be able to extend that control by campaigning in Arabia on the one hand and in the area between the Caspian Sea and the Black Sea on the other hand. At an early stage Parmenio had advised Alexander to accept the upper Euphrates as his eastern frontier, and then at Persepolis he had warned Alexander that it was dangerous to give the Asians the impression that he was 'merely going ahead conquering'. In mid-August 330 Parmenio was in command at Ecbatana; but there must have been Friends and Companions in

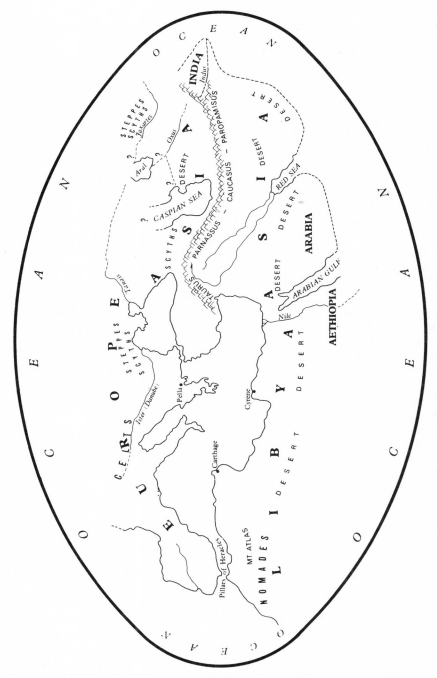

15. Alexander's world in 327 BC

Parthyaea who would have preferred to stop there and to consolidate a clearly defensible kingdom in Asia.

The other policy was to advance eastwards into areas which were beyond the range of Greek mercenaries and so little known to Greek thinkers. But they were familiar to many of the Asian courtiers of Alexander, who will certainly have warned him that it was a vast region of difficult terrain with high mountains and extensive deserts, and that its warlike peoples would be determined fighters in defence of their lands. He had seen at Gaugamela how formidable their cavalry was when they were serving under Darius as subjects or as allies – Parthyaeans, Bactrians, Arachosians, Sacae, Dahae, Massagetae, Scythians and Indians. How far to the east was it necessary for Alexander to go? The answer is related to Aristotle's concept of the inhabited earth (see Fig. 15). Aristotle had proved correct up to date. For at the edges of the earth there were areas of steppe country and desert facing Ocean in the north between the Black Sea and the Caspian and beyond the Caspian by hearsay as far as the Jaxartes river, and in the south in Libya, Arabia, Carmania and Gedrosia; and it was evident that a great range of mountains which Aristotle called 'Taurus-Parnassus-Caucasus-Parapamisus' divided northern Asia from southern Asia. What lay east of Parapamisus was not known even to the Asian courtiers of Alexander; for it seems that the Indian cavalry and the Indian elephants with their mahouts had come to Gaugamela from the westernmost region of Indian settlement. Alexander and his followers therefore believed that Aristotle was correct also in his description of 'India' when seen from the ridge of the Parapamisus as a small triangular promontory projecting eastwards into Ocean. Thus it was reasonable for Alexander to envisage the conquest of 'all Asia' as feasible in two stages, up to the Parapamisus ridge (our Hindu Kush) and then beyond it to Ocean. Once this was achieved, the Kingdom of Asia would be bounded by steppe and desert and by the waters of the Great Sea, and it would be easily defended against any enemies.

Alexander had long ago decided in principle in favour of the second policy, and he had persuaded his Macedonians in an Assembly at Hecatompylus to accept it (above, p. 123). It was a policy which he could have abandoned in mid-August, when he saw how strong a frontier could be drawn with the corridor as its central feature. Instead, he pressed on with the policy which he believed the gods had forecast for him: the winning of all Asia.

Scientific exploration was also a part of Alexander's plans. He was already in a part of the world which was largely unknown to Greek scientists. Thus he had been able to investigate the strange behaviour of the river Stiboetes (now Chesmeh-i-Ali) which flowed in and out of underground channels in Hyrcania and to send back to Greece a report, of which a summary is preserved in accounts by Diodorus and Curtius.

There is no doubt that he and his scientists and surveyors were in regular correspondence with Aristotle. It was probably in 330 that Alexander sent to him the huge sum of 800 talents, with which Aristotle was able to found in Athens for the first time in history a great library of literary texts on papyrus and to make the first collection of specimens for teaching (especially in the field of zoology). The advance eastwards was to provide a wealth of new discoveries.

CHAPTER XII

From Parthyaea to Kabul in Afghanistan

1. Forward planning by Alexander

Alexander showed his usual foresight during the summer of 330. Because the peoples between Parthyaea and the Parapamisus excelled in cavalry warfare, Alexander trained two new groups of light-armed cavalry: mounted javelin-men and mounted infantrymen. The personnel of the first were Medes and Persians, and that of the second group were Europeans. These units, together with the Scouts, who were armed with the lance, were to be deployed against the light-armed cavalry of the enemy and also to keep order in partially subjected districts. In addition he had considerable numbers of light-armed Thracian and Greek mercenary cavalry, which had been trained to act as flank-guards to the heavy cavalry in battle. They would now operate as independent light-armed units. The heavy cavalry, consisting of the Companion Cavalry and the Persian Euacae (above, p. 123), fought in formation against comparable cavalry and attacked infantry formations in the flank or in pursuit. Their task now would be to act in small numbers in support of the light-armed cavalry. He expected reinforcements – they reached him in the autumn at Artacoana on the border of Afghanistan – namely 130 Thessalian cavalry as allies, 500 Greek mercenary cavalry and 300 Lydian cavalry trained in the Macedonian manner.

For operations as far as the Parapamisus Alexander seems to have considered that his infantry forces, together with those he was expecting, namely 3,000 Illyrians and 2,600 Lydians, would be sufficient. He relied on the superb quality of his own experienced Macedonians, Agrianians and Archers, on his artillery and on his siege-train for attacks on enemy armies and strongholds, and he had an adequate number of Greek mercenaries and Balkan infantry to support them. He knew that he would not face any Greek mercenaries; for they preferred now to seek employment with him. In late spring 329 he sent orders for reinforcements, and these were brought by officers stationed in coastal areas of western Asia to Zariaspa (Balkh) in Bactria in early winter 329. They were as follows: 1,600 Greek mercenary cavalry, 11,400 Greek mercenary infantry, 500 Lycian cavalry, 4,000 Lycian infantry, 500 Syrian cavalry and 4,000 Syrian infantry.

The Lydian, Lycian and Syrian troops which have been mentioned were the first products of a training course which Alexander had established for selected boys in those countries, as also in Egypt (above, pp. 72, 78 and 101). He could now look ahead to a time when the Kingdom of Asia would be complete and he would have need of an army of Asian infantry. It was to this end that in late 330 and early in 329 he set up 'in his newly-founded cities and in the rest of the spear-won land' a complete system of training. Plutarch wrote as follows: 'He selected 30,000 boys (*paides*) and gave orders that they should learn Greek letters and be trained in Macedonian weaponry, and he appointed many supervisors.' In other accounts we are told that the boys when selected were 'utterly young', and that when the first draft of 'the new generation' (*Epigonoi*), 30,000 in number, paraded before Alexander in 324 they were already men, i.e. had reached manhood at twenty. It follows that the course started with boys aged fourteen and continued for four years until their eighteenth birthday. Alexander appointed teachers and trainers as well as supervisors to serve at his expense, so that he was providing what we may call a subsidised system of state-education for the brightest Asian boys in his kingdom. On completing the course they were to serve as soldiers under the command of the satrap of their region.

2. Campaigning in Afghanistan

Alexander's march from Parthyaea into Areia was unopposed. For the Persian satrap, Satibarzanes, came to meet him at Susia (near Meshed) and on behalf of himself and the Areians accepted his rule. Alexander continued Satibarzanes in the office of satrap, and sent to him a Companion with forty mounted javelin-men, whose task was to prevent any pillaging by the Macedonian army on the march. This is the first indication in the surviving accounts that Alexander's order on crossing into Asia that there was to be no pillaging might not be obeyed. As he marched on towards Bactra (in northernmost Afghanistan), he was met by some Persians. They reported that Bessus, a relative of Darius, was wearing royal dress as King of the Medes and Persians, renaming himself 'Artaxerxes', and claiming also to be 'King of Asia' as a direct challenge to Alexander; that he had a following of Persians and of Bactrians; and that he was expecting Scythians to come as his allies. Soon afterwards Alexander was joined by some of the troops who had been with Parmenio at Ecbatana and were sent forward by Parmenio (above, p. 120). The army, perhaps now of some 45,000 men, was proceeding on the line of the Persian royal road, which was itself being used by the wagons of the siege-train, baggage-train and supply-system. The great advantage of the road was that it was routed through fertile areas in which supplies could be purchased or requisitioned.

Alexander was still on the way to Bactra, when it was reported that Satibarzanes had killed the javelin-men and their commander, was calling the Areians to arms in support of Bessus, and was about to concentrate the rebel forces at Artacoana (near Herat), the capital of the satrapy. This was the first instance of rebellion after submission and acceptance of Alexander's rule as King of Asia. How was that acceptance ratified at the time? In Egypt Alexander was received into 'the cities and the country' and on his route 'the inhabitants put their places in his hands'; so too in Babylon he was welcomed by the Babylonians *en masse*, their priests and their magistrates, and 'each section of the inhabitants brought gifts and surrendered the city, the citadel and the treasure'. It is to be assumed that each unit of society within the satrapy not only made formal surrender, as these details in Arrian's account indicate, but also took formal oaths of loyalty to Alexander as their king and undertook to pay an annual sum as tribute and provide services. Rebellion thereafter meant the breaking of formal oaths and was punishable with justifiable severity.

Rebellion was in some ways more dangerous for Alexander's forces than open warfare. For once a satrapy had submitted, any troops in the satrapy were either acting as relatively small garrisons or operating in the countryside. They might easily be taken by surprise and liquidated, as presumably in the case of the forty mounted javelin-men. The risk too was that rebellion might spread rapidly, if the first outbreak was not nipped in the bud, and a widespread rebellion would cut the communications between the army with Parmenio and that of Alexander.

For such reasons Alexander acted with extraordinary speed. Taking the Companion Cavalry, the mounted javelin-men, two brigades of phalangites, the Agrianians and the Archers, he covered the 110 kilometres to Artacoana in two days. Satibarzanes fled, for he had not yet concentrated the troops of Areia. He escaped with 2,000 cavalry to join Bessus in Bactria. Alexander used the Persian road as the base from which operations were conducted against the insurgents by several detachments for a period of a month. Alexander commanded one such detachment. The ringleaders of the Areians were executed, and many of their followers were sold as slaves. The last city to be laid under siege was Artacoana. When the defenders saw the siege-towers coming up to the walls, they surrendered and asked for mercy. Alexander pardoned them and left them in possession of their property. He also made arrangements for the future. For he founded not far from Artacoana a new city, Alexandria-in-Areia, with a mixed population of Macedonians, Greeks and Areians, and he arranged for the teaching and training of selected Areian boys. The satrapy, comprising much of Afghanistan, was of great strategic importance, since routes radiated from it to Bactria in the north, 'India' in the east, and Drangiana in the south. Despite his experience with Satibarzanes Alexander appointed a Persian to be satrap of Areia.

3. The trial of Philotas and others

With the army reunited Alexander followed the Persian road southwards for 295 kilometres, according to his surveyors, and he made his headquarters at Phrada (Farah), the capital of Drangiana. The satrap had fled towards the Indians; for he was Barsaentes, one of those who had arrested and wounded Darius, and later, when the Indians sent him to Alexander, he was executed for that act of treason. While the army rested at Phrada for nine days, in October 330, a plot against the life of Alexander was reported.

One of the plotters was a Macedonian soldier of no particular distinction, named Dimnus. He boasted of the plot to his boy-lover, forced him to take an oath of secrecy, and named some leading Macedonians who were planning with him to kill Alexander. The boy told his brother Cebalinus, who went at once to Alexander's headquarters. He waited outside, as he had no authority to enter, and he accosted Philotas, a son of Parmenio, who came out alone from an audience with the king. Cebalinus told Philotas of the plot and asked him to report it at once to Alexander. On that evening and again next day Cebalinus asked Philotas if he had made the report, and Philotas put him off with excuses. This made Cebalinus suspect that Philotas was privy to the plot. So he approached one of the Royal Pages, who smuggled him into the armoury of the headquarters. There he told Alexander what he knew of the plot and of Philotas' failure to pass on his report of it.

As Alexander had done when Alexander Lyncestes was suspected of treason (above, p. 79), he now convened his Friends and sought their advice. They thought that the case should be submitted to trial. Alexander gave orders for the arrest of those under suspicion. Dimnus managed to commit suicide. Philotas did not resist. Next day the Macedonians were summoned to assemble under arms as judges. They were the Companion cavalrymen, the Hypaspists and the phalangites, and of them some 6,000 were present. Ptolemy, a participant at the time and writing when some other participants were still alive, gave an account which Arrian summarised as follows:

> Philotas was brought before the Macedonians. He was prosecuted vigorously by Alexander, and he made his own defence. Those who had reported the matter came forward and convicted Philotas and those with him with clear proofs, and particularly with the fact that Philotas himself agreed that he had heard that some plot against Alexander was being prepared and that he was convicted of saying nothing of it to Alexander,

although he visited Alexander's headquarters twice daily. Philotas and all who took part in the plot with him were shot down by the javelins of the Macedonians. ... At the same time four sons of Andromenes were accused of complicity in the plot, but they were acquitted by acclamation.

The centre of interest in this account was Philotas, because he was the Commander of the Companion Cavalry and a son of Parmenio. 'Those with him' were serving officers, for whom the form of execution was by javelin rather than by stoning. The 6,000 Macedonians, being full citizens of the Macedonian state, formed what may be called a 'People's Court'; they decided the verdicts, whether condemnation or acquittal. A People's Court was not unusual in Greek city-states. In contemporary Athens cases of treason were tried by the Assembly in which for some items of business a quorum of 6,000 was required, and Athens was proud of her system of law and justice.

Other writers – Diodorus, Strabo and Justin – had both Philotas and Parmenio (*in absentia*) undergo trial and Parmenio be condemned as an accomplice. There is no reason to doubt that this was so; moreover, it was customary that male relatives of a man condemned for treason were also put to death (Curtius 8.6.28 *Macedonum more*). In Arrian's summary of Ptolemy's account the executions of Philotas and others were coupled together in one sentence as results of the trial. At the time Parmenio was at the base at Ecbatana in command of a force of 6,200 Macedonians and 5,600 Greek mercenaries and in charge of 180,000 talents. If he should hear of the verdict of the Assembly in time, he might rebel and carry the army with him. Accordingly, an officer disguised as an Arab and with an Arab escort went on fast camels by the direct route through the desert and gave Alexander's written orders for the execution of Parmenio. He was killed without being aware of his son's trial and death. A statement by Alexander was read out to the Macedonians, who were about to mutiny. Arrangements were made for them to march the 2,000 kilometres to Arachosia and join their compatriots there.

Alexander had had a narrow escape. Had Cebalinus not been so persistent, Alexander would have been killed on the day when in fact the trial took place, and the conduct of affairs would have passed into the hands of Philotas as commander of the Companion Cavalry and of Parmenio as senior general. Alexander commemorated his escape by founding a city in Drangiana and naming it 'Anticipation' (Prophthasia). Further enquiries led to the execution of Demetrius, a Bodyguard, as a conspirator. The whole experience had a lasting effect on Alexander. He knew now that he could not trust even his closest Macedonian Friends. He never again placed so large a force of Macedonian soldiers under a separate commander, and he split the command of the Companion Cavalry between two officers, one being his friend from youth

Hephaestion and the other an older man, Cleitus. Alexander must have realised that what had prompted Philotas, Parmenio, Demetrius and other officers was opposition to his policy of partnership with Asians (for he had appointed only Asians as satraps since the Battle of Gaugamela), of dressing up as an Asian and holding an Asian court, and of advancing farther and farther eastwards.

In his account Ptolemy noted what he himself speculated were Alexander's inner thoughts on the subject of Parmenio. 'Possibly he thought it incredible that Parmenio was not a partner of Philotas in the plot; possibly too, if Parmenio had not participated, he was too dangerous to survive his son's execution' in view of his position and his popularity. This speculation had nothing to do with any arguments which Alexander had advanced as prosecutor. It is rather an indication that Ptolemy himself had an open mind on the question of Parmenio's innocence or guilt, and that Ptolemy could see, he thought, two ideas which had 'possibly' influenced Alexander.

According to Arrian, who cited Ptolemy and Aristobulus as his sources, Philotas had been suspected of plotting against Alexander in Egypt, i.e. in 331, but Alexander had not thought it credible at the time. Plutarch, drawing probably on Aristobulus, added the interesting point that Alexander did not reveal that suspicion for 'more than seven years'. It follows that when Alexander was prosecuting Philotas in 330 he did not mention this earlier suspicion, although it would have strengthened the case against Philotas. Plutarch added the just comment that Alexander made 'the fairest and most kingly use of his authority' in this case.

While the Assembly was in session, it was proposed by Atarrhias, a Commander, that Alexander Lyncestes should be brought in for trial; for he had been under arrest for some four years by the order of Alexander but had not been tried (above, p. 80). The Assembly approved. Alexander Lyncestes was prosecuted on a charge of treason, presumably by the king. He failed to muster words in his own defence, and he was killed by the Assembly's javelins. It is unlikely that he received any sympathy; for the Friends of Alexander had judged him guilty of treason in 333, and the evidence of the letter carried by Sisines (above, p. 79) was still available.

The knowledge that there was opposition among his Friends and Commanders to his policy seems to have made Alexander more anxious to gain the support of his Asian courtiers. He therefore developed at this time his use of Asian dress and ceremonial by appointing the most distinguished Asians to be his personal guards – corresponding to the seven Macedonian Bodyguards – and by giving to some of his Companions Persian cloaks to wear and Persian harness for their horses. Hephaestion was one who willingly supported Alexander in this policy. Then it was noted that Alexander used 'his ancient seal-ring' for correspondence sent to Europe, and that of Darius for correspondence within Asia. The wearing of a seal-ring was a general practice among Macedonians of some standing, and in Alexander's case he wore the traditional seal-ring which had been handed down in the Temenid dynasty; for that is the meaning of 'ancient' (*veteris anuli*) in the context. Now within Asia he began to use the traditional seal-ring of the Achaemenid dynasty for correspondence within Asia (especially correspondence with his Asian satraps), because that seal had long been recognised and accepted. The fact that he was drawing an official distinction between his position as King of Macedonia and his position as King of Asia may have given offence to those Macedonians who disliked the sharing of power with the Asians.

4. Operations in Afghanistan and Baluchistan

During three or four months into January 329 Alexander conducted extensive operations, of which his historians tell us little. We know that he founded two cities in this period, Alexandria probably at Kandahar and Alexandropolis at Kalat-i-Ghilzai. From Drangiana he advanced south into the very fertile land of the Ariaspi (Sistan), famous for its lakes and its production of cereals. These people were called 'Benefactors', because they had saved the starving army of Cyrus the Great by sending to him 30,000 wagon-loads of grain from their country. They accepted the rule of Alexander, and he treated them with generosity, adding land to their territory and giving them presents. His base camp was established there for some sixty days, during which stocks were accumulated for the winter months. The people of Gedrosia (Makran) made their submission, recognised Alexander's rule and were given presents by him. Alexander made sacrifice to Apollo, and he appointed a Persian to be satrap of Arimaspia and Gedrosia.

Meanwhile another rebellion in Areia threatened his line of communications; for Satibarzanes with his 2,000 cavalry had returned and raised an army of Areians in the name of Bessus. Alexander sent a force mainly of cavalry under the joint command of the Persian Artabazus and of Erigyius and Caranus, and he ordered the Persian satrap of Parthyaea to invade Areia at the same time. There was fierce fighting, which was brought to an end when Erigyius killed Satibarzanes in hand-to-hand combat, probably in November. While the rising in Areia was being suppressed, Alexander campaigned in Arachosia where he forced the people to submit. Because this satrapy in eastern Afghanistan was of great strategic importance, he departed from his usual practice and appointed a Macedonian to be satrap with a force of 600 cavalry and 4,000 infantry. In Arachosia he was joined by the army which had marched from Ecbatana (above, p. 133). It consisted of 200 Companion Cavalry, 6,000 Macedonians, 600 Greek mercenary cavalry and 5,000 Greek mercenary infantry. Then, if not earlier, the Spartan envoys and hostages arrived from Greece and made their appeal for clemency after their defeat (above, p. 117). Alexander pardoned them but required Sparta to become a member of the Greek Community and thus his ally.

He now advanced northwards with his united army on a route along a high flank of the mountain which the Macedonians called the Caucasus (Hindu Kush). It was now midwinter and there was deep snow and intense cold which caused frostbite and snow-blindness. Supplies were short for the troops, and there were casualties among them and among the camp-followers, who were not on the ration-strength but managed their own affairs. The native people lived in huts under the snow and had stocks for the winter months, and the Macedonians were saved from disaster by identifying the villages from the smoke and obtaining shelter and food from them. When they crossed the Sher-Dahan pass, they saw the crag where Prometheus had been chained and the cave in which the eagle nested that fed on his liver. On the northern side of the pass the weather was less severe, and the army spent the rest of the winter near Kabul where supplies were available. Alexander 'sacrificed to the gods to whom he usually did', and he founded Alexandria-in-Caucaso near Begram and some other cities in this region. The settlers near Begram numbered 7,000 Asians of the locality, 3,000 camp-followers and any volunteers among his Greek mercenaries, of whom many had Asian concubines and children. In these cities selected boys were enrolled in the four-year course. Alexander appointed a Persian to be satrap of the area, which was called Parapamisus. Routes from it led to Parthyaea, Bactria and 'India'.

The scale of these operations may be measured by the fact that they covered an area comparable to Asia Minor in extent and mountainous in character. The ethnic groups had a strong nationalistic feeling; they fought not for a continuation of Persian rule but for their own independence. Some he won over to his Kingdom of Asia by persuasion and with a courteous exchange of gifts. Others he had to overcome by force, and he succeeded mainly through the skilful deployment of his excellent cavalry in rapid sweeps. Whether he prevailed by persuasion or by force, he applied his usual principle, that the land was 'spear-won' and in his possession. Generally he gave it to the current inhabitants to cultivate on payment of a tax, which we call 'tribute'. Where there was a reason, he might confer additional territory, e.g. on the Ariaspi, or take territory away, as he did from the Areians. The peace on which he insisted brought economic advantages. In the six or more cities which he founded there was a prospect of collaboration between Europeans and Asians, and in particular the schools for selected Asian boys were evidence of Alexander's desire for the Asians to share in the future administration of the Kingdom. There was a danger of interference by outside powers. Bessus might try to stir up trouble again, and that was one reason for Alexander leaving so strong a garrison force in Arachosia. The other danger was that the Indians might invade. Alexander had made contact with the most westerly Indians who were neighbours of the Areians. It seems from a passage in Strabo 724 that Alexander annexed a border area between the two peoples and planted in it some military settlements (*katoikiai*) presumably of Greek mercenaries with their families.

CHAPTER XIII

The advance to the river Jaxartes

1. The system of supply and the crossing of the Hindu Kush

The Alexander-historians tell us little of Alexander's system of supply. It may be considered as having two departments: the maintaining of a central reserve and the provision of rations and fodder for forays. The Macedonians, like the Spartans, had a supply company or 'commissariat'. Its commander or director had the title 'Skoidos' according to Pollux, a late lexicographer. He had to purchase or requisition a huge stock of basic supplies, which were transported on four-wheeled wagons, drawn by horses, mules or oxen. He therefore needed all-weather hard-surfaced roads. The Macedonians and the Thracians had a long tradition of road-making, and there was probably a pioneer-brigade of Thracians who made and maintained roads. It was fortunate for Alexander that the Persians also were famous builders of roads. Thus the supply-column, like the baggage-train and the siege-train, followed the Persian roads as far as Arachosia and Areia. So also did the camp-followers, who made a living by selling food and goods to the soldiers and travelled with their families on their own wagons.

The provision of rations and fodder from the central reserve for expeditions into enemy country was much more difficult. The amounts had to be calculated in advance, even when the duration of an expedition was very uncertain. Philip trained his infantrymen to carry a month's supply of flour (bread being the staple diet), and Alexander ordered each man to carry four days' supply of water in desert country – these in addition to weapons and equipment. They were physically tougher than any modern soldier of the western hemisphere. A cavalryman had a groom, who also had to be mounted on a cavalry expedition and presumably carried the rations for two men and oats for two horses. Fresh fodder was most desirable for warhorses and was usually obtained by foraging, as near Pelium (above, p. 37). The most remarkable achievement was the feeding of men and horses during Alexander's racing pursuit of Darius, when two days' rations had to be spread over four days.

A new problem faced Alexander in the Hindu Kush. For there was no road from Kandahar over the Sher-Dahan pass to Kabul, and again from Kabul to Kunduz. At Kandahar Alexander must have learned through interpreters of the difficulties he would face in crossing the Sher-Dahan pass in the winter; but he overcame them thanks to 'the customary boldness and endurance of the Macedonians'. The description of the crossing which was given above (p. 136) applied to the vanguard which went ahead and chose a route for the main body and the baggage-train and siege-train, which would follow later. Alexander commanded that vanguard, and there were stories of him helping men who fell by the wayside. The supplies of the vanguard were carried by the men, their horses and pack-animals. When he was at Kabul, Alexander was aware that the crossing to Kunduz would be even more difficult under wintry conditions. Nevertheless, he undertook it in March 329 in order to anticipate any attempt by Bessus to defend the Khawak pass, which attains some 3,300 metres. Accounts of the hardships suffered by Alexander and the vanguard stem from Aristobulus. During the crossing, which took some sixteen days through thick snow, supplies ran short and the order was given to kill the pack-animals and season the raw meat (for there was no kindling) with the 'silphium' (possibily asafoetida) which grew abundantly in the spring. To this the soldiers added herbs and trout as they descended the north face of the mountain. 'Even so Alexander continued to advance.'

Bessus had never thought that Alexander would cross the mountain and invade Bactria so early in the year. He was beginning to lay waste the countryside on the Bactrian side of the mountain with a force of 7,000 Bactrian cavaly and a group of Dahae cavalry when the news of Alexander's approach reached him. Although the Bactrians were said to have 30,000 cavalry, Bessus had failed to muster them, and he now added to his incompetence by taking flight precipitately. He crossed the river Oxus (Amu-Darya) and burnt every boat in the hope that Alexander would be unable to pursue. As Bessus was abandoning their country, the Bactrian cavalry went home. Bessus depended now on the Sogdians and their allies, the Dahae.

2. The crossing of the Oxus, the Branchidae and the failure of Bessus

For some weeks Alexander made his base at Drapsaca (Kunduz) at the foot of the Hindu Kush. During this time the main body, the baggage-train and the siege-train were making the crossing from Kabul in improving weather. The country ahead of Alexander consisted of two satrapies which formed the northeastern frontier of the Persian empire, and beyond them lived the numerous nomadic peoples of the steppe country. The Bactrians, the Sogdians and the Areians were interrelated and had a common language with local variations, and for that reason the Bactrians had supported the risings in Areia. The territory of the

Bactrians and the Sogdians consisted of extensive, fertile plains and arid deserts. There were few cities but very many villages, mountain fastnesses and nomadic tribes in desert regions. Society was organised on an aristocratic basis. The barons and their retinues were superb cavalrymen in a countryside famous for horse-breeding, and it was they who organised resistance to the raids of the mounted Scythian tribesmen or entered into alliance with them.

When he had sufficient troops, in April or May, Alexander attacked the two greatest cities of Bactria, named Aornus and Bactra, and he captured them at the first assault. Whether there were other operations we do not know. Arrian was very brief: 'He left a garrison in the citadel of Aornus ... and as satrap over the rest of the Bactrians who readily came over to him he appointed Artabazus the Persian.' The surrender of the Bactrians will have involved the recognition of Alexander as King of Asia, the taking of oaths of loyalty by the barons and other magistrates, and the preliminary assessment of tribute. When these arrangements were complete, Alexander led a select force across an arid desert towards the river Oxus. In the intense heat of early summer he marched mainly at night, guided by the stars, and the men suffered great distress from the scarcity of water. When a cup of it was offered to Alexander by a soldier, Alexander told him to give it to his sons. On reaching the Oxus he encamped for some days, during which he selected the oldest Macedonians, now unfit for active service, and he sent them homewards, together with some Thessalians who had been serving as volunteers. He gave to all of them a generous bounty, and he urged them to beget children. In view of their departure Alexander convened an Assembly of the Macedonians in his force, and 'they promised that they would serve for the remainder of the war'.

Because he was afraid of a renewal of trouble in Areia, he sent Stasanor, a Companion of Cypriote origin, to be satrap in place of the Persian Arsaces, who in Alexander's judgement had been remiss in dealing with the revolt. The army crossed the Oxus, a huge river a kilometre wide, in five days on rafts buoyed up by the soldiers' leather tent-covers, which were filled with chaff and sewn up to be watertight. Soon after the crossing the army came upon a little town occupied by people who were bilingual in Greek and Persian and called themselves Branchidae. Their ancestors had been the priests and guardians of Apollo's oracular shrine at Didyma near Miletus, a shrine as famous then as those of Delphi and Dodona. But in 479 'the Branchidae had handed over the monies and the treasures of the god' to Xerxes, who had burnt the temple, and then they had 'willingly' accompanied him to Persia, where they had been given a new home. 'Their sacrilege and their treason' were heinous and infamous. Moreover, although the oracle was consulted after their departure, the god was silent until Alexander freed Miletus and Didyma. Then Apollo declared that Alexander was 'born of Zeus' and forecast events of his future career (above, p. 103).

How were the Branchidae of the little town to be treated? Whereas Arrian and Plutarch did not even mention the place, Curtius gave a highly sensational account. In it Alexander referred the question to the Milesians in the army as Didyma was in their territory; and when they disagreed among themselves, Alexander himself decided to destroy the place. Since the writer on whom Curtius relied for his account was Cleitarchus, and since ancient critics condemned Cleitarchus as 'notoriously untrustworthy' (above, p. 46), most scholars have rejected Curtius' account. However, Strabo in writing of places in Bactria and Sogdiana made the statements which are quoted in the previous paragraph, and he added that Alexander 'destroyed the town of the Branchidae in his disgust at the sacrilege and the treason' of their ancestors (Strabo 518; cf. 634 and 814). Strabo's sources were Callisthenes at 814 and most probably Aristobulus at 518 and 634, both participants in the campaign writing for contemporaries. As they cannot have been mistaken, it is evident that Alexander did destroy the town, killing the adult males and probably enslaving the remainder, as Curtius following Cleitarchus reported.

Why should Alexander have destroyed the place? He attached great importance to the sacrilege of the Persians in the wars of 499-479 and to his role as avenger of the gods and the Greeks for the Persian atrocities. His destruction of the palace of Xerxes at Persepolis was such an act of vengeance. The guilt of those Greeks who took the side of Persia was inherited by their descendants; for in the discussion about the treatment of the Thebans in 335 the treason of their ancestors was advanced as a reason for destroying Thebes (above, p. 48). So too the Branchidae in 329 were still polluted by the infamous conduct of their ancestors, which so disgusted Alexander. Moreover, in his role as champion and avenger of Apollo he was bound to punish these polluted Branchidae. We may recall that Philip as champion and avenger of Apollo of Delphi had drowned 3,000 prisoners of war, who as mercenaries had accepted money stolen from the god (above, p. 17). Alexander may well have had that precedent in mind when he killed the adult male Branchidae.

Alexander's aim was to engage the forces of Bessus. He therefore marched at speed, but he slackened his pace, when a message came that the arrest of Bessus was being planned by his associates, Spitamenes and Dataphernes, and that they would hand him over to a Macedonian officer in command of a small force. Alexander selected Ptolemy for this mission but gave him a considerable force of élite cavalry and infantry. Arrian's account follows that of Ptolemy. In four days of very rapid marching they reached the camp which Spitamenes had occupied a day before, and they learned that there was some doubt about the intentions of Spitamenes and Dataphernes. So Ptolemy pressed on with his cavalry and came to a village where Bessus was in the custody of a few soldiers. After negotiations with the villagers Ptolemy took possession of Bessus, and in accordance with instructions from Alexander placed him, bound, naked and wearing a wooden collar to the right of the road which the army was about to take. When Alexander came up, he questioned Bessus about the murder of his king Darius, and Bessus replied that he was only one of several who had intended to please Alexander. Then Bessus was scourged, while Alexander had a herald announce the crimes which he had committed.

'The king handed Bessus over to the brother of Darius and the other Kinsmen for punishment.' One of Alexander's principles was that offenders should be tried by their own nationals in accordance with their laws. Thus he had handed over the captured tyrants to the Greek islanders, and the Branchidae to the Milesians according to Curtius. The Persian courtiers met under the presidency of Alexander as King of Asia, and they decided to mutilate Bessus in the Persian manner by cutting off his nose and ear-lobes. Alexander sent him under escort to Ecbatana, where 'the Council of the Medes and Persians' would decide on the form of execution. When Arrian reported the treatment of Bessus, he censured Alexander as if it was he and not the leading Persians who made the decisions.

The history of Bessus illustrates the success of Alexander's policy in relation to Persia. We have seen that Alexander appointed Persians or at least Asians as satraps in almost every area east of the Euphrates as far as Bactria, and that after the death of Parmenio he left very few troops in Persis and Media. His confidence that the Medes and Persians would not rise against him was justified. Yet it is very surprising. No one was better qualified to lead resistance than Bessus, a member of the ruling house and satrap of Bactria, who brought to Gaugamela the forces of Bactria and Sogdiana and the Indians neighbouring Bactria. In the battle they had done him great credit, and it was the Bactrian cavalry which covered the escape of Darius. When Bessus disposed of Darius and declared himself King of the Medes and Persians, he must have hoped for a national rising; but nothing of the sort occurred. It was only the Areians, being related to the Bactrians and Sogdians, who rebelled with help from Bessus. When he too failed, some Persians in the northeast area fought on, but the future of Media and Persia lay with the Council of the Medes and the Persians and with the members of the royal family whom Alexander had left at Susa. It is doubtful if any conquered people in medieval or modern history has shown to any similar degree not only acceptance but also collaboration; for some leading Asians entered at once into the service of the conqueror, the Persians formed a Cavalry Guard to protect him, and the Persian mounted javelin-men played their part in the extension of the Kingdom of Asia.

3. Risings in Sogdiana and Bactria in 329

Alexander made good his losses in horses and advanced unopposed to the capital of the satrapy, Samarcand, where he placed a garrison of 1,000 men in the citadel, and then to the river Jaxartes, which formed the frontier of the Persian empire. In Aristotle's geography (see Fig.15) this river was thought to be the upper part of the Tanaïs (Don), which separated Europe from Asia. Alexander saw that it did indeed flow in a westerly direction, and one theory was that it flowed through the Caspian Sea, left the Caspian with the name Tanaïs, and entered the Maeotid Lake (Sea of Azov). Whatever was the truth of the matter (and Alexander planned to explore the Caspian Sea), he accepted the Jaxartes as the border between Asia and Europe, and he regarded the steppe country north of it as the edge of 'the inhabited earth'. He realised how extensive the steppe country was when he entered into diplomatic relations with two groups of Scythians, the Abii south of the river and the Sacae on the far side of the river. As a precaution against the Scythians he placed garrisons in the Sogdian cities south of the river.

The ease with which Alexander had taken possession of Bactria and Sogdiana was to prove misleading. The spirit of independence was first shown when some Macedonians who were foraging were seized and killed by members of a large tribe which mustered 30,000 men and occupied a mountain fastness. Alexander, leading the attack against them, was struck by an arrow which broke part of his fibula, and many others were wounded by missiles, before the summit was captured. Of the Sogdians 8,000 escaped; the others were killed in the fierce fighting or committed suicide by throwing themselves over the cliffs. While his wound was healing, Alexander began to draw up the plans of a new city at Khodjend on the Asian side of the Jaxartes, which was to be called Alexandria Eschate, that is Alexandria of the frontier. He intended also to establish his authority more firmly in the two satrapies, and he sent instructions to the leading men to attend a meeting which would be held at Bactra (Balkh).

'At this point the native people captured and killed the soldiers who had been placed as garrisons in the cities', i.e. in those which lay south of the river. Most of the Sogdians rose in sympathy; some of the Bactrians, instigated by Spitamenes and Dataphernes, joined the insurrection; and the Scythians on the north side of the Jaxartes began to muster an army for an invasion. If they had time to coordinate their actions, they would pin down the army of Alexander and encourage the peoples west of the Hindu Kush as far as Media to rise against the

Macedonians. Alexander realised that the very existence of his army was at stake. An immediate example must be made of the insurgents near at hand. Five cities were captured by assault in two days; for their defensive walls of mud-brick were pounded by catapults, while slingers, archers and javelin-men cleared the walls of defenders. On Alexander's orders all the men were killed and the women and children were part of the loot which was given to the troops. The largest city, called Cyropolis, had stronger defences, but Alexander led a select group through a dry torrent-bed into the city and opened some gates from the inside. The defenders concentrated their attack on Alexander's group. Alexander himself was struck on the neck by a stone and fell unconscious, and many officers were wounded; but they rallied and captured the market-place, while the rest of the army was coming through the gates. In the fighting 8,000 Sogdians were killed, and the remaining 7,000 surrendered. The seventh city surrendered, according to Ptolemy as cited by Arrian, and the men were deported to another part of Sogdiana.

These measures checked any would-be insurgents in the vicinity. But it was reported that the garrison at Samarcand was being besieged by Spitamenes. Alexander sent to its relief a force of 60 Companion Cavalry, 800 mercenary cavalry and 1,500 mercenary infantry, and he himself stayed to face the greater menace, a large army of Scythians on the far bank of the Jaxartes. During twenty days his army built the circuit-wall of Alexandria Eschate, which was twelve kilometres in length, and he planted as settlers some Macedonians who were unfit for active service, some Greek mercenaries and local Sogdians who volunteered. He purchased the liberty of some Sogdians whom his soldiers held as slaves, and he made them free settlers in the city, an act of kindness which was long remembered. The foundation of the city was celebrated by competitions in horsemanship and athletics, and Alexander sacrificed to the usual gods.

He made plans to cross the river on rafts buoyed up by tent-covers and attack the Scythians, but the omens when he sacrificed were pronounced adverse by Aristander. A second sacrifice was little better; for Aristander said that the omens portended danger to Alexander, and he refused to change the interpretation. Alexander mounted an attack nevertheless: his catapults drove the Scythians back from the far bank, his first rafts crossed with him and the archers and slingers, who covered the crossing of the phalangites, and then the cavalry followed. He had had experience in Europe (above, p. 19) of the dreaded Scythian horsemen, who withdrew, encircled their pursuers and rode round them while firing their arrows. He therefore made a series of attacks in quick succession. The first group, numbering perhaps 1,500 cavalry, charged the enemy who withdrew and surrounded them in a wide circle. Then a second force of cavalry intermingled with Archers, Agrianians and javelin-men and led by Alexander attacked at a point in the circle and stopped the encircling movement, whereupon two groups of his cavalry, one on either side of the second force, charged the Scythians as they were turning back. Alexander took command of one group and attacked with his squadrons each in column formation. The Scythians fled in confusion. They lost 1,000 men killed, 150 taken prisoner and 1,800 horses, whereas the losses of Alexander were 60 cavalry, 100 infantry and 1,000 wounded. During the pursuit Alexander drank dirty water, had violent diarrhoea, and was carried back to the camp. 'Thus the prophecy of Aristander came true.'

This brilliant victory brought an apology from the Scythian king and an offer to comply with Alexander's wishes; and Alexander gained some goodwill by releasing the prisoners without ransom. The Sacae sent envoys to offer submission, and Alexander opened negotiations with them. But he was distracted by bad news from Samarcand. The force which he had sent raised the siege of the citadel and then pursued Spitamenes, who led them into Scythian territory. There Spitamenes was joined by some 600 Scythian mounted archers and went into the attack. 'Riding round and round the phalanx, the archers fired volleys of arrows.' The cavalry of the Macedonians tried to drive them off, but since their horses were jaded and lacked fodder they made little impact. Spitamenes' cavalry returned to shoot at the infantry, which changed its formation into a hollow square and withdrew towards the river Polytimetus, where cover might be available. It was the duty of the cavalry to protect the flanks and rear of the infantry, and especially when it was crossing the river; but the cavalry commander tried to get his own men across the river first. This left the rear ranks of the infantry at the mercy of the enemy archers, and all the infantrymen rushed in disorder into the river. There they were surrounded and destroyed. Any prisoners were killed. Only 40 cavalry and 300 infantry escaped.

When Alexander learned of the disaster, he set off at once with half the Companion Cavalry, the Archers, the Agrianians, and some commando infantrymen, and he covered 278 kilometres in a little over three days to approach Samarcand at dawn. But Spitamenes who had the citadel under siege fled in time and could not be overtaken. Advancing to the river Polytimetus Alexander 'ordered the bones of the dead to be covered with a mound and made sacrifice in their honour in accordance with ancestral custom'. He then turned back and captured the strongholds in which Sogdians who had attacked the Macedonians had taken refuge. Those who survived the assaults were put to death as rebels. The main body of the army under the command of Craterus joined him at Samarcand. He made a show of strength by traversing all the area watered by the Polytimetus. It was now late in 329, and the army went into winter quarters at Bactra. There Alexander received larger reinforcements than ever before, 2,600 cavalry and 19,400 infantry (above, p. 129).There was no doubt that he would need them for the double task of putting down rebellions and defeating Spitamenes in the next campaigning season.

CHAPTER XIV

The subjugation of the northeastern
area in 328-327

1. Operations against rebels and the
Cleitus episode

During the winter the Persian satrap of Parthyaea, Phrataphernes, and the Cypriote Stasanor brought under arrest Arsaces, whom Stasanor had superseded as satrap of Areia, and the leaders of the Areians who had supported Bessus. They were able to assure Alexander that his communications with the west were now secure from danger. The negotiations, which the king of the Sacae had opened after Alexander's defeat of the Scythians, bore fruit. Ambassadors came with gifts to Alexander and with the offer of the king's daughter in marriage as a guarantee of a treaty of friendship and alliance. While Alexander did not take up the offer of marriage or a further offer of marriages between leading Macedonians and leading Scythians' daughters, it is to be assumed that he accepted the treaty; for it would ensure that the Sacae would not cross the Jaxartes and help the rebels in Sogdiana. At this time another Scythian king came in person, accompanied by 1,500 horsemen, to offer collaboration with Alexander in a campaign which he proposed they should undertake from his own kingdom, Chorasmia, which lay east of the Caspian Sea, towards the Black Sea. A summary of Alexander's reply, which Ptolemy probably consulted in the *Journal*, was given by Arrian. 'My concern at present is with India. If I reduce the Indians, I shall indeed possess all Asia, and with Asia mine I shall return to Greece and march from there via the Hellespont and the Propontis into the region of the Black Sea with all my naval and military forces. Your proposal should be reserved for then.' He made a treaty of friendship and alliance with the king (his name was Pharasmanes) and commended him to Artabazus, the satrap of Bactria, and to the other satraps whose provinces neighboured Chorasmia. On the other hand there were no envoys from the Scythian tribes between the Jaxartes and Chorasmia, of which the most dangerous were the Massagetae.

At the beginning of the campaigning season Alexander deployed his forces against the rebels in Bactria and Sogdiana, who relied on speed

of movement as cavalrymen and on the strength of the forts which
formed their bases. Because the rebels did not combine but were
widespread, Alexander had to divide his army into separate detachments. He left four commanders of such detachments in Bactria, led
another detachment into Sogdiana, and put four other detachments
there under the command respectively of Coenus and Artabazus together, and of Hephaestion, Ptolemy and Perdiccas. The detachments
had some success in capturing forts by assault and killing the defenders, and also in granting terms to those rebels who surrendered, but
their tasks were far from completed when Alexander recalled them to
meet him at Samarcand and made new plans. He commissioned
Hephaestion to found new cities in settled parts of Sogdiana. He himself
attacked and reduced some parts of Sogdiana which the rebels still
held. And he sent Coenus and Artabazus to his northern border, because there were reports that Spitamenes had taken refuge with the
Scythians.

Spitamenes moved first. With a company of fugitives from Sogdiana
and 600 Massagetae he took a fort in Bactria by surprise, killed the
garrison and carried off the commandant. A few days later they raided
the countryside round Bactra and acquired much booty. The small
garrison of Bactra made a bold sortie, recaptured the booty, but were
ambushed on the way back and suffered losses. On hearing of this
Craterus, being in command of a detachment, marched with great
speed and intercepted the troops of Spitamenes, which had been reinforced by 1,000 more Massagetae. Craterus defeated them. But the
Scythians escaped into the desert with the loss of only 150 men.

It was autumn 328, when Alexander returned to Samarcand for a
respite from warfare. The Sogdians, like the Macedonians, were keen
hunters, and they had a safari park full of wild beasts near Samarcand.
So Alexander mounted a great hunt, during which he personally killed
a lion and his soldiers were said by Curtius to have slaughtered 4,000
animals. Another diversion was a banquet to which Alexander invited
his leading Macedonians. Such banquets were a traditional feature of
the Macedonian court, and they provided an occasion for the king and
his guests to drink neat wine and to engage in frank discussion. Women
were not present. The king and his guests were not armed, but the king
was under the protection of armed men, namely his seven Bodyguards
and some soldiers of the Macedonian Guard. The banquets were held in
the palace at Aegeae, for instance, and on this occasion in the palace
inside the citadel of Samarcand. The Royal Hypaspists were stationed
outside the palace but within the citadel.

One of the most distinguished guests was Cleitus. He had saved the
life of Alexander during the Battle of the Granicus (above, p. 67), and
he had been in command of half of the Companion Cavalry since 330.
At Samarcand he was nominated to be satrap of Bactria and Sogdiana

in succession to Artabazus, who had just resigned on account of his advanced age. Cleitus too was a generation older than Alexander; for his sister had nursed Alexander as a baby, and she was much loved by Alexander. Thus there was trust and affection between the two men. However, during the heavy drinking a singer ridiculed the Macedonian officers who had fallen in the recent disaster near Samarcand (above, p. 146). This gave offence to the older men, but Alexander and those with him encouraged the singer to continue. Then contention arose between the older men, who judged the achievements of Philip to be the greater, and the younger men who flattered Alexander and put him on the same level as Heracles. This led to further recriminations in which Cleitus as the chief spokesman of his generation denounced the Asian policy of Alexander and mocked his pretension to be the son of Ammon. Personal insults followed. Alexander then threw an apple at Cleitus, tried to find his dagger which one of the Bodyguards removed, and shouted in the Macedonian dialect for the Hypaspists to come to his aid. He also ordered a trumpeter to sound the alarm, and he struck the man when he refused to obey. Cleitus was still blustering; but Ptolemy and others pushed him outside, took him over the ditch of the citadel, and deposited him beyond it.

When Cleitus was alone, he could not bear it but went back. He met Alexander just when Alexander was calling out 'Cleitus'. As Cleitus said 'Here I am, Cleitus, Alexander', he was struck by Alexander's pike and fell dead. Alexander saw that Cleitus was unarmed. He was immediately appalled at what he had done and tried to turn the pike against himself. But the Bodyguards disarmed him and carried him off forcibly to his room, where he lay lamenting for the rest of the night and next day.

The account which I have given is taken mainly from the narrative of Plutarch. His source in my opinion was Aristobulus, who was particularly interested in Alexander's personality and conduct. There is no doubt that fear of assassination was always in Alexander's mind (for he had seen his father killed by a Bodyguard), and that was why he called for the help of the Hypaspists and struck the trumpeter. He thought that there was a plot, and that he was acting in self-defence when he killed Cleitus. It was the sight of Cleitus unarmed that brought him to his senses. According to Aristobulus, as cited by Arrian, the fault which led to the tragedy (the *hamartia*) was that of Cleitus in returning to the banqueting-room – not that Alexander was thereby exonerated. Plutarch recorded his own opinion that the killing was not a matter of deliberation (*apo gnomes*) but due to an unfortunate chance (*dystychia*), when the king's passion and drunkenness provided the opportunity for the evil destiny (*daimon*) of Cleitus.

The terrible remorse and the despair of Alexander lasted for three days, during which he fasted and paid no attention to his bodily needs.

His Friends were alarmed and brought philosophers and diviners to argue with him. The most successful was Aristander, who argued as follows. It so happened that the day of the banquet was the day dedicated to Dionysus, and on that day each year Macedonians made sacrifice to Dionysus. Alexander for some unknown reason sacrificed instead to the Dioscuri. Cleitus began to sacrifice to Dionysus, but he answered a summons from Alexander and failed to complete it. When he was going to join Alexander, three sheep on which libations had been poured as a preliminary to the sacrifice followed after Cleitus. This was reported to Aristander and another diviner, who interpreted it as a bad omen. Alexander accordingly ordered them to sacrifice for the safety of Cleitus. But the banquet started, and instead of completing his sacrifice to Dionysus Cleitus went to the banquet. Aristander argued that the tragedy was due to 'the wrath of Dionysus', who had not been honoured by Alexander and Cleitus, and that it had been predetermined by the god (*katheimarmenon*). Alexander was convinced by Aristander. He sacrificed to Dionysus and began to take food.

The whole episode revealed the tensions between the older Friends and the younger Friends, and their respective feelings towards Alexander. The older men felt that they had been slighted by Alexander's promotion of young men over their heads. For instance, of the exact contemporaries of Alexander, Hephaestion had been put in command of half of the Companion Cavalry at the age of 26 and was now being given important commissions, and Leonnatus had been promoted to be a Bodyguard at an equally young age. Alexander's friends whom Philip had exiled were given military and administrative posts (Ptolemy, Nearchus, Erigyius and Harpalus), and Alexander's policy of appointing Asians to be satraps deprived the older Macedonians of advancement in the administrative field. It seems too that it was the older men who particularly resented Alexander's granting of a military command to an Asian. Thus it could be argued that the disaster at Samarcand had been due to Alexander's appointment of a Lycian rather than a senior Macedonian officer such as Caranus to be commander of the detachment.

During the banquet Alexander was made rudely aware of dissension among his Friends and of the hostility of the older men towards his Asian policy. It was within his power to appease his older Friends by giving them promotion and by modifying or abandoning his Asian policy. Compromise, however, was not in Alexander's nature. He was determined rather to pursue his Asian policy, and, if need be, to depend less on his Macedonians and more on the Asians. The killing of Cleitus would always be a terrible memory for Alexander, and he must have blamed himself for his heavy drinking and his passionate anger. But he probaby came to see, as Aristobulus did, that the death of Cleitus was largely due to accident in human circumstances, and that it had been predetermined on the divine plane.

2. Operations in the northeastern area

During the summer of 328 Alexander was able to recruit Bactrian and Sogdian cavalrymen. This was a sure sign that many leaders preferred the law and order which Alexander was imposing to the raiding tactics of Spitamenes with his Bactrian and Sogdian refugees and his Scythian allies. Alexander had been able to seal off the desert to the west of Bactria by founding Alexandria-in-Margiana in the Merv oasis and by linking it to a line of hill-forts which he garrisoned. The effect was that Spitamenes could direct his raids only into Sogdiana. For winter quarters Alexander settled with his main body at Nautaca in central Sogdiana, and he posted Coenus with a select force near the Sogdian frontier facing the Massagetae. His order to Coenus was to intercept any raiders. Early in the winter Spitamenes invaded with his Bactrian and Sogdian followers and with 3,000 Massagetae as allies, and Coenus advanced to meet him with 400 Companion Cavalry, the mounted javelinmen, the Bactrian and Sogdian cavalry, and two phalanx-brigades. In a fierce battle Spitamenes lost 800 cavalry, whereas Coenus lost only 25 cavalry and 12 infantrymen, and the Bactrians and the Sogdians deserted to Coenus, when their baggage was plundered by some Massagetae. Spitamenes and his allies fled into the desert. But when it was rumoured that Alexander himself was coming up from Nautaca, the Massagetae killed Spitamenes and sent his head to Alexander. The Dahae handed over Dataphernes, the partner of Spitamenes, and themselves recognised the rule of Alexander.

In midwinter Alexander concentrated all his forces at Nautaca. He made some new appointments. As Mazaeus had died, Stamenes became satrap of Babylonia; Stasanor was moved as satrap from Areia to Drangiana; and Atropates was sent to Media to replace the satrap Oxydates, who had been slack in administration. The trusted satrap of Parthyaea, Phrataphernes, was sent to arrest Autophradates, the satrap of Mardia and Tapuria, who had failed to answer Alexander's summons; and these two areas were taken over by Phrataphernes. Three officers were sent to Macedonia with orders to bring out reinforcements.

Early in 327 Alexander decided to attack the so-called 'Sogdian Rock', in which many rebels and their families had taken refuge, because it was thought to be impregnable. If he could take that, no refuge would be safe. The rock was precipitous on all sides, and heavy snow had just fallen. The defenders refused to negotiate, and they laughed at Alexander, saying that he needed winged soldiers to succeed. 'In his passionate pursuit of glory' Alexander offered immense rewards, ranging from twelve talents down to three hundred gold darics, to any who could reach the top of the rock. Many Macedonians were experienced rock-climbers, and three hundred men now volunteered to climb the rock at night. They chose the most precipitous face because it was not guarded, drove iron tent-pegs into frozen snow or clefts, and pulled themselves up on ropes. Thirty fell to their death, but by dawn most of the rest were on the top and unfurled the flags which they had worn. Alexander's herald proclaimed that he had found 'the winged soldiers', and that they were there to see on the summit of the rock. The enemy, thinking that the men on the summit were very numerous and fully armed, panicked and surrendered themselves and their families.

In the family of one of the Sogdian leaders, called Oxyartes, there was a young girl second in beauty, it was said, only to the wife of Darius. Her name was Roxane. Alexander fell in love with her at first sight. 'Despite his passion his wish was not to ravish her as a prisoner of war; rather he thought it not unseemly to marry her' (the marriage was later). This was the observation made at the time by those close to Alexander. They may have been surprised by his self-restraint; but it was in keeping with the respect he had shown for the wife of Darius. The love-life of Alexander was no doubt of interest to them. In the past Alexander had neglected the advice of Parmenio to marry and beget an heir before leaving Macedonia. In Asia he had formed a liaison – on the advice again of Parmenio according to Aristobulus – with Barsine, a daughter of Artabazus and the widow of Memnon, a mercenary captain from Rhodes who had served under Darius. This relationship started in 332 and resulted in the birth of a son, Heracles, probably in this year, 327. Alexander did not regard the child as an heir to the throne, since he was born out of wedlock, and he must have realised the need now to beget an heir. His choice of Roxane as his future wife was not only timely. It was politically appropriate; for it was in line with his Asian policy, and his chivalry towards Roxane won the approval of his Asian subjects. Alexander took Oxyartes into his entourage and treated him with suitable honour.

Alexander turned next to the vast and precipitous 'Rock of Chorienes', held by Chorienes and other local rulers. As an outer defence it was surrounded by a deep ravine. It seemed impossible to take it, but that only made Alexander more determined. He directed operations all day, and Leonnatus, Ptolemy and Perdiccas did so at night; for the entire army worked in shifts despite heavy snow and a shortage of provisions. Ladders were made from felled pine-trees and lowered into the ravine; the workers went down and drove stakes into the sides of the ravine at the requisite height; and on these stakes they constructed a bridge of wicker-work and soil on top of it. As they were within the range of enemy missiles, screens were erected for protection.

But when the bridge was completed and carried higher, they themselves were able to bring their arrow-firing catapults into action. Astounded by the Macedonians' progress, Chorienes asked Alexander to send Oxyartes to give him advice. That advice was to surrender; for Alexander and his army were irresistible, and Alexander was a man of good faith and integrity. So Chorienes surrendered. Alexander left the Rock in his hands and continued him as the local ruler. In gratitude Chorienes issued to the victors enough wine, grain and dried meat to feed them 'tent by tent' for two months.

A separate operation with a large force was carried out by Craterus in mountainous country. He killed or captured all the rebel leaders, who lost 120 cavalry and 1,500 infantry, and he then joined Alexander who had advanced to Bactra. The northeastern area was now pacified after two years of fighting under difficult conditions. The eight newly-founded cities were in operation, and the training of selected boys was under way. The peoples of the plains enjoyed an unparalleled freedom from raids by the hill-tribes and by the Scythian nomads, and agriculture and commerce developed rapidly as the peoples of the hills adopted a settled life. For his next campaign Alexander took large forces of cavalry from the Bactrians, Sogdians, Massagetae and Dahae; and he left behind with Amyntas, the satrap of Bactria, an unusually large garrison force of 3,500 cavalry and 10,000 infantry.

3. The conspiracy of the Pages

It was while he was at Bactra that an old friend of Alexander, Demaratus of Corinth, came to pay a visit and died a natural death. In his honour Alexander had a great mound built, 40 metres high. It was a cenotaph; for the corpse was cremated and the ashes were carried by a magnificent four-horse chariot on the long journey to his home. In Greek eyes such a cenotaph was an example of Asiatic extravagance.

At Bactra too a plot against the life of Alexander was discovered. According to Arrian it originated in the punishment of a Royal Page, Hermolaus, for breaking a rule of the Royal Hunt. He had killed a boar which Alexander was about to despatch, and for that offence he had been caned in the presence of the other Pages and had been deprived of his horse. Bitterly incensed, Hermolaus persuaded his lover and four other Pages to join him in seeking revenge. The plan was that one of them, whose duty it was to guard the king on a particular night, would admit the others and they would kill him in his sleep. The night came. But Alexander did not return. Some said that he stayed all that night at a drinking-party, but Aristobulus gave a fuller account, which has the ring of truth. There was at the court a Syrian woman, who sometimes went into ecstasy and was thought then to be possessed by a god; for she made prophecies which came true. Alexander had faith in her, and he allowed her access to him at any time. During this particular night Alexander was returning to his bedroom when she met him and begged him to go back and make it an all-night party. He did so and thus escaped assassination.

Next day one of the Pages, Epimenes, told his lover about the plot, and the lover mentioned it to Epimenes' brother, who went at once to Ptolemy and made a report. Ptolemy as a Royal Bodyguard had immediate access to the king. He therefore informed Alexander, who ordered the arrest of the Pages who had been named as conspirators. They were subjected to torture, admitted the plot, and gave the names of certain others. The Macedonians among them (for one Page was a Thracian) were prosecuted by the king before the Assembly of Macedonians, found guilty and stoned to death in accordance with Macedonian custom. The account I have given comes from Arrian, who was drawing on Ptolemy and Aristobulus, and it is confirmed as accurate by statements in two *Letters* of Alexander which mentioned the confession of the Pages (*paides*) under torture and the stoning of them by the Macedonians. On the other hand, Curtius provided a much longer account, which included speeches allegedly delivered during the trial by Hermolaus and by the king. His version is clearly fictitious; it was written to please his own contemporaries on the theme of liberty and tyranny.

It was clear at the time, as it is to a reader today, that the Pages in the conspiracy cannot have been motivated solely by a desire to seek revenge for the punishment of one of their number. They knew that caning was usual in the School, and that the removal of Hermolaus' horse was not permanent but temporary. They might well have sympathised with Hermolaus, but not to the extent of risking almost certain death themselves; for had they succeeded in killing Alexander they would have been the first to be suspected. It was therefore natural to suppose that the Pages had been inspired by others who hoped to benefit by the death of Alexander and proposed to protect his killers from retribution. Who could those others have been? According to Arrian some denounced Callisthenes as having 'participated' (*metesche*) in the plot, and others said that Callisthenes 'incited them (*eperen*) to the plotting'. To Arrian's second group Aristobulus and Ptolemy belonged: for Arrian reported them as agreeing that the Pages said 'Callisthenes incited them (*eparai*) to the daring deed'. There was, of course, a great difference between being a conspirator and being a persuasive figure in the background. Thus what the Pages said at the time of the trial was not sufficient in the judgement of the Macedonians for them to condemn Callisthenes.

After the trial there was further investigation, as there had been after the trial of Philotas (above, p. 133). This led to the arrest of Callisthenes, the court historian and philosopher. In the second *Letter* of Alexander, written to Antipater in Macedonia, Alexander wrote as follows, according to Plutarch: 'I shall punish the sophist and those who sent him out and those who accept in the cities the men who are plotting against me.' He was himself confident that Callisthenes had been involved as a conspirator; but because Callisthenes was not a Macedonian, he was to be tried not in the Assembly of Macedonians but 'in the presence of Aristotle in the Council' (of the Greek Community), the quotation being from Chares, a Greek courtier. This procedure was as it had been for some Chians (above, p. 99). In fact Callisthenes died seven months later 'of a disease', according to Chares and Aristobulus. The version of Ptolemy, that Callisthenes was tortured and hanged, is to be rejected; for the case of Callisthenes was still *sub judice*. It seems that Ptolemy, as a Macedonian, was less interested in the fate of the Greek philosopher.

We do not know the grounds on which Callisthenes was arrested. There are, however, 'stories' about him which may provide clues. As the philosopher who taught the Pages, Callisthenes was said to enjoy a particularly close relationship with Hermolaus. The story went that when Hermolaus asked Callisthenes how he might become most famous Callisthenes replied, 'By killing the most famous man.' The fact that exactly the same story was reported by Diodorus in reference to Philip's assassin does not add to its credibility. Other 'stories' showed Callisthenes giving offence to Alexander by feeble consolations after the killing of Cleitus and later at a banquet when in response to a challenge he listed the faults of the Macedonians only too freely. More to the point were the 'stories' of Callisthenes leading the opposition to Alexander over the matter of prostration (*proskynesis*). One of them, as reported by Arrian, gave Callisthenes a clearly fictitious speech in which he described it as a characteristic of oriental despotism and as anathema to freedom-loving Greeks and Macedonians.

There may be some truth in the 'story' that Alexander held a banquet for some courtiers who had agreed to prostrate themselves and then exchange kisses with Alexander, and for a number of leading men who would be asked only at the banquet to follow suit. Callisthenes was one of the first group. But because Alexander was talking to someone else, Callisthenes did not prostrate himself but went forward for the kissing. Alexander, however, was told of Callisthenes' misconduct and would not kiss him. Whereupon Callisthenes exclaimed in a loud voice: 'Well, then, I shall go away the poorer for a kiss.' His mockery, it seems, brought the experiment in prostration to an end.

After his death Callisthenes was portrayed by philosophers of Aristotle's 'Peripatetic' School as a martyr who had defended liberty against oriental despotism. At the time Alexander saw Callisthenes as a leading figure in a network of conspirators which included 'those who sent him out' (presumably Aristotle and other philosophers) and malcontents in Asia who later found shelter in cities of the Greek mainland. That at

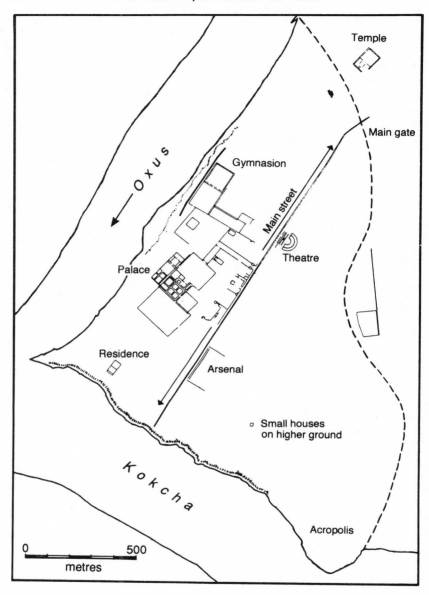

16. The Alexander-city at Ai Khanoum

least was what he wrote subsequently to Antipater. He must have realised that there was growing opposition to his Asian policy among representatives of the Greek city-states, both in Greece and in Asia, and among the leading Macedonians and among the Pages.

One cause of discontent was a change in the composition of the Companion Cavalry. After the death of Darius Alexander had recruited very large numbers of Asian light-armed cavalry in the area from Parthyaea to Sogdiana. Most served in their own ethnic units, but the best were incorporated into the Companion Cavalry, which had hitherto, apart from a few Asians, been the preserve of the Macedonians. The new Companion Cavalry consisted of eight 'hipparchies', each 500 strong and composed probably of one almost entirely Macedonian squadron and two light-armed squadrons (mainly of Asians but including the Scouts, for instance). Thus a Companion hipparchy was well fitted to act against light-armed enemies, whether Bactrian or Scythians. However, this large-scale adulteration of the Companion Cavalry offended nationalist Macedonian feeling.

When Alexander decided to cross the Hindu Kush, he left Amyntas in Bactria with 10,000 infantry and 3,500 cavalry, the latter perhaps including a Companion hipparchy. Alexander's allocation of forces between the control of the northeastern region and the invasion of the Indus valley was justified by the results. For in Bactria and Sogdiana trade and urbanisation developed under settled conditions. Two centuries later it was reported by Chinese invaders that they found men living there in a thousand walled cities. The excavation at Ai Khanoum has revealed one of them.

CHAPTER XV

The Indus valley

1. The advance to and the crossing of the river Indus

For two years Alexander had campaigned continuously winter and summer alike. Now, in 327 as 'spring was on the way out', the army had to make the arduous crossing of the Hindu Kush and return to Alexandria-in-Caucaso. The weather was less harsh and Alexander had discovered 'shorter routes' than in March 329, but even so the army had to climb as high probably as 14,300 feet over the Kaoshan Pass. It was therefore important to reduce the size of the baggage-train, which had been swollen by loot acquired during the sack of rebel centres. Alexander and his Companions set the example by burning some of their possessions, and the Macedonians destroyed what was superfluous to the needs of themselves and their families (for most of them were accompanied by Asian concubines and their children). The leading troops crossed in ten days, but the transportation of heavy material continued through the summer months. Meanwhile Alexander was training his multiracial army. He enlarged Alexandria by adding unfit soldiers and local people, and he replaced an incompetent administrator with one of his Companions. On his departure he left a garrison; for it was to be his advanced base. The satrap of the region 'Parapamisus' was Tyriespis, a Persian, and Alexander added land in the upper valley of the river Kabul to his satrapy.

In winter 327 Alexander sacrificed to Athena and embarked on the conquest of 'Indike', the land of the Indus and its tributaries, which constitutes today Pakistan and Kashmir. Aristotle had stated (above, p. 127) that 'India', being the region east of the Indus (Arrian *Ind.* 2. 5), was a peninsula pointing eastwards into the outer Ocean, an area so small that from the ridge of the Caucasus a man could see the Ocean on a clear day. Alexander knew now that 'Indike' was much larger, but his trust in Aristotle led him to direct his campaign continually eastwards in order to reach the Ocean. If he should acquire this 'India', he would possess 'all Asia', as he had told Pharasmanes (above, p. 149). The peoples of the region, called collectively the 'Indi', were known to be excellent fighters. Their infantry was armed with exceptionally long and powerful bows, javelins or sometimes long spears, and they all had swords. The cavalry attacked with javelins. Infantry and cavalry alike carried small shields of hide and had little or no protective armour. Fortunately for Alexander the 'Indi' were disunited; for tribe fought against tribe, and king against king. Where the caste-system prevailed, the soldiers were a separate class, father being succeeded by son, and they did not attack the caste of cultivators. Alexander had still to learn that the population within his 'Indike' was extremely large.

During the summer Alexander's emissaries had gone ahead and secured the submission of the tribal communities west of the Indus and of one community east of the river, and their rulers – mostly kings – had given sureties of allegiance. Now he summoned them, and they came bringing gifts and promising to hand over their war-elephants. But Alexander was not deceived. Taking a large striking force under his own command he entered the mountainous area which was to be the Northwest Frontier of British India. The first group of tribes, the Aspasians, defied him. When they took to their fortified cities, Alexander captured one after another by assault; and when they concentrated their forces, Alexander defeated them, taking 40,000 prisoners and carrying off 230,000 oxen according to Ptolemy. The next group, the Guraei, accepted his rule. The Assaceni mustered an army of 2,000 cavalry, 30,000 infantry and 30 elephants, but on his approach they dispersed to defend their cities. They resisted into the early months of 326. The fighting was as fierce as it had been in Bactria and Sogdiana, and Alexander employed the same methods, destroying the first centres and the inhabitants as rebels, then pardoning others, and in the final stages establishing new cities (e.g. at Arigaeum and Bazira), garrisoning some existing cities and setting up guardposts at strategic points.

Alexander owed his success to his speed of movement with cavalry forces (for he used mounted archers, mounted javelin-men and infantry called 'dimachae'), his artillery and his assault troops in sieges, and the skill of subordinate commanders such as Craterus and Ptolemy. Set battles were rare, and then the phalanx in formation was unstoppable. The number of Macedonians killed was small, but very many, including Alexander twice, were wounded by arrows. The toughest resistance was at Massaga, where the Assacenians were reinforced by 7,000 mercenaries from east of the Indus. When the Assacenian commander was killed by a catapult-bolt, his widow opened negotiations, during which the 7,000 mercenaries came out and camped close to the Macedonians. In the night a breach of the agreement occurred – Ptolemy and/or Aristobulus attributing it to the mercenaries, and other writers to Alexander – and the result was that the mercenaries were surrounded and killed. Finally, in order to show that resistance could never succeed, Alexander attacked the 'Rock Aornus' (Pir-Sar), which Heracles, it was said, had twice failed to take. Alexander felt a 'longing' (*pothos*) to outdo Heracles. Alexander and Ptolemy, commanding separate forces, captured a way up by a pincer movement; then a ravine was bridged, as at the rock of Chorienes, and from the bridge a peak was captured 'with incredible audacity'; finally of two climbing parties at night seven hundred men reached the top (Alexander arriving first) and routed the enemy. As Sir Aurel Stein commented, success was due to 'Alexander's genius and the pluck and endurance of his hardy Macedonians'. For in all these operations the King's Men and their traditional support-troops played the leading part.

In the course of this campaign Alexander and his Macedonians believed that they had been preceded not only by Heracles but also by Dionysus. The Indians themselves promoted the idea by claiming that Dionysus had founded a city of theirs called Nysa, and that Dionysus had planted the ivy which grew there and in no other Indian land. The Macedonians were delighted to see the ivy and other supposed signs of Dionysus' presence, and Alexander himself was seized with a 'longing' to visit the sacred places. Sacrifices were made to Dionysus; Alexander declared Nysa to be a free city; and 300 cavalrymen from Nysa served with the Macedonians until the autumn of 326. Thus the idea took root that Dionysus and Heracles had fought in the area west of the Indus, but that they had never crossed the great river. Alexander and his Macedonians planned to surpass them.

At Aornus Alexander was close to Kashmir, the realm of Abisares, who had helped the Assacenians and now gave refuge to survivors from Aornus. Alexander did not pursue them. He turned south, captured a number of war-elephants, found suitable timber and built ships which were floated down the Indus. As satrap of the whole area Alexander appointed a Macedonian, Philippus, and as guardian of the Rock Aornus a loyal Indian, Sisicottus. They proved dependable; for when a rising occurred in Assacenia late in this year, Alexander was informed by Sisicottus, and Philippus and Tyriespis restored order. As elsewhere, Alexander imposed peace and provided promise of progress in his new cities.

On setting out from Nicaea near Alexandria-in-Caucaso Alexander had sent the bulk of the army, commanded by Hephaestion and Perdiccas, on the direct route via the Khyber Pass to the Indus. They took over by surrender or captured by assault all inhabited centres (for they were to be on Alexander's main line of communication); and they fortified and garrisoned one of these, Orobatis. When the Indian ruler of the district Peucelaotis rebelled, his city fell after a siege of thirty days. An Indian was appointed governor of the city. Hephaestion had been instructed to bridge the Indus, and he therefore built boats which could serve as pontoons. These were made with local timber in sections, which could be transported overland and reassembled, and the largest were a pair of triaconters. When Alexander arrived in the spring of 326, the united forces held a great festival with athletic and equestrian games. Alexander sacrificed to the usual gods, and sacrificial offerings for the soldiers were provided by an Indian ruler, Taxiles, to the number of 3,000 cattle and above 10,000 sheep. The omens in the sacrifices were favourable. At dawn Alexander himself crossed first into 'India', a land totally unknown to the Greek world.

The army which crossed the Indus numbered some 75,000 combatants, of whom the bulk were infantry from Macedonia, the Balkans and Western Asia. Of the cavalry the Companions were so reconstituted that the four hipparchies accompanying Alexander consisted predominantly of Macedonian Companions; for he would need them to attack as heavy cavalry in any set battles. The ethnic units of light cavalry were highly trained. Our sources mention the mounted javelin-men who were Persians, the Dahae mounted archers, the Bactrians and the Sogdians, and there were certainly other units, for instance the Thracians.

2. The Battle of the Hydaspes

The rule of Alexander had been accepted in advance, and gifts had been exchanged on the most lavish scale between Alexander and Taxiles, on whose death at this time his son took the same dynastic name. This younger Taxiles placed his capital, Taxila (Bhir), at the disposal of Alexander, and he provided 5,000 soldiers to serve with Alexander. At Taxila Alexander received envoys and gifts from lesser rulers in the vicinity and from Abisares, ruler of Kashmir. He sacrificed to the usual gods, celebrated a festival with athletic and equestrian contests, and made his administrative arrangements. Philippus, a Macedonian, was appointed satrap over the region. Taxiles was rewarded with additional territory. A Macedonian garrison was placed in Taxila; unfit soldiers were left there; and the boats of the Indus bridge were transported in sections to Alexander's next objective, the Hydaspes. For no envoys had come from the ruler beyond that river, an enemy of Taxiles called Porus.

The army which advanced to the Hydaspes numbered some 75,000 soldiers, drawn from many parts of Alexander's dominions, and it was spearheaded by not more than 15,000 Macedonian citizen troops. The problem of supply was eased by the extraordinary fertility of the alluvial plains, which produced reserves of grain. On the far side of the river an army of some 35,000 men and 200 war-elephants had been assembled by Porus. It was not possible for Alexander to cross the river and force a landing, as he had done at the Jaxartes, because the sight and the smell of the elephants would make his cavalry horses unmanageable. By several masterpieces of deception Alexander masked his preparations for a crossing at a point some 27 kilometres upstream from his own camp. Then, despite many difficulties during a stormy night in May, Alexander landed 5,000 cavalry and 6,000 infantry on the

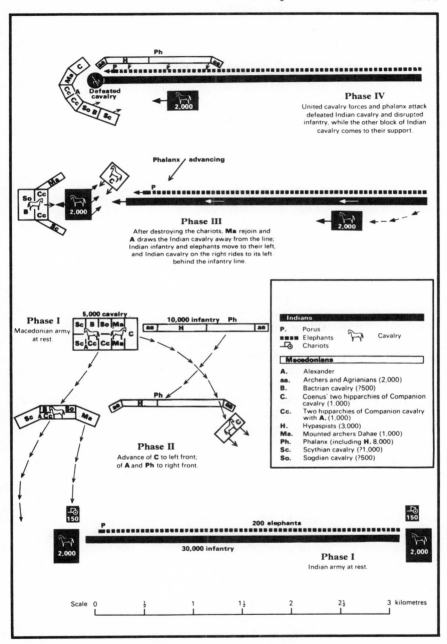

Phase IV
United cavalry forces and phalanx attack
defeated Indian cavalry and disrupted
infantry, while the other block of Indian
cavalry comes to their support.

Phalanx / advancing

Phase III
After destroying the chariots, **Ma** rejoin and
A draws the Indian cavalry away from the line;
Indian infantry and elephants move to their left,
and Indian cavalry on the right rides to its left
behind the infantry line.

Phase I
Macedonian army
at rest.

5,000 cavalry

10,000 infantry

Phase II
Advance of **C** to left front;
of **A** and **Ph** to right front.

Indians
P.   Porus
▪▪▪▪ Elephants   🐎 Cavalry
⊸ Chariots

Macedonians
A.   Alexander
aa.   Archers and Agrianians (2,000)
B.   Bactrian cavalry (?500)
C.   Coenus' two hipparchies of Companion
      cavalry (1,000)
Cc.   Two hipparchies of Companion cavalry
      with **A.** (1,000)
H.   Hypaspists (3,000)
Ma.   Mounted archers Dahae (1,000)
Ph.   Phalanx (including **H.** 8,000)
Sc.   Scythian cavalry (?1,000)
So.   Sogdian cavalry (?500)

200 elephants

30,000 infantry

Phase I
Indian army at rest.

Scale 0   ½   1   1½   2   2½   3 kilometres

17. The Battle of the Hydaspes River

far bank soon after dawn. Detachments of troops had taken up positions between the crossing-point and the camp, and their orders were to cross when they should see the Indians engaged in battle. At the camp Craterus was to be ready to cross with his force, but only if 'Porus should take all his elephants with him against me'. Those were Alexander's words.

When the landing was reported by scouts, Porus sent his son in command of 120 chariots and 2,000 cavalry to meet the enemy. The chariots were bogged down on the wet ground, and the cavalry were routed with the loss of their commander and 400 men. Porus left some elephants to deter Craterus from crossing, and deployed his army on sandy ground away from the bank. His 30,000 infantry formed a line ten men deep and some three kilometres long. In front 200 elephants were posted at intervals of 50 feet, and on each wing 150 chariots in front and 2,000 cavalry behind them were in column. He expected Alexander to make a frontal attack with forces which he knew would be outnumbered on foot. As Alexander advanced, he was joined by some of the detachments from the other bank and he gave them a breather before launching his attack not frontally but against one wing.

Alexander sent 1,000 cavalry under Coenus towards the right wing of Porus' line in order to deceive Porus and make him keep his 2,000 cavalry there. At the same time the mounted archers (1,000 Dahae) attacked the chariots on Porus' left wing and caused confusion, whereupon Alexander with 1,000 Companion Cavalry appeared on the left flank of the column of Indian cavalry which wheeled left to face him. By attacking and retreating, squadron by squadron, he drew the Indian cavalry away from the infantry line. That was the moment for Coenus, in accordance with his orders, to change direction and charge the flank and rear of the Indian cavalry. Attacked on every side, the Indian cavalry fled to the protection of the elephants (to which their horses were accustomed). Meanwhile Porus had ordered his elephants and infantry line to move to their left and support the cavalry, but the movement was slowed down by the elephants and some confusion arose. As Alexander had ordered in advance, his infantry in phalanx formation (Hypaspists, Phalangites, Agrianians, Archers and others, perhaps 10,000 strong) attacked the left part of Porus' line, using pikes against the mahouts and arrows and javelins against the elephants. At first the battle hung in the balance; for the elephants trumpeted and charged, the cavalry now reinforced by those from the right wing attacked, and the Macedonians' horses were terrified by the elephants. It was the infantry which prevailed by forming close order, advancing with bristling pike-points and driving the stampeding elephants onto their own troops, while the Macedonian cavalry attacking from behind Porus' line routed the Indian cavalry. The defeated troops and elephants collided with the rest of Porus' line, which all broke and fled. Craterus meanwhile had crossed the river and joined in the pursuit, during which the Indian losses of killed and captured were estimated at two-thirds of their total force.

Porus and his mahout fought on despite wounds until an Indian persuaded him to dismount and meet Alexander. 'Treat me, Alexander,' said Porus, 'like a king.' Alexander let Porus retain his kingdom as a vassal-king and gave him additional territory; and later he persuaded Porus and Taxiles to end their enmity towards one another. Of the force which had made the original crossing 80 Macedonian infantry were killed and 20 Companion Cavalry; and of the other troops 720 infantry and 280 cavalry. Alexander sacrificed to the usual gods and to the Sun-God, who had granted 'the conquest of the lands towards his rising'. He told an Assembly of his Macedonians that the wealth of India was theirs and that they had only to advance 'to the farthest East and the Ocean'. The Assembly promised to complete the task; for they too thought that the Ocean was not far away to the east.

Alexander rested his army for a month. During it he drew up plans for two new cities which he later named Nicaea and Bucephala – the latter in memory of his war-horse, which died of old age soon after the battle. In celebration of his victory Alexander issued silver medallions of decadrachm size. In that which is shown in Plate 13 Alexander, wearing cavalry uniform and diademed, holds a lance in his left hand and a thunderbolt in his extended right hand, and Nike is about to crown him with the wreath of victory. On the obverse side Alexander mounted attacks Porus and his mahout on an elephant which is withdrawing. The diadem proclaimed Alexander as King of Asia, and the thunderbolt implied that Alexander was the vicegerent of Zeus.

3. Advance to and halt at the Hyphasis

For Alexander and his scientists there were two routes to the Ocean. One was southwards down the Indus. It had been thought that the Indus was the upper Nile because the flora and fauna of the rivers were the same, but the Indians then reported that the river flowed into the sea, presumably the Ocean. The other was eastwards to the tip of Aristotle's peninsula. While the army rested, Alexander began to build the fleet for the southwards voyage. But his first choice was to go eastwards to 'the end of the land mass' (*finem terrarum*).

At first the numerous tribes surrendered or were easily subdued by Alexander and Hephaestion in command of advance-detachments, while the main body followed. Lives were lost in crossing the Acesines (Chenab), swollen by the monsoon rains which had just started. It was beyond the next river, the Hydraotes, that he met well-organised forces at Sangala (near Lahore). The siege cost him 100 killed and 1,200 wounded, but the enemy losses of 17,000 killed and 70,000 captured soon ended all opposition, and he reached the bank of the last river, the Hyphasis (Beas). Beyond it Alexander and his Macedonians had been led to believe that they would find 'the end of Asia and the Ocean'.

The truth was reported by the local Indians, that farther east was the populous valley of the Ganges and the greatest number of elephants 'remarkable for size and courage'. Bitter disillusion set in among the Macedonians, who were suffering from exhaustion and the effects of seventy days of continuous rain; for they had been misled and 'the end of Asia' was not at hand. They made it clear by their behaviour that they intended to go no further. On the other hand, Alexander was determined to advance and to reach, as he believed, the Ocean beyond the Ganges valley. He therefore consulted a meeting of the regimental commanders. His appeal was heard in silence. Then Coenus, a senior general, spoke 'on behalf of the majority of the army': their desire was to return home. The anger of Alexander was apparent. Next day he reconvened the meeting and announced his intention of going forward with those who were willing to follow; others could go home and say they had deserted their king. He stayed incommunicado in his tent for three days, hoping that the mood of the army would change. When silence persisted, he emerged to make sacrifice as for a crossing of the river. The omens were unfavourable. Through his Friends he announced that 'he had decided to turn back'. The soldiers shouted for joy, and some went to his tent and blessed him. Alexander had failed to impose his will. But he had avoided a confrontation, and he emerged with the goodwill of the Macedonians. The *anabasis*, the drive eastwards, was at an end.

On the bank of the Hyphasis 'he divided the army regiment by regiment and ordered them to set up twelve altars as high as the highest towers ... in thanksgiving to the gods who had brought him so far victorious and as memorials of his own labours'. The altars were dedicated to the twelve Olympian gods of the Greek pantheon, for they had guided the army, and Zeus had given Alexander the victory, as he had claimed on the Porus medallion. The mention of his labours invited comparison with Heracles, who had commemorated his labours by erecting at the western limit of the world 'the Pillars of Heracles'.

CHAPTER XVI

Southern Asia

1. To the delta of the Indus

It was characteristic of Alexander that as he advanced to and returned from the Hyphasis he made his arrangements for the governance of the territory. After the victory at the Hydaspes he extended the realm of Porus to the north into Kashmir, where the Glausae surrendered their thirty-seven cities and very numerous villages with a total population of something like half a million. Beyond them was the realm of Abisares, who after much prevarication finally submitted and sent lavish gifts and thirty elephants. Alexander confirmed him in his rule and made a neighbouring ruler subject to him. The region between the Acesines and the Hydraotis, and then most of the territory between the Hydraotis and the Hyphasis were added to the realm of Porus, who had loyally served with 5,000 Indians and many elephants under Alexander's command and had supplied the army. That realm was said finally to include more than 2,000 cities, which implied a population in excess of ten million. The area round Sangala was entrusted to some Indians who had come over voluntarily. The new cities which he founded, two by the Hydaspes and one by the Acesines, were on lines of communication. Thus he relied almost entirely on the native rulers to control the large and populous region up to the foothills of the Himalayas. His bond with them was personal and he treated them as 'allies', provided that they accepted his overall rule and paid to him the financial tribute which he assessed. For Alexander realised that he did not have the manpower to exercise direct rule over this northeastern area, and his trust in the native rulers was justified at the time.

The area of the greatest strategic importance was the kingdom of Taxiles, who had shown as staunch a loyalty as Porus had done. Alexander gave him additional territory, treated him as an 'ally', and expected him to cooperate with his neighbour, Philippus; but to make doubly sure Alexander maintained a garrison in Taxila, which Taxiles had entrusted to him (above, p. 164). Philippus as satrap controlled the areas through which communications with Macedonia ran, namely the route of the Khyber pass, the valleys of the Kabul, Cophen and Choaspes (Swat), and an enclave east of the Indus. Thus the entire hinterland was under control, and he could advance southwards with safety.

18. The southeastern satrapies

Moreover, for the new venture he was joined by large reinforcements: 6,000 cavalry from Greece and Thrace, 7,000 Greek mercenary infantry, and 23,000 infantry from his allies in Greece and in Asia (i.e. from the Greek cities). Together with them came two and half tons of medical supplies and 25,000 panoplies (sets of armour) inlaid with gold and silver – the product of Macedonian workshops. The total of combat troops available for the advance southwards was about 120,000 men, according to Nearchus. We may estimate the constituent numbers as follows: 13,000 cavalry; 55,000 front-line infantry of which the King's Men, Agrianians and Archers numbered about 15,000; and 50,000 supporting infantry, of which 15,000 were Indian troops. The fleet which awaited him on the Hydaspes was very large (the numbers in our texts vary widely). There were 80 triaconters and all sorts of other vessels, specially designed for the transportation of the army, its equipment and supplies.

Alexander's plan of campaign was unprecedented. He intended to use the Hydaspes, Acesines and Indus not only to carry the supplies which Taxiles and Porus had assembled but also to provide the base for military operations; for troops could be moved faster downstream than on land, and any opposition could therefore be outmanoeuvred. Expert crews were needed to cope with the rapids and other hazards. These were found among the soldiers from the Aegean islands and the Greek cities of Western Asia, and among camp-followers who hailed from Phoenicia, Cyprus and Egypt; for the Indians ventured on the rivers only for local fishing. Alexander had his own ship and helmsman, Onesicritus, and he appointed as his senior naval staff thirty-four leading officers – Macedonians, Greeks, Cypriotes, and one Persian. The role of most of them was honorary, and their title 'trierarch' did not involve an actual command.

On the eve of departure in November 326 a festival was held with competitions in the arts and in athletics, and victims for sacrifice were issued to the army. Alexander himself sacrificed then to his ancestral gods, the gods whom the diviners enjoined, the three river gods, Poseidon, Amphitrite, the Nereids and Ocean. At dawn on the day of departure he sacrificed on shore to his usual gods and to Hydaspes, and on shipboard to the three river gods, Heracles, Ammon and his usual gods. Then the bugle sounded, the fleet set out in formation, and the riverbanks rang with the cheers of the oarsmen. Alexander sailed in command of the Hypaspists, the Archers and the Royal Squadron of the Companion Cavalry. Two detachments of the army had started in advance, the larger with 200 elephants on the left bank under Hephaestion, and the other on the right bank under Craterus; and a third detachment under the satrap Philippus was to follow. The fleet and the detachments met at prearranged points. Most of the Indian tribes surrendered, and the others were subjugated as far as the confluence of the Hydaspes and the Acesines. There in the troubled waters some oared ships were damaged and lives were lost, but those vessels which went with the current came to no harm.

Alexander had early intelligence that the two largest and most warlike tribes in the central region, the Malli and the Oxydracae, were preparing to join forces and engage him in set battle. That was a daunting prospect; for their huge numbers would be effective, and a single defeat for the Macedonians might be disastrous. He must be first in the field, before they could combine. While the fleet sailed down to the border of the Malli, Alexander raided the country of their northern neighbours. On rejoining the fleet he made his dispositions. Craterus, proceeding down the right bank, was to be in command of the elephants. Hephaestion on the left bank was to move five days ahead of Alexander's own force, and Ptolemy was to follow three days behind Alexander's force, so that they could deal with any fall-out following on Alexander's attack. Alexander himself in command of the Hypaspists, one phalanx-brigade, the Agrianians, the Archers, half the Companion Cavalry and the mounted archers (totalling 6,500 infantry and 2,000 cavalry), marched through desert country deep into Mallian territory. In a day and a night he covered over 90 kilometres.

The attack by his cavalry at dawn was a complete surprise. Many Mallians were killed defenceless in the fields, and when the infantry came up they forced their way into the city and drove the enemy into the citadel. 'Alexander appeared here, there and everywhere in the action.' The citadel was captured by assault, and the 2,000 defenders were killed. The inhabitants of a nearby city fled, but many were overtaken and killed by the cavalry. After another night march he overtook a force of Mallians which was crossing the Hydraotes, killed many and took some prisoners, and then captured their stronghold. The survivors were enslaved. Another city was strongly held by Mallians and by Brahmans, members of a fanatical religious sect. The Macedonians gave covering fire with their catapults while the sappers undermined the walls (as elsewhere in the plains, these were of brick), and Alexander was the first to mount the wall of the citadel, in which some 5,000 Mallians fought to the death. 'Such was their courage that few were captured alive.' Other cities were abandoned. Alexander ordered a detachment to comb the woods and 'to kill all who did not voluntarily surrender'.

The heavy losses of the Mallians were due partly to the fanatical resistance of their soldiers and partly to the killing of refugees on Alexander's orders (e.g. in Arrian 6.8.3, derived through Ptolemy from the *Journal*). Since panic was now widespread, the only organised army of the Mallians, 50,000 strong, left their main territory and crossed the Hydraotes, intending evidently to join the Oxydracae. In close pursuit Alexander forded the river with his cavalry only and halted the Mallians by riding round them until his infantry appeared. At the sight of the phalanx the Mallians fled to a strongly fortified city, and next day when the Macedonians attacked they took refuge in the citadel. Alexander as usual was in the forefront. As he thought his soldiers to be slow, he himself propped a ladder against the citadel wall and led the way up, being followed by Peucestas, who was carrying the sacred shield of Athena of Troy, and by Leonnatus, a Bodyguard. Another ladder was raised alongside, and the first man up was Abreas. Behind them both ladders broke under the weight of the troops. The leaders were alone. Alexander forced the defenders off the top of the narrow wall and was joined there by Peucestas, Leonnatus and Abreas. Since he was a standing target, he jumped to the ground inside, killed some who attacked him, and was joined by the other three. Abreas was killed by an arrow fired at short range. Alexander was struck by another arrow which pierced his lung. He collapsed, but Peucestas and Leonnatus protected him with their shields. Now the Hypaspists arrived, some scaling the walls and others breaking down a gate, and in the belief that Alexander was dead the army killed everyone inside the citadel.

Alexander survived with much loss of blood. When he showed himself to the army, they shouted for joy and wreathed him 'with such flowers as India was then producing'. All the forces were now united at the confluence of the Hydraotes and the Acesines. While Alexander convalesced, the terrible losses he had inflicted on the Mallians had the effects he had foreseen. Mallians, Oxydracae, Sogdae and other tribes and communities as far as the confluence of the Acesines and the Indus sent envoys and gifts and accepted his rule. The only tribe which refused was reduced by Perdiccas. At the confluence he set the southern limit of the satrapy of Philippus, to whom he gave a garrison force which included all the Thracians, and a new city, Alexandria-in-Opiene, was to be built with dockyards. For Alexander foresaw the importance of the many navigable rivers for a water-borne trade which the disunited Indian tribes had never developed. Territory west of the Indus which Craterus overran was added to the satrapy of Arachosia.

Continuing down the Indus he received the submission of the tribes and founded another city with dockyards near the capital of the Sogdae (at Rohri). The river flowed not far from the desert of Thar, and the fertile country was to the west. There Musicanus reigned over what was said to be the richest kingdom of the Indus valley. Because Musicanus had sent no envoys, Alexander embarked a force on his now enlarged fleet, sailed swiftly downstream, and reached the kingdom before Musicanus even heard of his departure. Astounded, Musicanus came to meet Alexander. He brought lavish gifts and all his elephants, and he placed himself and his people at the service of Alexander. Pardon was granted, Musicanus was confirmed as vassal-king, and the citadel of his capital was garrisoned by the Macedonians. A neighbouring king, Oxicanus, had not negotiated. Sailing with a picked force to his realm, Alexander captured Oxicanus and two of his cities by assault. He gave all the plunder to his troops; but he kept the elephants. The ruler of the next kingdom to the south, Sambus, fled but his relatives surrendered the capital and the elephants.

Alexander was now close to the head of the Indus Delta. But behind him there broke out a mutiny, inspired by the Brahmans and led by Musicanus, and the danger was that the mutiny would spread. Alexander acted with his usual speed. The satrap he had appointed for southern 'India', Peithon, invaded the kingdom and captured Musicanus, while Alexander attacked the cities which were subject to Musicanus. 'Of some cities he enslaved the inhabitants and razed the walls, and in others he placed garrisons and fortified the citadels.' Any Brahmans who were captured and Musicanus were taken to their place of residence and were hanged as instigators of the rebellion. Another revolt occurred in the realm of Sambus (mentioned not by Arrian but by other writers). Alexander treated the cities in the same way, except that he pardoned those who surrendered, most notably at the chief city of the Brahmans, Harmatelia.

The king of the Delta, Soeris, came to Alexander, accepted his rule and was ordered to prepare supplies for the army. As the subjugation of 'India' seemed to be complete, Alexander prepared for the next phase by sending Craterus on the route through Arachosia and Drangiana to Carmania, which adjoined Persis. Craterus took any Macedonians who were unfit for active service, three phalanx-brigades, some of the Archers, all the elephants, and a baggage-train together with the families of the King's Men. His task was to confirm or extend Macedonian control of the areas through which he would pass. It was clear that Alexander intended to lead a more mobile army into unconquered territory, which had therefore to be south of Craterus' route.

After the departure of Craterus in June 325 Alexander sailed rapidly to Pattala at the head of the Delta, because Soeris was said to have fled with his tribesmen. It was true, but most of the tribesmen came back on the assurance that they would work their own lands (see above, p. 71, for a similar assurance). Alexander enlarged the cultivable area by having wells dug in the desert. At Pattala he planned his chief naval base: a large basin was excavated for the bulk of the fleet; dockyards were built; and both were included together with the citadel in a fortified complex. From Pattala he explored both arms of the Indus. He lost some ships through a storm from the sea and then a powerful ebb tide, of which he had had no experience. He found the eastern river to be more navigable. He arranged for the building of another basin and dockyards there, with a fort for a garrison, which would mark his eastern frontier. No doubt he hoped to develop trade by sea eastwards.

During his first voyage he landed on a river island and then on an island in the sea, and at each of them he sacrificed not to the usual gods but to special gods with special rituals, as he had been instructed to do by Ammon at the oracle of Siwah (above, p. 102). He then sailed out to sea, sacrificed bulls to Poseidon, and as a thank-offering cast vessels of gold upon the waters. He was confident that he had reached the Ocean – something which Ammon had presumably forecast – and he set up altars to Oceanus and to Tethys.

The conquest of 'India' south of his cities on the Hydaspes within seven months was an amazing example of Alexander's audacity, originality and planning and of his leadership of a multiracial army. His Macedonians were at the peak of their form. Because Arrian wrote of Alexander and the King's Men, we know little or nothing of the achievements of his Greek and Asian troops, of whom the Persian, Bactrian, Sogdian, Scythian and Indian cavalry must have played a leading part. Alexander was undeterred by the vastness of the plains, the huge populations, the elephants and the war-chariots; and his use of the rivers gave him a speed of execution which prevented his enemies, traditionally disunited, from combining their forces. Nor was it merely a matter of conquest. He had brought about acceptance of his rule. Polyaenus, a military commentator who drew on Ptolemy's account, observed that Alexander's mixture of the harshest methods as at Sangala and then of pardon and clemency to the neighbouring tribes (above, p. 167) had the effect that the reputation for clemency 'becoming current persuaded Indians to accept Alexander willingly' (4.3.30). Alexander later remarked that he had left Indians 'to maintain their own forms of government in accordance with their own customs' (Arrian 7.20.1). What he brought to Indians who had been split into warring communities was peace and with it the promise of economic development. We have seen the new use of the rivers, the digging of wells and the excavation of harbours. In Alexander's cities Indians had new opportunities, and their sons were eligible for a Greek form of education. Greek scientists and Greek adventurers with Alexander had much to teach the Indians in practical matters such as the mining of salt and the smelting of metals. The conditions were set for a new age.

2. The conquest of the southern regions

When Alexander sacrificed at sea, he prayed 'that Poseidon would escort safely the naval force which he intended to send with Nearchus to the Persian Gulf and the mouths of the Euphrates and Tigris'. This force would sail through uncharted seas. Indeed it was not known whether such a voyage was possible; for little credence was given in 325 to the report by Herodotus, which Alexander will have read, that almost two centuries earlier the Greek captain of a merchant ship, dependent on sail only, had voyaged from the Indus to the Red Sea in thirty months (4.44). It was thus an open question whether the sea off the Indus was an inner sea, like the Mediterranean Sea, or was the Ocean which in Aristotle's belief encircled the inhabited land mass. The voyage of Nearchus would solve that question.

The fleet was selected from the three classes of warships which were fastest under oar: triaconters (open boats with fifteen oars a side), *hemioliai* (light ships with one and a half banks of oars), and *kerkouroi* (skiffs). These ships had the advantage over merchant ships that they were faster under most conditions, were not held up by lack of wind, and could land on open beaches. Their disadvantage was that they could carry very little water and food. What alarmed Alexander was the danger of disaster during a voyage of unknown length (in fact some 1,200 miles), if the coast was harbourless, uninhabited, or deficient in natural foodstuffs. Indeed he had reason to think that some of the coast would be uninhabited, because Ocean was believed to be fringed by desert or steppe country. Nearchus made the shrewd comment that Alexander's apprehensions 'were overcome by his desire to achieve something new and extraordinary always'.

The voyage of the fleet was to be helped by an army which would start two months earlier, dig wells or mark water-points, dump supplies where they would be needed, and subjugate any hostile tribes. The army would soon be marching through unknown country. There was merely a tradition that an Assyrian queen, Semiramis, and Cyrus the Great had emerged from that country with only a handful of men, because it was deserted and difficult to traverse. Nearchus said later that Alexander had been aware of the tradition and intended to succeed where they had failed. The nature and the scale of the difficulties were not known. Alexander set off in August with an army of perhaps 20,000 men and four months' supply of grain; for he had sent home most of the numerous Asian cavalry and the Indian infantry. The first two tribes, Arabitae and Oreitae, planned resistance but capitulated. Alexander founded two cities, appointed Apollophanes as satrap, and left Leonnatus in command of the Agrianians, some of the Archers, and cavalry and infantry who were mainly Greek mercenaries. After the departure of Alexander Leonnatus put down a rising in a set battle, when the enemy losses were 6,000 and his were trivial but included Apollophanes. He welcomed the fleet on its arrival, provided substitutes for some of the crews, and gave Nearchus supplies for ten days.

With some 12,000 soldiers, mainly Macedonians, the supply-train and the camp-followers, who were traders with their families, Alexander entered Gedrosia in October, the month during which the fleet had been ordered to start. The first shortage was water, and Alexander was forced to go inland; but he still managed to send to the coast some supplies, which were reaching him from Apollophanes; but these dwindled with his death. Alexander then faced an agonising choice: either to take his army inland on an easy route to the capital, Pura, or to march near the coast through what was reported to be desert. He chose the latter course, in order to provide help for the fleet where it might need it most.

The army suffered dreadfully from intense heat, shortage of water and exhaustion. Where the sand was soft, it was impossible for the animals and men to drag the wagons uphill. To supplement their rations the troops killed the animals, broke up the wagons and used the wood to cook the flesh. With no means of transport the sick and the exhausted were left to die. When it rained inland, a flash flood at night swept away 'most of the women and children of the camp-followers, the king's property and most of the surviving transport animals'. Alexander's leadership held the troops together. He walked in front, and when he was given some water he poured it on the ground to show that he would drink only when they all could drink. Finally the native guides lost the way in the featureless desert. It was Alexander who reached the sea and discovered fresh water in the shingle. The army followed the coast for a week, drinking this water. It then turned inland into inhabited territory and headed for Pura, the capital of Gedrosia. It is to be noted that during the crossing of the desert food supplies, though short, were maintained for the army. It was the camp-followers who suffered most, for they were not on the ration strength.

After resting at Pura the army marched into Carmania, and there it was joined by the army of Craterus, who had carried out his task (above, p. 174). The reunion was an occasion for a festival of the arts and of athletics, and Alexander made 'sacrifices of thanksgiving for the victory over the Indians and for the salvation of the army in Gedrosia'. His anxiety now was for the fleet. On learning that Nearchus and a few others were being brought to him, he thought the fleet had been lost and they were the sole survivors. So when they appeared, he asked, 'How were the ships and the men lost?' Nearchus replied, 'Your ships and your men are safe, and we have come to tell you of their safety.' Alexander wept with relief. He mounted another festival of the same kind and made 'sacrifices for the salvation of the fleet to Zeus the Saviour, Heracles, Apollo averter of evil, Poseidon and other gods of the sea'. He was right to do so; for where we might say that luck was on his side he knew that the gods had saved him.

The fleet too had had a hard passage, which lasted from early October into January. During it, in accordance with Alexander's orders, Nearchus listed the inhabitants, anchorages, water supplies, and fertile and barren parts of the coast, and this information was the basis of a *Mariner's Guide* for what was to be a regular route for traders. After Alexander's death Nearchus published an account of the adventures of himself and his crews, which makes excellent reading in the version abbreviated by Arrian. In it he paid little attention to the army's support. Yet without it there is no doubt that the fleet would either have been lost or would have turned back for lack of food or water.

Nearchus had left his fleet in Harmozia near the entry to the Bay of Hormuz. He continued his voyage of exploration, moving mainly from island to island, and was able to rest and restock at the mouth of the river Sitaces (Mand), where Alexander had deposited a large quantity of grain. From there he sailed to the mouth of the Euphrates, which Alexander had set as his goal (above, p. 175), and then turned back to the mouth of the Pasitigris. On this part of the voyage also he recorded information for a *Mariner's Guide*. He then joined Alexander at a bridge over the Pasitigris in February 324. A festival was held with sacrifices for the safety of the ships and men, and Alexander placed crowns of gold on the heads of Nearchus for his services to the fleet and of Leonnatus for his victory in Oreitis (above, p. 176). It was a triumphant conclusion to a large-scale operation in which the four divisions of Alexander's forces had conquered the southern provinces and opened communication by sea between India and Persia.

3. Southwestern Asia

The success of Nearchus opened up new vistas for Alexander. Was there a route by sea from the Persian Gulf to the Egyptian Sea (our Red Sea), or if the Egyptian Sea was an internal sea was there a route by sea round the southern side of Libya to the Pillars of Heracles? During the next twelve months three expeditions, each in a triaconter, worked their way down the east coast of the Arabian peninsula, and the last reached Cape Macetia, a good Macedonian name for the Oman peninsula. Another expedition set out from Suez and reached Yemen; for that was 'as far as the water in their ships permitted'. Had Alexander lived longer, he would have completed, in the opinion of Arrian, the circumnavigation of Arabia.

From the Pasitigris Alexander marched to Susa where there was another reunion, and he then sailed with a select force down the river Eulaeus to the sea. With the fastest ships he explored the coast to the mouth of the Tigris. The Persians had built weirs on the Tigris, in order to prevent any enemy from coming upriver. Alexander had them removed and proceeded to Opis. The Euphrates on the other hand had not been blocked by the Persians and was navigable very far inland to Thapsacus. Aristobulus wrote of Chaldaean traders, settled at Gerra on the Arabian coast, who sent cargoes of Arabian spices on rafts to Babylonia, whence they went by river to Thapsacus and were then distributed overland. Alexander appreciated the importance of this route. He assembled a great fleet at Babylon. To the ships of Nearchus were added Phoenician naval vessels, from quinqueremes (in which the upper and middle oars were each rowed by two men, the lower by one man) to triaconters, which had been transported in sections from Phoenicia to Thapsacus, were reassembled there, and then sailed down to Babylon. Other ships were being built from local cypress in dockyards there. To accommodate the fleet a basin was excavated to hold 1,000 warships, and naval personnel were recruited from the Mediterranean area, some voluntarily, some hired in advance, and others 'bought', i.e. redeemed from slavery and liberated. Moreover, 'Alexander intended to found settlements on the coast and the islands of the Persian Gulf, since he thought it would become as prosperous as Phoenicia'.

The prosperity of Babylonia was due to a system of irrigation, which Alexander personally investigated and improved. A particular problem was posed by the control of the flood water of the lower Euphrates, which was carried off by the Pollacopas canal and formed marshlands on the coast; for during most of the year the water had to be diverted away from that canal and used for irrigation. The Persians had achieved this by employing 10,000 labourers for two months each year to dam the outlets from the river into the canal. Alexander discovered a deposit of boulder clay, constructed a permanent dam, and used sluices to control the flow from the Euphrates into the canal. The head of the Persian Gulf has altered greatly since ancient times, but its general nature is the same. The marshlands, extending towards what is now Kuwait, were regarded as part of the natural defences of Arabia. Alexander visited them and founded a city, in which he settled Greek mercenaries, in Kuwait, before he returned to Babylon in 323. There the fleet had been under constant training with competitions in oarsmanship and helmsmanship and between ships. Alexander intended to command it himself and to join the main army in Kuwait for the invasion of Arabia. He was planning the details of the voyage and the Arabian campaign during his final illness. Had he lived, there is no doubt that he would have conquered at least part of Arabia.

CHAPTER XVII

The Kingdom of Asia and the Macedonians

1. The organisation of the Kingdom of Asia

We have seen that in the central provinces Alexander appointed Asians, mainly Persians, to be satraps. Four of these had commanded large contingents in the Battle of Gaugamela: Mazaeus, Phrat<!---->aphernes, Atropates and Satibarzanes. The first three were outstandingly loyal to Alexander. Satibarzanes rebelled and led an actual revolt in 330. Thereafter Alexander spent five years in Bactria and India, during which it was not possible for him to supervise the conduct of his administrators, both European and Asian, in the area from the Hellespont to Parthyaea. As in Macedonia, every subject of the King of Asia had the right of appeal, but this was an effective safeguard against maladministration only when the king was within range. This was so in 325 when complaints were lodged against the satrap of Parapamisadae, Tyriespis, and he was brought to south 'India', put on trial and executed for peculation and oppression of his subjects; his satrapy was transferred to the Sogdian Oxyartes, the father of Roxane. But when he returned from India, a number of complaints reached him. In Carmania, the satrap, Astaspes, came under suspicion; an inquiry was held and on being found guilty he was executed. Advancing from Carmania to Persis, Alexander learned that the satrap of Persis, Phrasaortes, had died a natural death, and a Persian, Orxines, who had been a commander at the Battle of Gaugamela, had taken control of the satrapy 'for Alexander', then in India. Complaints were now made by Persians against Orxines for misgovernment; he was tried, found guilty and was hanged. At Susa Alexander arrested on charges of maladministration Abulites, satrap of Susiane since 331, and his son Oxyartes, satrap of Paraetacene since 330 (he had been a commander at Gaugamela), and both were executed.

Arrian, drawing on Ptolemy and Aristobulus, wrote that the satraps of the region (i.e. Astaspes, Abulites, Oxyartes and the self-appointed Orxines) did not believe that Alexander would survive, particularly in the Gedrosian desert, and that this belief led them to misgovern. The implication, and probably the fact, was that these Persian satraps had

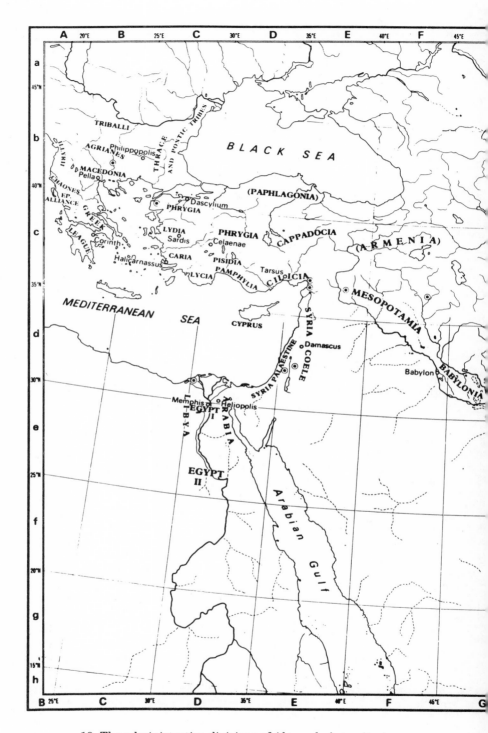

19. The administrative divisions of Alexander's territories.

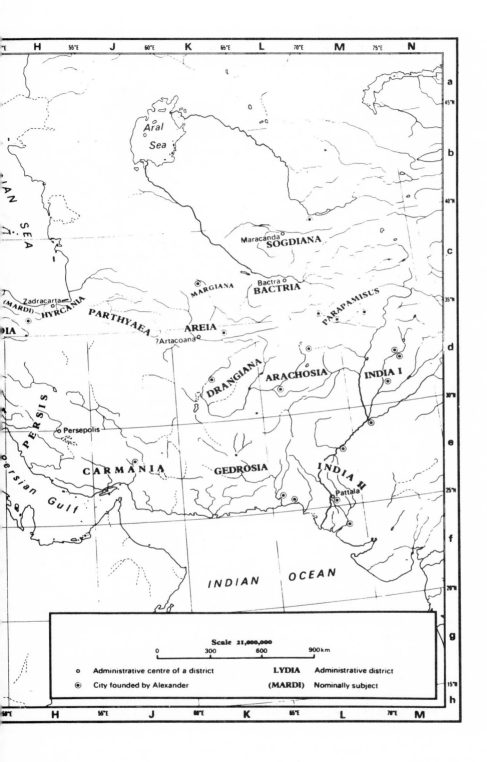

a

45°N

Aral
Sea

b

40°N

Maracanda ○   c
SOGDIANA

MARGIANA ◉   Bactra ○
BACTRIA   35°N

Zadracarta   PARAPAMISUS
(MARDI)   HYRCANIA   PARTHYAEA   AREIA

?Artacoana ○   d

DRANGIANA   ARACHOSIA   INDIA I   30°N

○ Persepolis   e

CARMANIA   GEDROSIA   INDIA II   25°N

Pattala

Persian Gulf   f

INDIAN   OCEAN   20°N

g

Scale 21,000,000

0   300   600   900 km   15°N

○   Administrative centre of a district   LYDIA   Administrative district
◉   City founded by Alexander   (MARDI)   Nominally subject

h

previously governed satisfactorily. When we remember the size of the Kingdom of Asia and the installation of satraps from 334 to 325, we should not be surprised that there were four cases of maladministration. As regards the policy of appointing Asians as satraps, it had succeeded remarkably in that there had been no risings in the central satrapies during the long absence of Alexander. Some Persians who were not satraps were found guilty of intending to start rebellion, for instance two arrested in Drangiana by Craterus, but the only pretender who claimed to be 'King of the Medes and Persians', Baryaxes, was arrested by Atropates, the satrap, and delivered with some associates to Alexander in 324. In all cases those found guilty of rebellious behaviour were executed.

Misconduct by European troops was on a larger scale. As we have mentioned (above, p. 72), the troops in a satrapy were commanded not by the satrap (in Media the loyal Atropates) but by an independent officer. Thus a force of some 10,000 men in Media was commanded by a distinguished Macedonian, Cleander a brother of Coenus, and on his staff were two officers, who like him had held commands at the Battle of Gaugamela – Sitalces and Agathon. In response to complaints, Alexander ordered these officers to bring the bulk of their army to him in Carmania. Asians and soldiers laid numerous charges of robbery and rape, and Cleander and Sitalces, being held reponsible, were executed. After an investigation in Media 600 soldiers were found guilty of misconduct. They too were executed. So striking an example of justice did more than anything else, as Arrian reported from Ptolemy and Aristobulus, to persuade 'the peoples of the spear-won lands to be orderly ... for they knew that it was not possible in Alexander's Kingdom for his subjects to be wronged by those in power'.

Since Alexander was looking forward to campaigning in Arabia and then in the Mediterranean, he had to ensure that the Kingdom of Asia would be 'orderly' during his long absence. Most of his actions in 324-323 were directed to that end. The centre of military and economic control was to be located in the region between the Persian Gulf and the Caspian Sea. For that reason he developed the thalassocracy in the Gulf and made the fleet's base at Babylon. His only military operation was against the tribesmen who lived in high villages and raided the lowlanders. Alexander defeated them in the winter and founded cities 'so that they should no longer be nomads but become agriculturists and cease from raiding others'. It was from these tribes, led by the Cossaei, that Peucestas recruited a considerable number of warriors in 323. In Hyrcania Alexander arranged for the building of warships, which were to explore the Caspian Sea and discover whether it was a part of Ocean – in which case on Aristotle's theory there would be a passage by sea to 'India' – or whether it had communication by river with the Black Sea.

The Kingdom of Asia would be self-sustaining and orderly during his absence in the West only if the policy of cooperation with the Asians and particularly with the Persians were to continue successfully. Hephaestion was to be his deputy as King of Asia with the title 'Chiliarches' (Arrian *Succ.* 1a 3), and Peucestas was to be satrap of Persis. Both men were close friends, entirely loyal and in sympathy with Alexander's policy. Unfortunately Hephaestion died in 324, and Alexander did not appoint anyone in his place before his own death. 'Peucestas alone of the Macedonians adopted Median dress, learned the Persian language and in all respects assimilated himself to Persian ways ... to the gratification of Alexander and to the delight of the Persians.'

For the defence of the Kingdom and for the maintenance of law and order within it Alexander's deputy would need a large army which could not be provided by Macedonia. Greek mercenaries were unsuitable for this purpose. They were willing to serve any paymaster, and they had been recruited by some satraps who had thought that Alexander would not return from 'India'. Moreover, they were unruly and even fought among themselves, for instance in Bactria in 325. Nor were the Thracians dependable; for example, they assassinated the satrap Philippus in 'India' in 325. Alexander therefore created in May a mixed army of Macedonian and Persian infantry, 26,700 strong, in which each file contained four Macedonian pikemen and twelve Persian archers and javelin-men (the latter from Cossaea and Tapuria). Each file was commanded by a Macedonian, and there was higher pay for the Macedonians. It was shortly before his illness that Alexander presided at the integration of these Persians and Macedonians. At the same parade he allocated Lydian and Carian troops which had arrived as reinforcements. He had for some years had units of cavalry in which Macedonians, Persians and other Asians fought alongside one another. He intended to leave a considerable number of these in Asia. He was joined probably by a reinforcement of Companion Cavalry who came from Macedonia under the command of Menidas.

'Alexander thought that Asia could be held together by an army of modest size, because he had posted garrisons at many places and because he had filled the newly founded cities with settlers who were eager to maintain the *status quo*.' The garrisons were stationed at strategic points in the web of all-weather roads which enabled troops to move rapidly. The new cities numbered seventy, each starting with at least 10,000 male citizens, and it was in these cities that 'boys' were trained in Greek literacy and in Macedonian weaponry. In addition there were militias in the towns which would resist raiders. One should think therefore of the mixed army, consisting of Macedonians and Asians, as a mobile force which could move rapidly to defeat any considerable rising and so hold Asia together. The defence of the Kingdom of Asia against outside enemies hardly figured in Alexander's calculations; his frontiers were mainly desert and steppe, the Scythian tribes had entered into alliance, and his fleets ruled over the waves of the Indian Ocean, the Red Sea, the Eastern Mediterranean and the Black Sea.

The greatest threat to peace within Asia came from unemployed Greek mercenaries. During Alexander's long absence many of these mercenaries had been hired by ambitious satraps and military commanders, who hoped to carve out a kingdom for themselves if he should be killed. On his return they were dismissed on his order, and they joined the huge number of mercenaries who had lost their employment with the defeat of Darius and his satraps. Before he fell ill Alexander was planning to settle 50,000 of them together with their Asian women and their children in Persis, and no doubt to train their 'boys' to be his soldiers later. It is probable that his plan became known at the time; for a considerable number preferred to move to Greece, where there was still hope of employment. He must have been glad to see them go.

As a military area Persis was second to Media. For the overland communications between east and west all ran through Media; it had provided the best soldiers of the Persian Empire; and its pasturelands bred the finest horses in Asia. The dependable satrap Atropates had kept the Medes loyal during Alexander's absence, and many of them were serving in his Companion Cavalry. According to Polybius, 'it was on the initiative of Alexander that Media was ringed round with Greek cities'. The process probably began before his death (it was completed by his general Seleucus). It seems that these foundations were not mixed in population, but that city-populations were transplanted from the Greek mainland or islands; and their place there was taken by Asian city-populations. For in the plans which were made known after his death Alexander intended 'to establish cities and transplant populations from Asia to Europe and conversely from Europe to Asia'.

The other factor which was to hold Asia together was economic growth and prosperity. Alexander encouraged the transition from pastoralism to agriculture by creating urban centres for native peoples, for instance the Cossaeans and the subjects of Musicanus, and Greek methods of intensive agriculture were introduced by the settlers of his new cities. His concern is seen in flood-control, irrigation and the digging of wells in barren land. Trade expanded rapidly with secure, peaceful conditions and no tariffs over the entire area from the Greek mainland to the river Hyphasis. Overland communications were eased by the maintenance of all-weather roads and bridges, the siting of the Alexander-cities, and the suppression of brigandage. The carriage of goods on a large scale on the great rivers of Mesopotamia and of Pakistan, and the development of sea-borne trade between the Persian Gulf and the Delta of the Indus were innovations which added enormously to inter-regional exchange and the distribution of surplus foodstuffs. Whereas Persia had made only limited use of coined money,

Alexander issued a gold and silver coinage of real value which was valid throughout the Kingdom of Asia and beyond its eastern frontier. The chief mint was at Babylon, 'the metropolis' as the M on its coins indicated. Alexander was able to stabilise the relationship between gold and silver and to avoid inflation by his control of the output of coinage. The change from barter to capitalism was rapid and effective.

Some have suggested that if Alexander had lived longer he would have reorganised the system of government in Asia. This seems not to be so. The only alternative was the representational system of the Greek Community. But that system could not have succeeded in Asia; for whereas the members of the Greek Community had a common language and lived close to one another, the Asians spoke innumerable languages and were widespread. The combination of an autocratic king with an improved satrapal system and full local self-government was in Alexander's lifetime effective and acceptable. For his purpose was understood, as we see in a passage of the *Alexander Romance*, in which after the death of Darius Alexander was represented as saying to the Persians as follows:

> You are each to observe the religions and customs, the laws and conventions . . . which you observed in the days of Darius. Let each stay Persian in his way of life, and let him live within his city . . . for I wish to make the land one of widespread prosperity and employ the Persian roads as peaceful and quiet channels of commerce.

Such a prospect of peace, prosperity and progress is lacking in many parts of the modern world.

2. Macedonians and Asians

A decisive factor in the policy of Alexander was the small number of Macedonian citizen troops in Asia. The only firm figures we have are for 324, when the infantry totalled 23,000 and the cavalry more than 2,000, and there were in addition perhaps 1,400 Macedonians unfit for active service in the Alexander-cities. An army of this size would have been swamped by the forces of Darius. From the start Alexander had to add Balkan troops, Greek allies, Greek mercenaries and after his first victory Persians and other Asians, and for the future he set up the training of young Asians for service with Macedonian weapons. The recruitment of Asians and particularly Persians was possible only if they accepted Alexander's rule willingly (as he had prayed in 334; above, p. 64). In consequence, the policy of cooperating with Asians and of treating them as equals was essential for Alexander and became a *sine qua non* with the expansion of the Kingdom of Asia. The process began with the drafting of Persians into the Companion Cavalry and the ranking of the Persian Royal Cavalry Guard on a par with the Companion Cavalry Guard. The adoption of Median dress and Persian ceremonial in audiences for Asians was a mark of respect for them, even if very few Macedonians followed Alexander's example.

Alexander's chivalry towards the Persian Queen Mother and towards the Sogdian princess, Roxane, whom he did not rape but married, made a great impression on the Asian aristocracy. In 324 at Susa he arranged the weddings of more than eighty Persian, Median and Bactrian aristocrats to the leading Macedonians. A daughter of Darius and a daughter of his predecessor, Artaxerxes Ochus, were taken in marriage by Alexander. The weddings were conducted in the Persian manner, in which the bridegroom kissed the bride. Also at Susa Alexander converted into official marriages the liaisons which some 10,000 Macedonian soldiers had formed with Asian women; and he gave them wedding presents. It was known that many Macedonians owed money to Asian traders, who had little hope of recovering it. Alexander paid the money *in toto* without requiring the soldiers in debt to reveal their identity. In all these ways Alexander was treating his Macedonians and his Asians as equals in status and in obligation.

He was still at Susa in February 324 when 'the satraps came to him bringing from the newly founded cities and from the rest of the spear-won land 30,000 boys (*paides*) already reaching maturity and all of the same age'. These were the 'Epigonoi' (above, p. 130), whose training Alexander had started in 330/329. They were now in their twentieth year. 'They were equipped with Macedonian weapons and they were practised in the arts of war in the Macedonian manner.' When they were paraded before the king, 'they showed amazing dexterity and agility in their manoeuvres'. Trained as pikemen and serving as a parallel unit to the Macedonian phalanx, they were superior in number and bound to outlive the ageing Macedonians. That was why 'Alexander called them Epigonoi' – the next generation, the successors. He needed them for the campaign in Arabia, for which he would have few Macedonian phalangites; and he was also implementing his policy of placing Asians and Macedonians on the same level of respect.

The Macedonian phalangites, however, took a very different view. They were the acknowledged élite of Alexander's army, and they had held that position through many years of devoted and exacting service. They resented the arrival of the Epigonoi, and they were alarmed by the fear that they would ultimately be replaced by them. Their anger was focussed on Alexander. He had already offended Macedonians by his Median dress, his Persian ceremonial, his staging of the massed marriages, and his integration of Asians into the Companion Cavalry and even into the Cavalry Guard and the arming of them with the Macedonian lance. There was little that Alexander could do to placate them. He held many assemblies but found them unruly.

The crisis came at Opis in summer 324. Alexander had decided to send to Macedonia those Macedonians who were unfit for active service on account of their age or their injuries. They would number several thousand (in the event 10,000 went), and apart from some cavalrymen they would be phalangites rather than Hypaspists, who seem to have remained with him as a unit. He convened an assembly of the Macedonians and announced his decision. The reaction of those he had in mind was not pleasure at going home, as he may have expected, but fury that they were being despised as unfit and treated with contempt; and the reaction of those who did not feel themselves threatened was anger that Alexander was insulting his Macedonians once again and would replace them with Asians. In the general outcry Alexander was told to send them all home and go campaigning 'with his father', meaning Ammon. He and the commanders beside him leapt down from the dais into the crowd and ordered the arrest of the ringleaders by the Hypaspist Guards. Thirteen men were marched off to be executed for mutiny.

In the silence which ensued Alexander made a speech, of which the substance, not the words, was preserved by Arrian. In brief, he recounted the services of Philip and more especially of himself in raising the Macedonians from obscurity and poverty to be the leaders of the world, the conquerors of every land and sea, the owners of Persia's treasure and of India's good things. He had not exalted himself above his men; he had been wounded as often as any of them, lived more humbly than most, and had won everlasting glory for them and for those who had died in action. His intention had been to send home those unfit for war. Now they could all go home and report there that they had abandoned their king to the mercies of those who had been conquered.

After his speech he shut himself off from any Macedonian for two days, and on the third day he summoned the leading Persians and conferred on them the command of Asian troops which were not only brigaded in the Macedonian manner but were given the Macedonian names: Foot-Companions, Town-Companions, Companion Cavalrymen and so on. The Persian commanders were to be his 'Kinsmen' and they alone had the right to kiss him. He had turned his back on the Macedonians. But they could not bear it. They threw down their weapons at his door in supplication and begged him for mercy. He came out quickly, and 'seeing them so humble ... he too shed tears'. A leading Companion complained that Alexander was calling some Persians 'Kinsmen' and letting them kiss him but was not according that privilege to Macedonians. Alexander cried out: 'You are all my Kinsmen,' and the Companion and anyone else who wished kissed Alexander. The Macedonians went to their camp rejoicing and singing the victory song. 'Alexander thereupon sacrificed to the usual gods.'

At the start of the narrative which Arrian derived from Ptolemy and

Aristobulus it was clear that Alexander misjudged the situation. He thought that in announcing his decision 'he would of course please the Macedonians', and the reaction of the Macedonians was 'not unreasonable'. Ptolemy and/or Aristobulus realised that Alexander was out of touch with the Macedonians' feelings about the latest developments of his Asian policy. Their embittered and angry mood broke out into an uproar, which Alexander quelled by treating it as an act of mutiny. One dimension of the impasse was the Asian policy. The other dimension was the splitting of the Macedonian State. For throughout the campaign Alexander and the Assembly of Macedonians had acted as the Macedonian State in matters of policy, trials for treason and celebrations of festivals in honour of the gods. If the Macedonians went home and he stayed, the Macedonian State would be torn apart. Alexander exploited this fact. By showing that he would stay, he virtually forced them to stay with him. The emotional tension was understood and was shared by him, as his tears showed. Despite their singing the victory lay not with the Macedonians but with the King. They would stay with him, and they would accept such Persian customs as being 'Kinsmen' and 'kissing the king'.

Alexander did not let his victory dwindle. He staged a banquet of reconciliation for 9,000 guests. The Macedonians sat with him; and next to them were the Persians and representatives of the other races in Asia. The Greek diviners and the Persian Magi pronounced the omens favourable. Alexander 'prayed especially for concord and for the sharing of the rule between Macedonians and Persians'. All who were present poured the same libation and sang the victory song. It was the triumph of Alexander's Asian policy. Macedonians and Asians were to share as equals in the administration of the Kingdom of Asia.

CHAPTER XVIII

The plans and personality of Alexander

1. Arrangements affecting the Macedonians and Macedonia

After the reconciliation in late summer 324 Alexander offered his terms for any Macedonians who might volunteer to go home. They would be paid the normal wage up to their arrival in Macedonia, and each man would receive a gratuity of one talent. They were ordered to leave their Asian wives and children in Asia, where Alexander undertook to bring up the boys 'in the Macedonian manner in other respects and in military training'; and he said he would send them thereafter to their fathers in Macedonia. He made provision also for orphans of Macedonian soldiers in Asia. Some 10,000 Macedonians accepted these terms. 'He embraced them all, with tears in his eyes and tears in theirs, and they parted company.' They were being released from the campaign in Asia, not from military service. In summer 323 they reached Cilicia, where Alexander intended that they should winter. In spring 322 they were to be transported to Macedonia by his newly built fleet. By then Alexander expected to have completed his Arabian campaign and to be in Egypt or Cilicia. He was to be joined there by 10,000 Macedonians 'in their prime', who would be replaced in Macedonia by the returning veterans.

In summer 324 arrangements were made to change the representatives of the king's authority in Macedonia. Olympias had held the *prostasia*, which comprised the religious affairs of the state and the financial management of the royal property (above, p. 59); and Antipater had been 'General with full powers'. The two had become increasingly incompatible, and each of them accused the other of exceeding their powers in letters to Alexander. In 324 he moved Olympias to Molossia and brought their daughter Cleopatra from Molossia to hold the *prostasia* in Macedonia. At that time Molossia was almost a dependency of Macedonia. From 334 to 331 the Molossian king, Alexander, the husband of Cleopatra, had conducted his own campaign in Italy, and after his death Cleopatra held the office of *prostasia* in the Molossian state, which was a member of the newly formed 'Epirote Alliance'. As a member of the Molossian royal house Olympias was well qualified to take the place of Cleopatra. In recognition of Olympias' services in Macedonia Alexander announced that on her death she would be 'dedicated to immortality' (*immortalitati consecretur*), that is to receive worship at her grave as a deity.

Antipater had been entirely loyal to Alexander. In 324 he became seventy-three years of age, and Alexander decided to replace him. The commander of the returning Macedonians was Craterus, the most trusted and respected general of those who had served under Philip, and he was instructed to take over the duties of Antipater on reaching Macedonia in 322. Antipater was then to have the honour of commanding the 10,000 Macedonians 'in their prime' who were to join Alexander. 'No public act or statement by Alexander was reported which might have implied that Antipater was not as highly regarded as ever by Alexander.'

His other representative in Europe was the 'General of Thrace', Zopyrion, who exercised authority also over the Black Sea. It was no doubt on Alexander's order that he embarked on a major campaign by land and by sea against the Getae and then the Scythians of South Russia in 325. His large army, reported to be 30,000 strong, must have consisted mainly of Thracian troops. His fleet was destroyed in sudden storms, the army suffered a crushing defeat, and Zopyrion was killed. Thereupon the most powerful tribe in Thrace, the Odrysians, rose in revolt. 'Thrace was almost lost.' That it was recovered must have been due to an agreement at the time with the Odrysian king, Seuthes III.

2. Arrangements affecting the city-states

Alexander respected the sovereignty of the Greek Community in the settlement of affairs after the defeat of Agis and his allies (above, p. 117), and he continued to do so, for instance by sending captured works of art to the states in the Greek Community. His conduct in these years indicates that the allegations of exceeding his powers as *Hegemon*, which were made in a speech 'On the Treaty with Alexander' in 331, were groundless. Within the Greek Community only one breach of the charter was reported in our sources, the expulsion of the people of Oeniadae from their city by the Aetolians. It happened perhaps in 325; for Alexander said that he himself would punish the Aetolians, presumably on his return to the West. In the years of peace a large number of Greek allies went east to serve in Alexander's army (above, p. 171), and no doubt others emigrated to trade or settle in Asia. At Athens Phocion was re-elected general repeatedly as the advocate of compliance with the Charter, and Lycurgus used the prosperity which Athens enjoyed under the peace to complete the construction in stone of the auditorium of the theatre of Dionysus and to improve the naval shipyards.

In June 324, when Alexander was at Susa, one of his financial officers, Harpalus, fled to Greece in order to escape punishment for misconduct. He came to Cape Sunium with 5,000 talents, 6,000 mercenaries and 30 ships, and as an Athenian citizen (for he had been honoured earlier by a grant of citizenship) he proceeded to Athens and asked for asylum and in effect alliance against Alexander. The Assembly rejected his request. He and his forces went on to Taenarum in the Peloponnese, but he returned as a suppliant with a single ship and a large amount of money. The Assembly then granted him asylum as an Athenian citizen. Although he gave bribes freely in Athens, he did not win over the leading politicians. Meanwhile Antipater and Olympias made the demand that Athens as Macedonia's ally should extradite Harpalus; and envoys from Alexander came from Asia with a similar demand. On the proposal of Demosthenes the Assembly voted to arrest Harpalus, confiscate his money, and hold him and his money 'for Alexander'. During the debate Harpalus said he had brought 700 talents to Athens, but when his money was confiscated it amounted only to 350 talents. While the Council of the Areopagus was enquiring into the missing talents, Harpalus escaped, collected his forces at Taenarum and sailed to Crete, where he was assassinated. The attitude of Alexander was conciliatory. He did not demand the return to him of the 700 talents. Six months were to pass before the Areopagus Council delivered its report. During those months two general issues were raised by Alexander, as follows.

When his forces were assembled at Susa, Alexander announced to them that all exiles, except those under a curse and those exiled from Thebes, were to be recalled and reinstated. He chose this method of letting his intention be known, because he was acting on his own authority and not in collaboration with the Council of the Greek Community; for he was addressing a larger number of states than those of the Greek Community. An official announcement in the form of a letter was made by his envoy at the Olympic Festival in July, when 20,000 exiles were among the audience. The wording was as follows: 'Alexander to the exiles from the Greek cities ... we shall be responsible for your return ... we have written to Antipater about this, in order that he may compel any states which are unwilling to restore you.' This announcement to the exiles was not an order to the Greek states. We may assume that a separate statement was sent to them in the form of an 'ordinance' (*diagramma*), which could lead to a discussion between a state and Alexander. We see this in an inscription from Tegea in the Peloponnese. The purpose of Alexander was twofold: to resettle the floating population of exiles (we may call them refugees today), which caused instability and often led to mercenary service; and to reconcile the parties which had fought one another and caused the vicious circle of revolutionary faction (*stasis*; above, p. 10).

Such an act of statesmanship was and is unparalleled. It affected almost all Greek city-states to varying degrees, and it hit Athens and Aetolia hardest. For Athens had expelled the population of Samos in 365 and occupied the island herself; and now, forty years later, she would have to restore the island to its proper owners. And Aetolia had to hand back Oeniadae to the Acarnanians she had expelled. At the time Alexander could not be accused of restoring his own partisans; for the bulk of the exiles had been opponents of the pro-Macedonian regimes in power. According to Hieronymus, an objective historian born around 364, 'people in general accepted the restoration of the exiles as being made for a good purpose'. In many states the restoration had taken place at the time of Alexander's death, but Athens and Aetolia were still making objections.

Alexander addressed the Greek states individually with two other requests in 324: the granting of heroic honours to Hephaestion, who had died in October, and the granting of divine honours to himself. The distinction between the two forms of honours was basically one of a person's achievement in life being worthy of a hero or of a god. In the case of Hephaestion, Alexander consulted Zeus Ammon at Siwah, and he accepted the response that Hephaestion should be worshipped as a hero. In answer to his request many states, including Athens, set up cults honouring Hephaestion as a hero; for there were many precedents in the city-states. 'Divine honours' were on a different plane, and the request in this case was to grant them to a living man. In Macedonian practice the worship of a king or queen after death was a mark of special distinction, and the granting of divine honours to Philip II in his lifetime (above, p. 25) was exceptional and perhaps unique. Alexander felt himself to be in competition with his father. He therefore asked the Assembly of Macedonians in Asia to grant him 'divine honours' (*caelestes honores*), but they refused. On the other hand some city-states of the Aegean islands and on the Asian coast had already in 334/333 granted divine honours to Alexander and had set up a shrine, games and sacrifices to him. These had been spontaneous acts of gratitude for liberation from Persian rule. Neither in Macedonia nor in the city-states was a man so honoured thought to be literally a god on earth.

Alexander's request was granted by most, perhaps by all, of the city-states individually which he addressed. Athens, for instance, dedicated a shrine, an altar and a cult-image to him. A general act of recognition was staged at Babylon in 323, perhaps at the traditional spring festival of the Macedonians. 'The envoys from Greece came to Alexander, wearing crowns themselves, and they crowned him with golden crowns; for they had come indeed on a sacred mission to honour a god.' The analogy of the honours paid to Philip must have been in people's minds; for then 'not only distinguished individuals but also the majority of the important city-states, including Athens, crowned him with golden crowns'. Alexander himself must have felt that he had attained the same pinnacle of glory and was the equal of his father. The motives of the city-states were no doubt mixed. But it is evident that the majority in the democratic assemblies recognised that they owed to Alexander the stability of the Greek Community, the liberation of the city-states overseas, the overthrow of the Persian empire, the thalassocracy in the Eastern Mediterranean and the Black Sea, the opening of Asia to Greek enterprise, and the consequent peace and prosperity. The most bitter enemy of Alexander, Demosthenes, was found guilty by the Areopagus Council of embezzling money deposited by Harpalus. Unable to pay an enormous fine, he was imprisoned; but he escaped and went into exile.

When embassies came to Babylon, Alexander heard first those concerned with religious matters. Because the Olympian gods had granted victory to Macedonia and the Greek Community, Alexander planned to build magnificent temples to Apollo at Delos and Delphi, Zeus at Dodona and at Dium, Athena Alcidemus at Cyrrus (in Macedonia), Artemis at Amphipolis, and Athena at Troy. He intended also to pay a special honour to his father, Philip: 'to build a mound of proportions equal to the tallest pyramid in Egypt.' He did not live to achieve it, but one of his generals – probably Lysimachus – built the Great Mound over the tomb of Philip at Vergina. Thanks to the plan of Alexander the tomb survived intact until it was excavated in 1977 by Manolis Andronicos.

3. Preparations for the Mediterranean campaign

Alexander must have let it be known at Susa in 324 that he intended to campaign in the West; for envoys came to Babylon early in 323 from that area. The Libyan envoys congratulated Alexander on winning 'the Kingdom of Asia', and those from Italy – Bruttians, Lucanians and Etruscans – honoured him for his achievements. This information was transmitted from Ptolemy and Aristobulus by Arrian, and is to be accepted. The Libyans thought he would march along the African coast; the Italian peoples expected him to follow the example of his namesake, the king of the Molossians, and invade South Italy from Epirus. The plans which were made public after Alexander's death were more specific: to build a thousand warships larger than triremes in Phoenicia, Syria, Cilicia and Cyprus for the expedition which was to be undertaken against Carthage, the coastal peoples from Libya to Spain, and those of the coast from Spain to Sicily; to build a coastal road from Libya to the Pillars of Heracles; and to build harbours and dockyards to accommodate so large an expeditionary force. These were, of course, provisional plans which Alexander sketched out for an expedition two years ahead, and they are chiefly of interest in revealing the scale of his ambitions. It seems from a passage in Justin 13.5.7 that Alexander issued orders before his death for the construction of the thousand warships.

If the expedition had materialised, the forces at Alexander's disposal would have been of the following order. If he should leave the Macedonian fleet and that of the Greek Community to maintain order in the Aegean Sea, he could count on the fleets of Phoenicia, Cyprus and Egypt in addition to his thousand new warships. If he should conquer Arabia with small casualties, he would have some 16,000 Macedonian pikemen, 20,000 Asian pikemen, the Persian Infantry Guard, plenty of light-armed infantry, the Companion Cavalry and units of Asian cavalry. There is no doubt that he would have defeated Carthage, and that he would have advanced to the Pillars of Heracles.

4. Events leading to the death of Alexander

In October 324 at Ecbatana Alexander suffered a terrible blow in the death of Hephaestion, his closest friend from childhood days and his constant sympathiser and supporter. He lay in a paroxysm of grief for two days, fasting and inaccessible. The funerary games were on an unprecedented scale with 3,000 artists and athletes, and the ashes of Hephaestion were taken to Babylon, where work began on a ziggurat of colossal size (its completion was still on order when Alexander died). The place and the form of this memorial were chosen because Hephaestion had been appointed *chiliarches*, i.e. the second-in-command in the Kingdom of Asia, and if he and Alexander had survived long enough he would have ruled the kingdom from Babylon as its metropolis. Mourning in the Persian manner was ordered throughout the Kingdom. The Macedonians instituted a cult of Hephaestion as 'a hero', which lasted for centuries as an inscription from Pella reveals. Special tributes were paid to Hephaestion as Commander of the Royal Hipparchy of the Companion Cavalry, many Companions dedicated themselves and their weapons to his memory, and Hephaestion's standard continued to be carried in front of the Hipparchy. The city-states too were asked by Alexander to pay heroic honours to Hephaestion, and many did so (above, p. 194). Alexander did not appoint a successor to Hephaestion either as chiliarch or as Commander of the Royal Hipparchy; but in practice Perdiccas became second-in-command, and it was he who took the initiative when Alexander died.

The death of Hephaestion and the immoderate grief of Alexander were the subject of many sensational accounts, which Arrian judged to be often untrue. Writers critical of Alexander, for instance, said that he razed the temple of Asclepius at Ecbatana, and that he ordered worship of Hephaestion 'as a god'. Arrian cited from the account by Ptolemy a letter from Alexander to Cleomenes, in which memorials were to be erected to Hephaestion in Alexandria and on the offshore island,

Pharos, and Alexander promised Cleomenes pardon for any offences in the past and in the future, 'if I shall find the shrines in Egypt in good condition'. It was Ptolemy who added that Cleomenes was 'a bad man' (so Arrian), in self-justification because he executed Cleomenes in 322. Did Ptolemy invent and insert the promise of Alexander? Some have thought so. Let us summarise the little we know. Cleomenes had been appointed in 331 as the senior financial officer in Egypt, and during Alexander's absence he took control of Egypt under unknown circumstances. That may have been one offence which Alexander would pardon. The pardon for future offences was only until Alexander should arrive in Egypt, probably early in 322. It is thus possible that the letter is genuine, and that it is an indication of Alexander's passionate desire to commemorate Hephaestion in grand style.

'After the funeral of Hephaestion ... the divine power began to indicate the end of Alexander himself, for many strange omens and signs occurred.' Most of the prognostications were inventions of the numerous authors who wrote about the end of Alexander. The omens ranged from a donkey kicking to death the finest lion in Alexander's menagerie to an escaped convict sitting on the king's vacant throne. There was, however, one prognostication which did affect the march of Alexander and his army after the campaign against the Cossaei. As he crossed the Tigris on his way to Babylon, he was met by Chaldaean diviners who warned him not to enter Babylon from the east but to do so from the west. According to Aristobulus Alexander wished to comply with the warning and did march the army round to the Euphrates on the west side of the city, but he was then thwarted by coming upon marshes and open water and so he entered from the east side. 'Thus willy-nilly he disobeyed the god', i.e. Belus (Ba'al); for Aristobulus believed the Chaldaeans had been inspired by Belus to give the warning. During his stay in Babylon Alexander set the army to work on clearing the site for a temple to Belus (the earlier one having been destroyed by Xerxes). He himself sailed down the Pollacopas canal (above, p. 179), and on his return through the marshlands he entered Babylon from the east side, confident in the fact that nothing disastrous had occurred since his first entry.

Soon afterwards, in May 323, the preparations for the Arabian campaign were complete. As usual before embarking on a new enterprise (above, p. 51), Alexander sacrificed to the gods for their blessing and distributed sacrificial victims and wine to the army, unit by unit; and he entertained the Friends at a banquet far into the night. He prolonged the drinking as the guest of a Friend, Medius, and slept by day, as was probably usual in the heat of summer in Iraq. He did the same the following night and day, and it was on that day that the fever started. 'However, he was carried out on a bed to perform the sacrifices, as custom prescribed for each day, ... and as darkness fell he issued orders to his commanders for the march and the voyage'. This is Arrian's abbreviation of a fuller account in the *Journal* (Plutarch had provided his own abbreviation). Alexander acted in this way day by day until he lost the power of speech. The Macedonian soldiers forced their way into his room in their longing to see him. 'The *Journal* says that as the men filed past he was unable to speak but greeted them severally, with difficulty raising his head and indicating with his eyes.' Death came to him that night, on 10 June 323, at the age of thirty-two. All the symptoms suggest that he died of *malaria tropica*. Later allegations that his death was due to poisoning or the result of alcoholism are untrue, for they are not consistent with the detailed report in the *Journal*.

5. Alexander's beliefs and personal qualities

Alexander grew up in a kingdom which was continually at war, and he saw it as his duty to lead the Macedonians in war not from a distance but in the forefront of the fighting. He saw the destiny of Macedonia as victory in war, and he and his men made military glory the object of their ambitions. Thus he spoke of the victorious career of Philip as conferring 'glory' both on him and on 'the community of Macedonians'. His own pursuit of glory was boundless. As he declared to his Commanders at the Hyphasis, 'I myself consider that there is no limit for a man of spirit to his labours, except that those labours should lead to fine achievements.' He made the same demand on his Commanders and his men. They had committed themselves to following him when they had sworn the oath of allegiance (*sacramentum pietatis*), to be loyal and have the same friend and enemy as their king. If a man should be killed in his service, Alexander assured them that his death would bring him glory for ever and his place of burial would be famous.

Life was competitive for boys in the School of Pages and for boys being trained for the militia in the cities, and thereafter in civilian affairs and in the services. No Macedonian festival was complete without contests in such arts as dramatic performance, recitation of poetry, proclamation as a herald, and musicianship, and in athletic events which on occasion included armed combat. Alexander was intensely competitive throughout his life. He would be the first to tame Bucephalus, to attack the Theban Sacred Band, to mount a city wall or climb an impregnable rock. He was the inspirer and often the judge of competition in others. He alone promoted soldiers and officers, awarded gifts for acts of courage, bestowed gold crowns on successful Commanders, and decided the order in the hierarchy of military rank up to the position of Senior Friend and Leading Bodyguard. Competitions between military units and between naval crews were a part of training and of battle. Alexander himself believed that he must compete with

Philip, Cyrus the Great, Heracles and Dionysus and surpass them all, and as Arrian remarked, 'if he had added Europe to Asia, he would have competed with himself in default of any rival'.

His belief in the superiority of Greek civilisation was absolute. His most treasured possession was the *Iliad* of Homer, and he had the plays of the three great tragedians sent to him in Asia, together with dithyrambic poems and the history of Philistus. They were his favourite reading. He admired Aristotle as the leading exponent of Greek intellectual enquiry, and he had a natural yearning (*pothos*) for philosophical discussion and understanding. His mind was to some extent cast in the Aristotelian mould; for he too combined a wide-ranging curiosity with close observation and acute reasoning. His belief in the validity of the Greek outlook of his time was not modified by his acquaintance with Egyptian, Babylonian and Indian ideas. One mark of Greek civilisation was the vitality of the city, both in Europe and in Asia, and Alexander believed that the best way to spread Greek culture and civilisation was by founding cities throughout Asia. At the outset the leaders in these cities were the Macedonians and the Greek mercenary soldiers, who conducted the democratic form of self-government to which they were accustomed. At the same time the future leaders were being educated 'in Greek letters and in Macedonian weaponry' in the schools which Alexander established. The process was already well under way before Alexander died, as we see from a passage in Plutarch's *Moralia*: 'When Alexander was civilising Asia, the reading was Homer and the boys (*paides*) of the Persians, Susianians and Gedrosians used to chant the tragedies of Euripides and Sophocles ... and thanks to him Bactria and Caucasus revered the Greek gods'. Egypt has yielded a teaching manual of the late third century, which was designed to teach Greek as a foreign language and included selections from Homer and the tragedians. The excavations at Ai Khanoum in Afghanistan have revealed Greek temples, theatre and odeum (for music) alongside a very large Asian temple in the late fourth century (see Fig. 16). Alexander was the standard-bearer of Greek civilisation. His influence in education and so in civilisation has been profound, extending even into our own age.

Faith in the orthodox religion of Macedonia was deeply implanted in Alexander's mind. He sacrificed daily, even in his last illness, on behalf of himself and the Macedonians and on innumerable other occasions. He organised traditional festivals in honour of the gods in the most lavish fashion. He believed as literally as Pindar had done in the presence in our world of the Olympian gods, in the labours of heroes such as Heracles and the exploits of Achilles, both being his ancestors. The deities made their wishes or their warnings manifest to men through natural phenomena and through omens and oracles, which were interpreted and delivered by inspired men and women. It was an advantage of polytheism that the number of gods was not limited, and Alexander could see Zeus in the Libyan Ammon and in the Babylonian Belus, and Heracles in the Tyrian Melkart or the Indian Krishna. His special regard for Ammon was probably due to the prophetic oracles which he received at Siwah and which were evidently fulfilled *in toto* when Alexander reached the outer Ocean. He gave thanks time and again to 'the usual gods' (the twelve Olympians) for the salvation of himself and his army, and he must have thought that he owed his charmed life to them. Even in his last illness he believed that his prayers in the course of sacrifices would be heard and that he would live. For he died without arranging for the transition of power.

Of the personal qualities of Alexander the brilliance, the range and the quickness of his intellect are remarkable, especially in his conduct of warfare. At Gaugamela and at the Hydaspes he foresaw precisely the sequence of moves by his own units and the compulsion they would place on his enemies. As Ptolemy, himself a most able commander, observed of the first campaign, 'the result was as Alexander inferred that it would be', and after the last campaign 'not a one of the operations of war which Alexander undertook was beyond his capability' (*aporon*). In generalship no one has surpassed him. Arrian wrote that Alexander had 'the most wonderful power of grasping the right course when the situation was still in obscurity'. Thus he knew on his landing in Asia that he must set up his own Kingdom of Asia and obtain the willing cooperation of his subjects. Already at Sardis he began the training of boys who would become soldiers of that kingdom. The originality of his intellect was apparent in his development of the Indus, the Tigris and the Euphrates as waterways of commerce and his reorganisation of the irrigation of Mesopotamia. The boldness of his calculations was rewarded with success in many engagements and especially in the opening of navigation between the Indus Delta and the Persian Gulf.

His emotions were very strong. His love for his mother was such that one tear of hers would outweigh all the complaints of Antipater. He sent letters and gifts to her constantly, and he said that he would take her alone into his confidence on his return to Macedonia. His loyalty to the friends of his own generation was carried sometimes to a fault, and his passionate grief for Hephaestion was almost beyond reason. He loved his soldiers and they loved him; he and his veterans wept when they parted company; and he and they acknowledged that love in his last moments. When he killed Cleitus, his remorse was desperate. His compassion for the Theban Timoclea and for the family of Darius and his love for Roxane were deeply felt and led to actions which were probably unique in contemporary warfare.

As King of the Macedonians and as King of Asia he had different roles to fill. His way of life was on the same level as that of the Macedonians on campaigns and in leisure. As he said at Opis, his rations were the same as theirs and he shared all their dangers and hardships; and he enjoyed the same festivals and drinking parties as they did. He led them not by fiat but by persuasion, and a crucial element in that persuasion was that he should always tell them the truth, and they should know that he was telling them the truth. Thus he respected the constitutional rights of the Macedonians, and his reward was that he was generally able to convince them in their Assemblies that they should accept his policies. His role as King of Asia was almost the opposite. His court, like that of the Persian King of Kings, was the acme of luxury and extravagance. He gave audience in a huge pavilion which rested on fifty golden columns, and he himself sat on a golden chair, surrounded by so many richly-dressed guardsmen that 'no one dared approach him, such was the majesty associated with his person'. He accepted obeisance, and he ruled by fiat. The wealth at his command was beyond belief; for he had taken over the accumulated treasure of the Persian monarchy, and he received the fixed tribute which was paid by his subjects over a huge area. His expenditure was extraordinary by Greek standards, for instance on memorials commemorating Hephaestion, but it was in proportion to his wealth as King of Asia. The strength of his personality was such that he was able to keep the two roles separate in his mind and in his behaviour, and Ptolemy and Aristobulus were correct in seeing the real Alexander as Alexander the Macedonian.

Alexander combined his extraordinary practicality with a visionary, spiritual dimension which stemmed from his religious beliefs. As a member of the Temenid house he had a special affinity with his ancestors Heracles and Zeus, and he inherited the obligation to rule in a manner worthy of them and to benefit mankind. His vision went beyond Macedonia and the Greek Community. When he landed on Asian soil, his declaration, 'I accept Asia from the gods', and his prayer, that the Asians would accept him willingly as their king, were expressions of a mystical belief that the gods had set him a special task and would enable him to fulfil it. This spiritual dimension in his personality created in him the supreme confidence and the strength of will which overrode the resistance of the Macedonians to his concept of the Kingdom of Asia, and which convinced the Asians of the sincerity of his claim to treat them as equals and partners in the establishment of peace and prosperity. The power of his personality was all-pervading. It engaged the loyalty of Persian commanders and Indian rulers after defeat in battle and the loyalty of Asian troops at all levels in his service. It inspired *The Alexander Romance* in which Asian peoples adopted Alexander as their own king and incorporated his exploits into their own folk-lore. We owe to Plutarch, drawing probably on the words of Aristobulus, an insight into this spiritual dimension in Alexander.

Believing that he had come from the gods to be a governor and reconciler of the universe, and using force of arms against those whom he did not bring together by the light of reason, he harnessed all resources to one and the same end, mixing as it were in a loving-cup the lives, manners, marriages and customs of men. He ordered them all to regard the inhabited earth (*oikoumene*) as their fatherland and his armed forces as their stronghold and defence.

Appendix

The following articles support views expressed in the text, enumerated by chapters.

Abbreviations are as follows:

AG = N.G.L. Hammond, *Alexander the Great: King, Commander and Statesman* (1st edn. New Jersey 1980, London 1981; 2nd edn. Bristol 1989; 3rd edn. Bristol Classical Press 1994)

AJPh = *American Journal of Philology*

CQ = *Classical Quarterly*

GRBS = *Greek, Roman and Byzantine Studies*

JHS = *Journal of Hellenic Studies*

HG = N.G.L. Hammond, *A History of Greece to 322 B.C.* (Oxford, 1st edn. 1959, 2nd edn. 1967, 3rd edn. 1986)

HM = *History of Macedonia*, vol. 1 by N.G.L. Hammond (Oxford, 1972); vol. 2 by N.G.L. Hammond and G.T. Griffith (1979); vol. 3 by N.G.L. Hammond and F.W. Walbank (1988)

MS = N.G.L. Hammond, *The Macedonian State* (Oxford, 1989)

Sources = N.G.L. Hammond, *Sources for Alexander the Great* (Cambridge, 1993)

THA = N.G.L. Hammond, *Three Historians of Alexander* (Cambridge, 1983).

Chapter I. *Sources* 20 ff. (Bucephalus); *Historia* 39 (1990) 261 ff. (Pages).

Chapter II. *HG* 521-32 and 582-95 (Greek states); *HM* 1.59-123 (Upper Macedonia); *MS* 16-36 and 49-70 (Institutions).

Chapter III. *Philip of Macedon* (London, 1994); *HM* 3.471-9 (Greek Community).

Chapter IV. *GRBS* 19 (1978) 343 ff. (trial); *CQ* 38 (1988) 382 ff. (Calindoea); *JHS* 94 (1974) 66 ff. (Balkan campaign).

Chapter V. *Sources* 198-210 and *Historia* 37 (1988) 129 ff. (Sources of information); *AG*[3] 68 f. and *Antichthon* 20 (1986) 74 ff. (Crossing to Asia and Kingdom of Asia).

Chapter VI. *CQ* 30 (1990) 471 ff. (Europe); *Antichthon* 26 (1992) 30 ff. (Macedonian navy); *JHS* 100 (1980) 73 ff. (Granicus).

Chapter VII. *THA* 38 ff. (Miletus); 39 f. (Halicarnassus); 40 and 62 (Marmara).

Chapter VIII. *THA* 97, 120, 184 and *Sources* 47, 217 (Gordium); *AG*[1] 96-110 with Figs. 23-28, *Historia* 41 (1992) 395 ff., and *Prudentia* Suppl. Number, 1993, 77 ff. (Issus); *THA* 124 ff. and *Sources* 56 f. (Gaza).

Chapter IX. *Historia* 39 (1990) 275 ff. (King's Boys); *AG*[3] 132 ff. (Gaugamela); *CQ* 28 (1978) 336 ff. (Pursuit).

Chapter X. *CQ* 42 (1992) 358 ff. (Persepolis); *Historia* 39 (1990) 261 ff. (Pages); *JHS* 109 (1989) 63 ff. (Losses).

Chapter XI. *Sources* 74 f., 233 and *THA* 57, 101, 133 (Darius' death); *Historia* 39 (1990) 275 f. (Epigonoi).

Chapter XII. *Sources* 84 f., 180, 233 and *THA* 59 f., 103, 136 (Philotas).

Chapter XIII. *THA* 141 f. (Branchidae); *Ancient World* 22 (1991) 41 f. (Samarcand).

Chapter XIV. *Sources* 89 f., 180 f., 240 f. and *THA* 103 f., 146 (Cleitus); *Sources* 98 f., 245 f. and *THA* 148 (Pages' Conspiracy).

Chapter XV. *CQ* 30 (1980) 465 f. (Hipparchy); *Sources* 106 and *THA* 52 f., 104, 149 (Massaga); *Sources* 248 ff., 258, 314 (Nysa); AG^3 208 ff. (Hydaspes); *Sources* 258 ff. (Coenus' speech); *Sources* 114 f. and *THA* 64, 152 (altars).

Chapter XVI. *Sources* 115 ff., 268 ff. and *THA* 65, 105, 154 (city of Malli); *Sources* 124, 273 ff. and *THA* 68 ff., 155 f. (Oreitis and Gedrosia).

Chapter XVII. *CQ* 30 (1980) 469 f. and *JHS* 109 (1989) 64 ff. (Macedonians in Asia); *Historia* 39 (1990) 275 f. (Epigonoi); *Sources* 134, 287 ff. and *THA* 72 f., 106 f. (Opis mutiny).

Chapter XVIII. *CQ* 30 (1980) 471 f. and *JHS* 105 (1985) 303 f. (Olympias); *THA* 157 (Exiles); *Sources* 136 f. 294 ff., *THA* 73, 75, 107 f. (Hephaestion); *Sources* 140 f., 300 ff. and *THA* 74, 108 (Chaldaeans); *Historia* 37 (1988) 129 ff. and 40 (1991) 382 ff., and *AJPh* 110 (1989) 155 ff. (Journal).

Further articles are published in my *Collected Studies* IV (Hakkert, 1997).

Notes on illustrations

Figures

1. Cavalryman wearing helmet, cuirass and cloak practises with his double-headed lance. A thong attaches the back part of the lance to his wrist, so that if the lance breaks he can use the back part as a spear. He aims at a shield held by a negro groom. The pikemen are indicated by dots. The four front ranks have pikes at the ready, and the four rear ranks hold their pikes upright. See Plate 3(a).

7. The penteconter, about 120 feet long and 13 feet wide, had 25 oarsmen on each side, and the triaconter had 15 oarsmen on each side. Note the steering-sweep and the rigging for the sail, which is to be imagined.

9. See Plate 10 which is on the same scale.

15. The land-mass rested on the underworld and was surrounded by ocean. The length of the land-mass in proportion to its width was estimated by Aristotle to be 5 to 3.

16. Only parts of the site in north Afghanistan have been excavated. The public buildings and the fine residences were generally on the lower ground, and the bulk of the population lived on the higher ground east of the main street. The course of the fortification-wall is shown by the broken line.

Plates

1. (a) Roman gold medallions of Philip wearing the diadem and a cuirass similar to that of Alexander in Plate 3(b), and of Olympias, whose headband is suggestive of a diadem. Diameter 5.4 cm.

2. The Royal Hunt Fresco, 5.56 m long, on the façade of the Tomb of Philip. The central horseman is Alexander, and that on the viewer's right is Philip about to strike the lion with his spear. The page on the right wears the traditional dress which included the *kausia*. The marble door of the façade leads into the antechamber of the built-tomb.

3. (a) A phalanx of pikemen making a charge. The first five ranks present their pikes at the ready, and the other ranks hold their pikes aloft to intercept missiles.

(b) Alexander in action in the 'Alexander-Mosaic', protraying the Battle of Issus. He holds the lance at the point of balance in his right hand. His cuirass has shoulder-pieces like those of Plate 1.

4. (a) One of twenty silver vessels in Philip's Tomb. The Silenus was associated with the worship of Dionysus. Height 24.5 cm.

(b) The miniature head on a silver amphora from Philip's Tomb represents Heracles, wearing the lion-skin cap. His features may resemble those of Alexander. Height of amphora 36.4 cm.

5. (a) The gold larnax from Philip's Tomb contained his cremated remains, wrapped in purple cloth.

(b) The gold wreath of oak leaves and acorns in its present state weighs 714 g.

6. (a) The Mosaic of a Lion Hunt from a house in Pella is dated 'a little before 300'. The figures may represent Craterus coming to the aid of Alexander. 4.9 x 3.2 m.

(b) The Mosaic of Dionysus riding on a panther, from the same house, is evidence of the worship of Dionysus. 2.7 x 2.65 m.

7. The Boscoreale fresco is a reproduction of a Macedonian original. A youthful Alexander, wearing a *kausia* (as on Plate 2), plants his *sarissa* across the Hellespont into Asiatic soil, while Asia gazes at him with a look of acceptance. The Macedonian shield is the emblem of a defensive war, which is being waged against Persia. On the lefthand part of the fresco (not shown here) a philosopher, i.e. Aristotle, watches his pupil, Alexander. Other interpretations have been advanced.

8. (a) The photograph shows Lake Little Prespa and just below it the plain of Pelium. To the west of that plain is the plain of Koritsa.

(b) The knoll (right centre) is the site of Pelium, near which the river Eordaicus ran. Alexander's army on parade advanced towards the camera.

9. Alexander, wearing the lionskin cap, in action; from the 'Alexander-Sarcophagus', found at Sidon and dated c. 325-300.

10. The river Payas is visible low down on the right.

11. Paolo Veronese appreciated the remarkable charisma and the perfect manners of Alexander, which won the love of Sisigambis (and the loyalty of Taxiles and Porus).

12. The 'Alexander-Mosaic' (5.12 x 2.71 m) in the National Museum of Naples shows Alexander on the left and Darius on the right at the Battle of Issus. Behind Darius the pikes of the Macedonian infantrymen rise high in the air. This Roman mosaic copied a Macedonian fresco of the late fourth century BC.

13. The 'Porus Medallion' shows a cavalryman attacking Porus and his mahout, who are mounted on an armoured elephant. The Indian archer and the unarmoured elephant perhaps commemorate an elephant-hunt as in Arr. 4.30.8. Another interpretation is given by M.J. Price in *Studia Paulo Naster Oblata* I (Leuven, 1982) 75 ff.

14. The bronze crater from Derveni, dated c. 330, portrayed scenes with Dionysus, Ariadne, Maenads and Satyrs. Worship of Dionysus was associated with life after death for his followers. Height 90 cm.

15. A young Alexander, riding Bucephalus, is hastening to help Philip in the Royal Hunt Fresco (Plate 2 above). This contemporary portrait shows the piercing eyes, prominent nose and narrow face, which are features of the youthful Alexander in the Alexander-Mosaic (Plate 3 (b) above) and the Boscoreale painting (Plate 7 above). See M. Andronicos V Fig. 70 on p. 115.

16. A marble copy of a late fourth century original. This and similar portraits show a mature Alexander with deep-set eyes, a full face and hair brushed upwards from the forehead in the style called *anastole*. These features were probably idealised. This head is in the Pella Museum. Height 30 cm.

Chronological table of dates adopted in the text

336 BC	Spring	Vanguard invades Asia.
	October	Accession of A(lexander).
	Nov.-Dec.	A gains support of Amphictyonic Council; A appointed *hegemon* of Greek forces v. Persia.
335	Spring to Sept.	A campaigns in the Balkans; Memnon counter-attacks in Asia.
	Oct.	Fall of Thebes; arrangements for war v. Persia concluded with the Greek League Council.
	Nov./Dec.	Festivals at Dium and Aegeae.
334	May	A lands in Asia.
	May/June	Battle of the Granicus river.
	Summer	Capture of Miletus and isolation of Persians at Halicarnassus.
334/3	Winter	A conquers Caria, Lycia, Pamphylia and Phrygia.
333	March-June	Naval offensive by Memnon; he dies in June.
	April-July	A is based on Gordium and campaigns in adjacent areas.
	July-Sept.	Pharnabazus conducts his naval offensive.
	Aug.	A enters Cilicia; ill until late Sept.
	Oct.	Parmenio sent ahead to 'Syrian Gates'; A campaigns in Rough Cilicia.
	Nov.	Battle of Issus.
332	Jan.-July	Siege of Tyre; disintegration of the Persian fleet.
	Sept./Nov.	Siege of Gaza; Macedonia supreme at sea.
	Dec.	A enters Egypt.
331	Jan.	A founds Alexandria.
	Feb.	A visits Siwah.
	Spring	Festival at Memphis.
	Early summer	A in Phoenicia and Syria. Reinforcements leave Macedonia in July.
	Late July	A sets out for Thapsacus.
	Aug.-Sept.	A campaigns in northern Mesopotamia and southern Armenia.
	Sept. 20, p.m.	Eclipse of the moon.
	Oct. 1	Battle of Gaugamela; Agis raises a coalition in Greece.
	Dec.	A at Susa learns of Antipater's settlement of Thrace and of Agis laying siege to Megalopolis.
330	Jan.-March	A at Persepolis.

	March-April	A campaigns v. Mardi.
	April/May	Antipater defeats Agis.
	May	A leaves Persepolis.
	Summer	A campaigns in Tapuria, Hyrcania, Parthyaea and Areia. Pursuit and death of Darius in July.
	Oct.	Plot of Philotas.
	Nov.	A in Ariaspia.
	Late Dec.	Armies unite in Arachosia.
329	Jan.	A advances to Kabul and winters there.
	Spring	A crosses the Hindu Kush.
	Summer	A reorganises his cavalry. Crosses the Oxus. Captures Bessus. Advances to the Jaxartes.
	Autumn	Rising of Sogdians and Bactrians.
329/8	Winter	A at Bactra.
328	Spring/Summer	Campaigns in Sogdia and Bactria.
	Autumn	Death of Cleitus at Samarcand.
328/7	Winter	A at Nautaca. In late winter A captures the Sogdian Rock and the Rock of Chorienes.
327	Spring	Forces unite at Bactra. Plot of the Pages.
	Spring/Summer	Army crosses the Hindu Kush.
327/6	Winter	Hephaestion advances to the Indus. A campaigns in Swat, and late in the winter captures Aornus.
326	Spring	Forces unite at the Indus.
	May	Battle of the Hydaspes.
	Summer	A advances to and returns from the Hyphasis.
	Nov.	The fleet starts down the Hydaspes.
326/5	Winter	A campaigns against the Malli; is wounded in an assault on a Mallian city.
325	Feb.	Forces unite at the confluence of the Acesines and the Indus.
	Spring	The Brahman rebellion.
	June	Craterus starts for Carmania.
	July	Other forces unite at Pattala.
	Late Aug.	A starts for Carmania.
	Oct.	Nearchus starts on his voyage. A enters Gedrosia.
	Dec.	A meets Craterus in Carmania.
324	Jan.	A meets Nearchus in Carmania; A advances into Persis.
	Feb.	A's army and Nearchus' fleet meet on the Pasitigris.
	July/Aug.	Recall of exiles announced at Olympic Games.
	Late summer	Mutiny at Opis. Veterans set off with Craterus for Cilicia and Macedonia.
	Autumn	A at Ecbatana; Hephaestion dies there. Perdiccas takes main army to Babylon.
324/3	Winter	A campaigns v Cossaei.
323	April/May	A joins Perdiccas at Babylon.
	May	Final preparations for summer campaign against the Arabs.
	End of May	A falls ill.
	June 10	A dies.

Index

A stands for Alexander and D for Darius III. Place-names include their inhabitants, 'Sparta' for instance including Spartans.

Abii: 144
Abisares: 163 f., 169
Abreas: 173
Abulites: 112, 181
Abydus: 65
Acarnania: 35, 194
Acesines R.: 167, 169, 171 f., 208
Achaea: 17, 19, 64, 113
Achaemenidae, Persian royal house: 135
Achilles: 7, 11, 62, 64, 96, 199
Acrocorinth: 20
Admetus, officer: 95
Aeane: 56
Aegae, in Cilicia: 100, 112
Aegeae, in Macedonia: 3, 25, 50 f., 56, 150, 207
Aegean Islands: 99, 171, 194, 196
Aegean Sea: 75, 83, 85 f., 94, 97, 116, 125
Aelian: 42
Aëropus II, sons of: 27, 29; grandson of: 80
Aeschines: 117 f.
Aethiopia: 100, 103, 122
Aetolia: 44, 48, 192, 194
Afghanistan: 129-31, 135, 199, 205
Africa: 195
Agathon: 184
Agesilaus: 73
Agis III of Sparta: 94, 113, 117, 192, 207 f.
Agrianians: 36, at Pelium, 39; 45, 52, 60, 66, 81; enter Cilicia, 85; at Gaugamela 108; 114, 129, 131, 145 f.; at the Hydaspes, 166; 171 f.; in Oreitis, 176

Ai Khanoum: 158 f., 199
Alani: 43
Albania: 12
Aleuadae: 30
Alexander cities: 118, 170, 185, 187, 199
Alexander Letters: see Letters
Alexander I of Molossia: 22, 25, 191
Alexander III of Macedonia: 22
Alexander IV: 22, 55
Alexander V: 22
Alexander Lyncestes: 27, 29, 60, 79 f., 132; executed, 134
Alexander Mosaic: 205 f.
Alexander Romance: 187, 201
Alexander Sarcophagus: 206
Alexandria Eschate: 144 f.
Alexandria-ad-Issum: 100
Alexandria-in-Areia: 131
Alexandria-in-Caucaso: 136
Alexandria-in-Egypt: 43; founded, 100; 101 f., 112, 196, 207
Alexandria-in-Margiane: 153
Alexandria-in-Opiene: 173
Alexandropolis: 6
Alinda: 75
Amanus Mt.: 87
Ambracia: 20
Amisus: 83
Ammon: 99, 102, 151, 171, 175, 189, 200
Amphaxitis: 60 f.
Amphilochus: 100
Amphictyonic Council: 21, 30 f., 207
Amphictyonic League: 17 ff.
Amphipolis: 15, 32, 60 f., 195
Amphissa: 19

Amphitrite: 171
Amu-Darya R.: 140
Amyntas II of Macedonia: 28
Amyntas III of Macedonia: 4, 21, 28, 30
Amyntas IV of Macedonia: 15, 17, 22, 24, 27, 31
Amyntas, son of Antiochus, deserter: 79, 90
Amyntas, son of Nicolaus, satrap of Bactria: 155, 159
Anatolia: 77, 80 f., 123
Anaximenes: 55
Andromache: 64 f.
Andromenes: 133
Andronicos, M.: 3, 195
Andros: 94
Ankara: 81
Antalcidas, Peace of: 73
'Anticipation': 133
Antigonus Monophthalmus: 81, 90
Antilebanon: 95
Antipater: 4, 27, 32, 51; Deputy-Hegemon, 59 f., 113, 117; 156, 159; 85, 122 f., 156, 159; and Olympias, 191 ff.; 200, 207 f.
Antipater, son of Cassander: 22
Aornus: 141; Rock of, 162 f., 208
Aphytis: 102
Apis: 99
Apollo: 135; Averter of Evil, 177; of Didyma, 103, 141 f.; of Delos, 195; of Delphi, 7, 9, 17 ff., 195
Apollodorus: 112
Apollonia, in Mygdonia: 18, 31 f.
Apollophanes: 176
appeal, right of: 181
Arabia: 100, 102, 125, 127, 133; circumnavigation of, 178 f.; planned invasion of, 184, 179, 184, 188, 196 ff., 208
Arabitae: 176
Arachosia: 127, 133, 135-8, 173 f., 208
Aradus: 92
Aramaic: 92
Araxes R.: 114
Arbela: 109
Arcadia: 46, 48, 113, 116 f.
Archelaus, king of Macedonia: 28, 50, 55
Archers, unspecified: 37, 39; at

Thebes, 45; at the Granicus, 66; 114, 129, 131, 166, 171 f., 174, 176; Cretan, 87, 109; 'Macedonian' 108
Areia: 130 f., 135, 137 f., 140 f., 143, 149, 153, 208
Areopagus Council: 193, 195
Arethusa: 100
Argeadae: 60
Argos in the Peloponnese: 46, 72
Ariadne: 206
Ariaspi: 135 f., 208
Arigaeum: 162
Aristander, the seer: 53, 79, at Tyre, 94, 96; at Alexandria-in-Egypt, 100; 105; at the Jaxartes R., 145; re Cleitus, 152
Aristobulus: as a source, 23 f., 42-45; on Timoclea, 47, 52 f.; at the Hellespont, 68 f.; 75, 80; at Gordium, 83; 85, 91; at Gaza, 98; at Siwah, 102; 115, 121; re Philotas, 134; 140, 142; re Cleitus, 151 f., 154-7; 162, 181, 184, 190, 195; on entry to Babylon, 197; 201
Aristogeiton: 113
Aristotle: 5 f., 11, 28; on the Nile, 103; on 'Asia', 121 f.; on the Jaxartes R., 144; 157; on 'India', 161, 167; 176, 184, 199, 205 f.
Armenia: 105, 112, 116, 119, 207
Arrhidaeus: 6, 21 f., 24, 80
Arsaces: 141, 149
Arses: 91
Arsites: 71
Artabazus: 120, 123, 135, 141
Artacoana: 129, 136
Artaxerxes Ochus: 119, 123, 130, 188
Artemis: 73, 195
Arybbas, of Molossia: 4
Asander: 72
Asclepiodorus: 112
Asclepius: 86
'Asia': 121, 206
Asia: 111, 168, 186, 201; Gates of, 66
Asia, Greek cities in: 19, 171, 194 f.; limits of, 102, 127, 144, 149
Asia, king of: 73, 79, 82 f., 91 f., 101; acclaimed, 110; 112, 114, 119;

meaning of, 121 f.; 135, 141, 143 f., 161, 167, 181, 184-8, 190, 195 f., 200 f.
Asia, kingdom of: 73, 97, 100, 116, 119, 127, 132; claimed by Bessus, 130; 136, 203
Asia Minor: 73, 77, 83, 90, 136
Asian ceremonial: 134
Asian policy: 134, 141, 143 f., 159; triumphs, 190
Aspasia: 162
Aspendus: 78
Assacene: 162 f.
Assembly of Macedones: 7, 12, 28 f., 32; re Aspendus 79 f.; 123, 127, 132, 134, 141, 156 f., 167, 188 ff., 190, 194, 201
Assyria: 176
Astaspes: 181
Atarrhias: 134
Atheas: 21 f.
Athena: 64, 161; Alcidemus, 92, 195; of Athens, 69; of Lindus, 110; of Troy, 52, 72, 92, 173, 195
Athena of Pydna: 52
Athens: 9 ff., 15, 17; at Chaeronea, 19 f.; 25, 30, 35 f.; and Thebes, 44 ff.; courted by A, 48 ff.; 60, 75; her fleet, 85; loyal to the Greek Community, 85, 115-20; 99; state-ship of, 105; 122; 125; Library provided by A at, 128; People's Court at, 133; 192; and Samos, 194; honours A, 194
Atropates: 153, 181, 184, 186
Attalus: 21 ff., 26 ff., 31
Attic dialect: 100
Audata: 15, 22
Augustus: 72
Autariatae: 24, 26
Autophradates: 153
Azerbaijan: 43
Azov, Sea of: 122, 144

Ba'al: 92, 111, 197
Babylon: 111, 116, 125, 131, 153, 184, 208
Babylonia: 111 f., 119, 178 f., 186, 194 ff.
Bactra: 130 f., 141, 146, 150, 155, 159, 162, 175, 199, 208
Bactria: 68, 108 f., 119, 127, 129, 131, 136, 140-3; risings in, 144 f., 149 f., 153, 155, 181, 185, 208
baggage-train: 34, 52, 77, 81, 86, 115, 119, 130, 139 f.; lightened, 161; 164, 174
Bahce Pass: 87
Balkans: 12, 35, 41 f., 52, 54; forces at the Hellespont, 60; 62, 74, 81, 86 f., 112, 117, 164, 187; campaign in, 203
Balkh: 129, 144
Bardylis: 11, 15, 36
Barsaentes: 121, 132
Barsine: 22, 154
Baryaxes: 184
Batis: 96
Bazira: 162
Beas R.: 168
Begram: 136
Belus: 111, 200
bematistae: 122
'Benefactors': 135
Bessus: 120; 'King of Asia', 130 f.; 135, 137, 140, 142 f., 149, 208
Bhir: 164
Bisthanes: 119
Black Sea: 83, 97, 100, 122, 125, 127, 149, 184, 186
Bodrum: 75; *see* Halicarnassus
Bodyguards: 21, 25 f., 31, 37, 39, 43, 53, 134, 150 f., 173, 198
Boeotia: 17 f., 44 f.; League, 45
Bolbe L.: 32
Boscoreale Fresco: 65, 206
Bosnia: 24
Bosporus: 19, 36
Bottia: 100
Bottiaeans: 18
bounty: 79, 112, 118 f.
Brahmans: 172, 174, 208
Branchidae: 141 f., 204
Bucephala: 167
Bucephalus: 1-3, 6 f., 41, 167, 198 f., 203, 206
Byblus: 92
Byzantine Empire: 97

Cabiri: 4
Cadiz: 122
Cadmea: 45
Caïcus R.: 77
Calas: 65, 72

Calindoea: 31 f., 51, 203
Callipolis: 94
Callisthenes: 64, 78, 90; at Siwah, 102 f.; 111, 114, 142, 156 f.
Camacaea: 31
Cambyses: 99
Cambunia Mt.: 44
Cappadocia: 83, 90, 106
Caranus: 135, 152
Caria: 75, 78 f., 81 f., 86, 185, 207
Carmania: 115 f., 127, 174, 177, 181, 184, 208
Carthage: 92, 95, 195
Caspian Sea: 125, 127, 144, 149, 184
catapults: 39, 75 f., 94, 96, 145, 155, 162, 172
Caucasus Mt.: 127, 136, 161
Caunus: 86
Caÿster R.: 77
Cebalinus: 132
Celaenae: 81
Cephissus R.: 19
Chaeronea, Battle of: 19, 21, 48, 68, 116
Chalcidice: 102
Chalcidian League: 17
Chaldaeans: 178, 197, 204
Chares: 157
Charias: 76
Charidemus: 48
chariots: 90, 106 ff., 166
Chenab R.: 167
Chermah-i-Ali R.: 127
Chersonese, Thracian: 19
Chiliarches: 185
Chinese: 159
Chios: 83, 94, 99, 157
Choaspes R.: 169
Choerilus: 55
Chorasmia: 149
Chorienes: 142; Rock of, 154f., 163, 208
Cicero: 46 f.
Cilicia: 77, 83, 85 f.; Gates of, 85; 120, 125, 191, 195, 207 f.; Tracheia, 86
Cleander: 184
Cleitarchus: 46-50; defined, 48; 53, 62; re Halicarnassus, 75; 91; re Gaza, 96; 102; re Persepolis, 115; re Branchidae, 142
Cleitus: 36 f., 39, 51; at the

Granicus, 67; 120, 134; quarrels with A, 150 f.; 157, 200, 204, 208
Cleomenes: 102, 196
Cleopatra, daughter of Philip: 22, 25, 191 f.
Cleopatra, wife of Philip: 21-4, 31, 41
Coenus: 150, 153; at the Hydaspes, 166; 168, 184, 204
coinage: 36; (Thracian), 53, 55; (in 334) 91 f.; 167; 187, 206
Colophon: 46
Commandoes: 113
Common Peace: 46, 91, 99, 101, 111, 116 f.; Council of, 20 f., 59, 117
Companion Cavalry: 87, 108 f.; reorganised, 113; 120, 123; role in Bactria, 129; two commanders of, 132 f.; 135, 146, 150, 152; adulteration of, 159, 187; 164; at the Hydaspes, 166 f.; 171 f., 185 ff., 189, 196
Companions: 1, 12 f., 15, 19, 24, 32, 34; at Pelium, 36 f.; 51 f., 55, 60, 62, 64; at the Granicus, 66; 86, 92; consulted at Tyre, 94 f.; 114, 125, 134, 161; in reorganised cavalry, 164; 189
Cophen R.: 169
Corcyra: 10
Cossaea: 184 f., 197, 208
Corinth: 19, 30 f., 155
Cos: 94
Craterus: 66, 87, 114, 146; defeats Spitamenes, 150; 155, 162; at the Hydaspes, 166; 171-4, 177, 184, 192, 206, 208
Crete: 94, 97, 193
Croton: 111
Ctesiphon: 118
cupido: 103
Cyclades: 85
Cydnus R.: 85
Cyprus: 73, 90, 92, 94 f.; kings of, 103; 141, 171, 195 f.
Cynna: 22, 31
Cyrene: 100
Cyropolis: 145
Cyrrus: 195
Cyrus the Great: 116, 135; in Gedrosia, 176; 199; Tomb of, 44
Cyzicus: 65

Dahae: 127, 140, 153, 155, 166
daimon: 151
Damascus: 91
Dardania: 11, 15, 37, 59
Darius I: 115
Darius III Codomannus: 50, 68, 75, 77; and Alexander Lyncestes, 79 f.; 85 ff.; at Issus, 89 f.; offer by, 91; at Gaugamela, 105 f.; 119; flight of, 120 f. 139; death of, 121; 123; and Bessus, 142 f.; 154, 159, 166 ff., 204, 206, 208
Darius, family of: 90 f., 112 f., 116; A's plans for, 121; 143, 154, 188, 200.
Dascylium: 72
Dataphernes: 142 ff., 153
debts: of A, 52; of Macedonian soldiers, 185
deification and divine honours: for Philip, 25; for Olympias, 192; for Hephaestion and for A, 194; 196
Delos: 195
Delphi: 9 f., 17, 21, 105, 141, 195
Demades: 117
Demaratus: 23, 67, 150
Demeter: 100
Demetrius, Bodyguard: 133 f.
Demosthenes: 25; and Attalus, 31; and Thebes, 46; 49, 117; crowned, 118; and Harpalus, 193; 195
Derveni: 55, 206
Diades: 75, 94
Didyma: 103, 141 f.
dimachae: 162
Dimnus: 132
Dinar: 81
Diogenes: 6, 31
Dionysius of Syracuse: 5
Dionysus: 4, 10, 56, 60; re Cleitus, 152; in India, 163; theatre of at Athens, 192; 199, 205
Dium: 50, 195, 207
Diyllus: 9 f., 17, 21, 141
Dobruja: 19, 21
dockyards: 173 f., 179, 195
Dodona: 102, 141, 195
Don R. 121, 144
Drapsacus: 140
Drangiana: 132 f., 135, 153, 174, 184

Ecbatana: 119-22, 125, 130, 133, 135, 143, 196, 208
eclipse: 105
Egypt: 73, 90, 92, 94, 96 f.; A in, 99 ff., 116, 122 f., 125, 130, 134, 171, 178, 195 ff., 199, 207
eirenophylakes: 10, 52
Elaeus: 62 ff.
El Alamein: 112
Elburz Mt.: 125
elephants: 106, 127, 162 f., 164-9, 171-5, 206
Elimeotis: 15
Elis: 46, 48, 81, 113, 116 f.
Emathia city: 31
Eordaïcus R.: 206
Ephesus: 72 ff., 74, 100
Epigonoi: 130, 188, 204
Epimenes: 156
Epirote Alliance: 191
Epirus: 11, 59, 195
Erigyius: 23, 135, 152
Erythrae: 103, 122
Etruscans: 195
Euacae: 123, 129
Euboea: 119
Eukleia: 3
Eulaeus R.: 178
Euphraeus: 55
Euphrates R.: 100, 105, 119, 125, 143, 175, 178 f., 197, 200
Euripides: 55, 199; *Bacchae*, 4
Europe: 122, 129, 135, 144, 186, 199, 203
Eurydice: grand-daughter of Philip II, 22; grand-mother of A, 3 f.; wife of Philip II, 23 f., 28, 55 f.
Eurymedon R.: 78
Exiles decree: 193 f., 204

Farah: 132
fleets: Cyprian, 105; Greek, 61-4, 74, 81; recalled, 85; 97, 105; Macedonian, 51 f., 85, 94, 97, 105, 203; Persian, 52, 73 ff., 81, 86, 92, 94 f., 105
Foot-Companions: 40, 189
Friends: 12 f., 25, 31, 40, 51, 56, 79 f., 114, 123, 125, 132 ff., 152, 197 f.

Gadara: 100

Ganges R.: 168

Gaugamela, Battle of: 58, 106-9, 111, 113, 119, 122, 127, 134, 181, 184, 200, 203, 206

Gaza: 96, 103, 203, 207

Gedrosia: 127, 135, 176 f., 199, 204, 208

Gerasa: 100, 105

Gerra: 178

Getae: 21, 34 f., 192

Glaucias: 36 f., 50 f.

Glausae: 169

Gordium: 81, 83, 122, 203, 207

Grammus Mt.: 44

Granicus R., Battle of the: 65 f., 72, 77, 99, 203, 206

Greek Community, or 'The Greeks': set up by Philip, 20 f.; addressed by A, 30 f.; 36, 45, 47; re Thebes, 49 f.; 52; forces v. Persia, 60 ff.; 74, 85, 97, 116, 118; war with Persia ends, 119 f.; 122 f., 125, 136, 203; Council of, 48, 99, 207

Greek language: spread of, 32, 35, 100 f., 113, 119, 199

Gryneum: 65, 72, 150

Guard: Companion Cavalry, 89, 188; Hypaspist, 108, 189; Infantry, 87, 89, 113; Persian Cavalry, 89 f., 106, 123, 188; Persian Infantry, 106, 196

Guraei: 162

Gymnasion: 101

Haemus Mt.: 34

Halicarnassus: 75 ff., 85 f., 94, 203, 207

Hamadan: 119

hamartia: 151

Harmatelia: 174

Harmodius: 113

Harmozia: 178

Harpalus: 2, 7, 23, 120, 152; at Athens, 193; 195

Hecatompylus: 122, 127

Hector: 96

Hegemon: 91, 97, 99, 105, 117, 119, 192, 207

Hellanicus: 55

Hellespont: 19, 36, 59; A at, 62 ff.; 76, 83, threatened by Persia, 85 f.; 94, 112, 149, 181

hemioliai: 176

Hephaestion: 2, 64, 91, 134, 150; commands half of the Companion Cavalry, 152; 163, 167, 171 f.; death of, 185; 194, 196 f., 200 f., 208

Hera: 10

Heracles: 55, 62; altar to, in the Troad, 64, 90, 92; at Tyre, 94 ff.; 102, 151; and Aornus, 162 f.; worship of, in Carmania, 168; 171, 177, 199 f.; Patroüs, 6 f., 11; Pillars of, 122; in India, 163; 168, 178, 195 f., 205

Heracles, son of A: 22, 154

Herat: 131

Herculaneum, 56

Hermolaus: 155 ff.

Hermus R.: 137

Herodotus: 12, 55, 75

heroic honours: 194, 196

Hieronymus: 194

Himalayas: 169

Hindu Kush: 122, 127, 136, 139 f., 144, 159, 161, 208

Hipparchus: 159, 164

hipparchy: 77, 159, 164; Royal, 196, 204

Hippocrates: 55

Homer: 3, 5, 40, 64, 101, 199

Hormuz: 178

Hydaspes R.: 102; Battle of, 164 f.; 169, 171 f., 175, 200, 204, 208

Hydraotes R.: 167, 169, 172

Hyparna: 78

Hypaspists: 28, 37, 39 f., 45, 52; at the Granicus, 66 f.; 85, 87; at Tyre, 95 f.; 108 f.; 112 f. 123, 132; in the Cleitus episode, 150 f.; 166, 171; at the city of the Malli, 173; 189; see under 'Guard'

Hyphasis R.: 168 f., 208

Hyrcania: 120, 123, 127, 184, 208

Hyrcanian Sea (Caspian Sea): 125

Illyria: 11 f., 15, 24, 32 f., 36, 44, 50; with A, 60; at Gaugamela, 109; 129

'India': 122, 136; A enters, 164; 175, 181, 184 f.

India: 106, 109; Viceroy of, 112; 122, 127, 132, 136 f., 143, 149, 178,

181, 199; cavalry, 175; infantry, 176

Indian Ocean: 186

Indus R.: 122, 159, 161, 163, 171 f., 176, 200; Delta, 102, 174, 186, 200, 208

Iraq: 197

irrigation: 179, 186, 200

Isis: 100

Iskenderun: 86

Issus: campaign of 86-90; 92, 108, 203, 205 ff.

Ister: 35

Isthmus: 116

Italy: 191, 195

javelin-men: Thracian, 81, 87, 108 f., 131; mounted Persian, 129, 131

Jaxartes R.: 127, 144 f., 149, 164, 208

Jews: 105

Jonah, Pillar of: 86 f., 123

Journal: nature of, 42 f.; 48, 65 f.; Battle of Granicus, 69; 72; Halicarnassus, 75 ff.; 79 f., 91 f.; pursuit of Darius, 121; 149, 172; A's last illness, 198; 204

Kabul: 136, 139 f.; R., 161, 169, 208

Kalat-i-Ghilzai: 135

Kandahar: 135, 139 f.

Kaoshan Pass: 161

Kashmir: 161, 163, 169

Kasht-i-Kavir desert: 125

Katerini: 56

katoikiai: 137

kausia: 65, 205 f.

Kavir: 125

kerkouroi: 176

Kerman: 125

Khawak Pass: 140

Khodjend: 144

Khyber Pass: 163, 169

King's Boys: 101, 203

King's Eyes: 71

King's Men: defined, 12 f.; in assembly, 16; acclaim A, 27; 29, 32, 40, 60, 81, 163, 174 f.,

Kinsmen: 123, 189 f.

Koçabas R.: 206

koine: 100

koinon: 11, 20

Koritsa: 37, 206

Kosovo: 11, 36

Krishna: 200

Kunduz: 140

Kuwait: 179

Lade: 74

Lahore: 167

Lancers: 66, 87, 108 f., 113 f.

Laomedon: 23

Larissa: 17, 30

Lebanon: 95

Leocrates: 118

Leonidas, teacher of A: 5

Leonnatus: 26, 90, 152, 154, 173

Lesbos: 88

Letters of A: 48, 78, 102, 123, 156; to Antipater, 123

Library at Athens: endowed by A, 128

'Libya': 102

Libya: 100, 121, 127, 178, 195

Lindus: 110, 122

Lion Hunt Mosaic: 206

Longinus: 46 f.

Loudias L.: 56

Lucania: 195

Lut desert: 125

Lycia: 77 f., 82; troops from, 78, 130; 95, 123, 152, 207

Lycurgus: 192

Lydia: 72; troops from, 72, 129; 82, 86, 90, 123, 185

Lyncus: 4, 11, 15, 80

Lysimachus: 195

Lysippus: 68

'Macedones': citizenship of, 12 f., 15, 187

Macedonian Guard: *see* Guard

Macetia C.: 178

Maedi: 6

Maenads: 206

Maeotis L.: 122, 144

Magarsus: 100 f.

Magi: 190

Makran: 135

malaria tropica: 198

Malli: 172 f., 204, 208

Mallus: 86, 100 f.

Mand R.: 178

Mantinea: 9

manual for teaching Greek: 101

Mardia: 115, 123, 153, 208
Mareotis L.: 99
Mariner's guide: 177 f.
Marmara, Sea of: 36, 203
marriages, mixed: 188
Marsyas Macedon: defined, 1 f.; 28, 41
Massaga: 162, 204
Massagetae: 149 f., 153, 155
Mazaeus: 105, 111, 123, 181
Meda: 21 f.
Media: 91, 113, 117, 119, 121 ff., 125; dress, 125, 185, 188; 143 f., 153, 184 ff.
Mediterranean Sea: 96, 90, 92, 94, 97, 99 f., 122
Megalopolis: 207
Megara: 19
Melkart: 200
Memnon, officer: 113
Memnon, of Rhodes: 25, 71, 75 ff., 83, 85, 154, 207
Memphis: 97, 207
Menidas: 185
mercenaries: Arab, 96; Greek, 12, 17 f., 25: Theban, 48; 52, 54, 60, 62, 68, 74, 76 ff., 81, 83, 85 ff., 89 f., 102 f., 106, 108 f., 112 f., 117; Thracian, 120; 127, 129 f., 133, 135 f., 171, 176, 179, 185 ff., 193, 199; Darius' last, 125; settled in *katoikiai*, 137; Indian, 162
Mersa Matruh: 102
Merv: 153
Meshed: 130
Mesopotamia: 92, 105, 200, 207
Mesta R.: 17
Metohija: 11
Midas: 83
Mieza: 5
Miletus: 74 f., 100, 141 ff., 203, 207
militia: 12; Thracian, 35; 51, 59, 113, 185, 198
minerals: 12, 36, 52
Mithridates: 67
Mithrines: 72, 112
Molossia: 4, 11, 17, 23, 25, 65, 96, 191, 195
Muses: 86
Musicanus: 173 f., 186
Mycale C.: 74
Myndus: 75

Myriandrus: 81 f.
Mytilene: 83, 85, 99

Nautaca: 153, 208
Nearchus: 23, 152, 171, 175-8, 208
Neoptolemus, officer: 96
Neoptolemus, son of Achilles: 11, 64
Neoptolemus II, of Molossia: 22
Nereus: 87
Nereids: 87, 171
Nestus R.: 17, 60
Nicaea: 163
Nicesipolis: 17, 22
Nicias: 72
Nike: 92, 167
Nikisiani: 55
Nile R.: 97 f., 103, 121, 167
Nysa: 163, 204

oath of loyalty: to A, 40, 131, 198; to the Greek Community, 45
Ocean: 121, 125, 127, 161, 167 f., 171, 175 f., 184, 200
Ochus, son of D: 116
Odeum: 100
Odrysae: 12, 21, 109, 192
Oeniadae: 192, 194
Oesyme: 31
oikoumene: 202
Olympian gods: 168, 195, 199 f.
Olympias: 3 f., 6, 17, 22-5, 55 f., 60, 64, 102, 191 f., 193, 200, 204; medallion of, 205,
Olympic Festival: 193: Games, 2, 208
Olympus Mt.: 7
Olynthus: 17
Oman; 178
On the treaty with A: 192
Onchestus in Boeotia: 44
Onesicritus: 64, 171
Onomarchus: 17
Opis: 178, 189, 200, 204, 208
Orchomenus in Boeotia: 46 ff., 50
Oreitis: 176, 178, 204
Orestes, king of Macedonia: 24
Orobatis: 163
Orontes R.: 100
Orontobates: 75 f., 86
Oropus: 9
Orpheus: 4, 53
Orxines: 181
Oxicanus: 174

Oxus R.: 140 f., 158, 208
Oxyartes, father of Roxane: 154 f., 181; son of Abulites, 181
Oxydates: 153
Oxydracae: 172 f.

Paeonia: 11 f., 15, 32, 36, 66, 87, 108, 113
Pages: 1, 5 f., 13, 21, 27 f., 40, 56, 59, 101; join A, 114; 132; conspiracy of, 155 ff., 204, 208; 159, 198 f., 203
Pakistan: 106, 161, 186
Pamphylia; 77, 207
Paphlagonia: 83, 90
Paraetacene: 119, 181
Parmenio: 25, 36, 51, 60, 62, 66, 71 f., 74, 77, 79 ff., 85-8, 100, 106, 109, 115, 120, 123, 125, 130, 132 f., 143, 154, 206 f.
Parnassus Mt. in Asia: 127
Parapamisadae: 181
Parapamisus: 122, 136, 161
Parthyaea: 120, 122, 125, 127, 129 f., 135, 149, 153, 159, 181, 208
Parysatis: 22
Pasargadae: 44, 115 f.
Pasitigris R.: 178, 208
Patroclus: 64
Pattala: 174, 208
Pausanias, assassin; 26-30
Pausanias, officer: 72
Payas R.: 86 f., 89, 206
Peithon: 174
Pelagonia: 11, 15
Pelinna: 44
Pelium: 36-9, 50, 138, 206
Pella, in Macedonia: 4, 18, 56, 196, 206; Pellaios, 12
Pella, in Palestine: 100
Peloponnese: 76 f., 90, 94, 97, 105, 111 ff., 115, 117; League, 117
Pelusium: 96, 102
penteconter: 61, 205
People's Court: 133
Perdiccas III: 11, 24, 28, 52 f.
Perdiccas, Bodyguard: 26, 45 f., 150, 154, 163, 173, 196, 208
Perge: 78 ff.
Perinthus: 91
Peripatetic School: 157
Persephone: 4

Persepolis: 114; Palace at, 115; 117, 120 f., 125, 203, 207 f.
Perseus: 102, 116
Persia: 6, 11, 18-21, 30 f., 46, 48 ff., 52, 66, 74; at Issus, 90; 141-3, 161, 171, 175, 178, 184, 186 f., 189 f., 199, 201.
Persian ceremonial: 123, 125, 188; Gates, 114; Wars of the fifth century, 91, 111
Persian Gulf: 178, 186, 200; *see* Red Sea
Persis: 113, 115, 119, 208
Peucelaotis: 163
Peucestas: 173, 184 f.
pezhetairoi: 13, 40
Pharaoh: 99, 102
Pharasmanes: 149, 161
Pharnabazus: 85 f., 94, 207
Pharos: 196
Phaselis: 78
Pherae: 17
Phila: 15, 22
Philinna: 17, 22
Philinus: 42
Philip II: 1-6, 13-16; killed, 24 ff.; 28 f., 56, 77, 91, 116, 138, 142, 151 f., 157, 189, 192, 195, 198 f.; coinage of, 53; tomb of, 54-8, 205; medallion of, 205 f.
Philip III Arrhidaeus: 22
Philip IV: 22
Philip, doctor: 85
Philippus: 163 f., 169, 171, 173, 185
Philippeioi coins: 53 f.
Philippeum: 25
Philippi: 6, 17, 32, 51
Philippopolis: 7
Philippoupolis (Plovdiv): 35
Philistus: 199
Philonicus: 1 f.
Philotas: 36 f., 132 f., 204, 208
Phocion: 117, 192
Phocis: 9 f., 17 ff., 44 f.
Phoenicia: 73 f., 94 f., 97, 103 f., 171, 178 f., 195 f., 207
Phrada: 132
Phrygia, Greater: 77, 79, 81, 90, 207; Hellespontine, 71 f., 77, 83
Pinarus R.: 86, 92
Pindar: 101, 162
Pindus Mt.: 44

'Pirates': 97
Pisidia: 78, 80 ff.
Pitane: 65
Pixodarus: 24
Plataea: 43, 46, 48, 111
Plato: 5, 10, 28; *Laws*, 10
Pleurias: 24
Pluto: 4
Pollacopas: 179, 197
polygamy: 4, 23
Polytimetus R.: 146
Polyidus: 76
Pompeii: 56
Port Said: 96
Porus: 164-7, 169, 171, 206;
    medallion, 206
Porus, son of Porus: 166
Poseidon: 64, 87, 175, 177
pothos: 83, 100, 199
Priam: 64
Prespa L., Little: 39, 206
Priene: 100 f.
Prometheus: 136 f.
Prophthasia: 133
proskynesis: 125, 157
prostasia: 59, 191
Protesilaus: 62
Ptolemy, guardian of Alexander II:
    28
Ptolemy, officer: friend of A, 23 f.;
    43; at the Hellespont, 64; at the
    Rock of Chorienes, 154; 156;
    praises A, 200; as a source used
    by Arrian, 34; had access to the
    Journal, 42 f.; as a source, 43,
    45 f., 64 ff., 69, 72, 75, 77, 79, 91;
    re Gaza, 96; at Siwah, 102, 115,
    121; re Philotas; 133 f., 142 f.,
    145, 149 f., 151 f., 154; re
    Conspiracy of the Pages, 156 f.;
    162, 172; used by Polyaenus, 175;
    181, 184; re Opis, 189 f.; 195 ff.,
    200 f.
Pulvar R.: 114
Pura: 177
Pydna: 52; Battle of, 116
Pythion: 31

quinquereme: 178
Quintilian: 46 f.

Ra: 99, 102

'Red Sea' (Persian Gulf): 100, 176,
    178, 186
reinforcements: 77, 81, 103 f., 112 ff.,
    123, 129, 153, 171, 185, losses, 203
Rhodes: 95, 122, 154
Rhoesaces: 67
Rhoeteum: 65
roads: Royal, 77; 78, 105, 120,
    130 ff., 123, 129, 139, 185, 187
Rogozen: 55
Rohri: 173
Roman Empire: 97
Rome: 116
Rommel: 112
Roxane: 22, 154, 181, 188, 200
Royal Hunt Fresco: 155, 205 f.
Russia: 19, 192

Sacae: 106, 127, 144, 146, 149
Sacred Band of Thebes: 27, 68, 198
Sacred Wars: 7, 9, 11, 17, 19
Sagalassus: 80
Samarcand: 144 ff., 150 f., 204, 208
Samaria: 105
Sambus: 174
Samos: 74, 194
Samothrace: 4, 85
Sangala: 167, 169, 175
Sardis: 72, 77, 112, 115, 122, 200
Sari: 125
sarissa: 65, 206
Satibarzanes: 121, 130 f., 135, 181
Satyrs: 206
Satyrus: *Life of A*, 41; *Life of Philip*, 22
Scouts: 120, 159
Scythia: 21, 108 f., 119, 122, 127,
    130, 141, 144; A defeats, 145 f.;
    149, 153, 155, 159, 175, 185, 192
seal-ring: 134 f.
Seleucus: 186
Selge: 80
Semiramis: 176
Sestus: 50, 61 f., 64
Seuthes II: 192
Sevaste: 55
Sher-dahan Pass: 136, 138, 140
Sibyl: 103
Sicily: 10, 195
Side: 78
Sidon: 92, 95, 206
Silenus: 205
silphium: 140

Sindos: 56
Sinope: 83, 125
Siphnos: 85, 94
Sisicottus: 163
Sisigambis: 116, 121, 206
Sisines: 79, 134
Sistan: 135
Sitaces R.: 178
Sitalces, Odrysian king: 12
Sitalces, officer: 184
Siwah: 102, 122, 175, 194, 200, 207
Skoidos: 139
Sochi: 86 f.
Skopje: 36
Sochi: 86 f.
Sogdae: 173
Sogdia: 140 f., 145, 208
Sogdiana: 141-5, 150, 153, 155;
     Rock, 153 f.; 159, 162, 175, 181,
     188
Soli: 86
Sophocles: 199
Spain: 195
Sparta: 9, 11, 17, 19; defies Philip,
     20; 44, 73, 92, 94, 105; defeats a
     Macedonian force, 113; 115 ff.;
     Antipater defeats, 122; 125, 136,
     139
Spitamenes: 142 f., 144-7, 150, 153
Spithridates: 67
Stageira: 18
Stasanor: 141, 149, 153
stasis: 10 f., 35, 52, 73, 86, 100 f., 193
Stateira: 22
Stein, Sir Aurel: 103
Stiboetes R.: 127
Strabo: 115, 142
Strattis: 42
Strymon R.: 6
stylis: 92
Sudan: 122
Suez: 102, 178
Sunium: 193
Susa: 71, 90, 103, 111 ff., 116, 120,
     143, 178, 188, 195, 207
Susia: 130
Susiane: 112, 116, 181, 199
Swat R.: 169, 208
Syllium: 78
Syngeneis: 68: *see* Kinsmen
synoikia: 52
Syria: 85 f., 100, 105, 123; troops
     from, 130; 195, 207
Syrmus: 35

Taenarum: 90, 193
Tanaïs R.: 121, 144
Tapuria: 123, 125, 153, 185, 208
Tarsus: 85, 87, 92, 123
Taulantii: 36 f., 39
Taurus Mt.: 127
Taxila: 164, 169
Taxiles: 164, 167, 169, 171, 206
Tegea: 193
Temenidae: 6, 80, 135, 201
Tenedos: 85
Termessus: 80
Tethys: 175
Thaïs: 115
thalassocracy: 36, 94, 96 f., 116, 122,
     184, 195
Thamiscia: 31
Thapsacus: 178 f., 207
Thar desert: 173
Thebes: 9, 17-21, 44-9, 117, 142, 198,
     200, 207
Theopompus, *Philippica*: 21
Thermaic Gulf: 11
Thermopylae: 18, 44
Thespiae: 46 f.
Thesprotia: 11
Thessalonice: 22
Thessaly: 17 f., 66, 77, 79 ff., 85, 87,
     89, 108 f., 123, 129, 141; League,
     17; A President of, 30
Thetis: 87
Thrace: 6 f., 11 f., 17, 19; A
     campaigns in, 32 and 34 ff.; 46,
     50, 60, 66; coinage of, 53; 78, 81,
     87, 91, 101, 103, 108; rising in,
     111; 112 f., 120, 139, 156, 171,
     173; assassinate Philippus, 185;
     192, 207
Thrasymedes: 55
Thucydides: 10, 55
thunder: 73, 83, 167
Tigris R.: 105 f., 175, 178, 197, 200
Timoclea: 47 f., 200
Town-Companions: 189
triaconter: 61, 86 f., 163, 171, 176,
     178 f.
Triballi: 19, 21, 32 ff., 43, 59
tribute: 32, 35, 72; exemption from,
     72 f., 84, 100 f.; paid to

Macedonians, 78 f.; 83, 113, 131 f., 136, 141, 170
trierarch, 171
Tripoatis: 31
trireme: 74, 83, 94-7, 102, 195
Trogus: 47
Troy: 62, 72, 96, 100, 195
Tsangon Pass: 37
Tyre: 72, 96, 100, 200, 207
Tyriespis: 161, 163, 181

Uxii: 113

Vergina: 195
Veronese, P.: 91, 206
Vesuvius: 65

weirs: 178
wells: 174, 176, 186
Wolf's Pass: 37 f.

Xandica: 103
Xanthus: 78
Xenophon: 73
Xerxes: 111, 113, 115

Yemen: 178
Yugoslavia: 12

Zadracarta: 125
Zariaspa: 129
Zelea: 65, 72
Zeus: 50, 55 f., 73 f., 83, 90, 103, 111, 142, 167 f., 195, 201
Zeus Ammon: 102, 194; Apobaterios: 64; Basileus: 92, 103; Herkeios: 64; Olympius: 50, 55, 86; Soter: 177
Zeuxis: 56
ziggurat: 196
Zopyrion: 192